A
History of
WORCESTER
1674–1848

A
History of
WORCESTER
1674–1848

Kenneth J. Moynihan

Charleston   London

History
PRESS

Published by The History Press
Charleston, SC 29403
www.historypress.net

Cover image: *View of Worcester, Mass. Taken from Union Hill*, by P. Anderson, and R. Cooke, T. Moore's Lithography, Boston, 1838(?). *From the collections of Worcester Historical Museum, Worcester, Massachusetts.*

First published 2007

Manufactured in the United Kingdom

ISBN 978.1.59629.234.5

Library of Congress Cataloging-in-Publication Data

Moynihan, Kenneth J.
A history of Worcester, 1674-1848 / Kenneth J. Moynihan.
p. cm.
Includes bibliographical references and index.
ISBN 978-1-59629-234-5 (alk. paper)
1. Worcester (Mass.)--History. I. Title.
F74.W9M69 2007
974.4'3--dc22
                                2007035104

Notice: The information in this book is true and complete to the best of our knowledge. It is offered without guarantee on the part of the author or The History Press. The author and The History Press disclaim all liability in connection with the use of this book.

To Mary Jo

CONTENTS

ACKNOWLEDGEMENTS

My interest in Worcester's history stems from an interdisciplinary curriculum project begun in 1978 at Assumption College. Funded by the National Endowment for the Humanities, the project introduced students to the interdisciplinary study of real historical communities; with a single exception, the communities we studied were in Worcester. The faculty team included Kevin L. Hickey, a geographer; Charles W. Estus, a sociologist; historian John F. McClymer; and me. I want to thank those gentlemen for their creative collaboration and support. I want especially to thank Professor Estus for his generous friendship and in particular for joining me in leading an undergraduate seminar on Community Life in Pre-Industrial Worcester at the American Antiquarian Society in 1980. I am grateful also to NEH for a research fellowship at the American Antiquarian Society in 1992, and to the Faculty Development Program at Assumption for several summer grants.

Given the long gestation of this book, I cannot hope to list all the people who provided significant help along the way. Some more recent help I especially want to acknowledge. At the American Antiquarian Society, I received help from Georgia B. Barnhill; Andrew W. Mellon, curator of graphic arts; and from Jaclyn Donovan Penny, library assistant and rights and reproductions coordinator. William D. Wallace, executive director of the Worcester Historical Museum, supported the project and provided the expert services of Robyn Christensen, librarian, and Holly Izard, curator of collections, to both of whom I am grateful. I am also grateful to Jack Larkin, chief historian at Old Sturbridge Village, for his help. Donald W. Chamberlayne read early versions of these chapters and provided helpful commentaries. Mary Jo Moynihan read late drafts, continuing her principled campaign against ambiguity and other literary sins. Her work has significantly improved the book.

Finally, I am grateful for the pleasing company and valuable conversation of the Worcester History Group.

INTRODUCTION

The introduction to a book is an opportunity to explain why and how the work was done. This book was written to provide for twenty-first-century readers a modern account of what happened in Worcester in the seventeenth and eighteenth centuries and in the first half of the nineteenth century. The study of any community reveals odd things about it. About Worcester, one of the odd things has been the absence of a modern overview of the early years. Almost any local history book a reader might pick up, if it concerned early Worcester at all, would tend to rely on one source above all others: William Lincoln's admirable *History of Worcester*, published in 1837 and republished in 1862.

As the cultural generations have rolled past, Lincoln's account has remained remarkably informative and insightful, but it has not been joined on the bookshelf by other studies seeking a coherent overview of community life in the period that extends from Metacom's War (King Philip's War) to Worcester's official designation as a city. Writers of local history have reproduced Lincoln, but often they have seemed to regard the period as ancient (meaning dead) history. A conspicuous exception is *The First American Revolution: Before Lexington and Concord* by Ray Raphael (New York: The New Press, 2002). That work sheds welcome new light on the American Revolution, but it does not explore the earlier colonial experience in depth, nor does it venture into the nineteenth century. It might even be said that there was a need for a new book to cast a fresh eye on the years from 1674 (when the Nipmuc submitted to English "protection") to 1848 (the year the city charter was adopted).

Why was this book written? Because it wasn't there.

This is history in a narrative form. The information it conveys is couched in stories about the people who tried to find opportunity and security—and perhaps some adventure—in the social and political environments of their days. It is largely about what people thought they were doing. It is also the story of a world changing, in ways that sooner or later reached Worcester.

Chapter 1
NIPMUC COUNTRY

For the last three centuries, the hilly patch of North America known as Worcester, Massachusetts, has been claimed and ruled by people of European descent. The first among them were the English. Before that, for a hundred centuries, the land had been the domain of people whose ancestors had migrated from Asia. The last among them were the Nipmuc.

THE NIPMUC AND THEIR QUANDARY

By English reckoning, it was the seventeenth day of September 1674 when the Reverend John Eliot and Captain Daniel Gookin rode up to the principal Nipmuc settlement in the area. Situated on a hill called Pakachoag, it was home to around one hundred people living in twenty families. Eliot, seventy years old, and Gookin, sixty-two, were on their way to the wigwam of Horowaninit, who was called by the English "Sagamore John." Eliot represented the Puritan Church and Gookin its close ally, the civil power of the Colony of Massachusetts Bay. They had come to establish a new order at Pakachoag, and at the neighboring village of Tetaessit (Tatnuck).

More than five decades had passed since the beginning of English settlement in New England. Horowaninit of Pakachoag and Woonaskochu of Tataessit appeared ready to submit their people to the supervision of Eliot's church and Gookin's state. For three years, various Nipmuc villages had been visited by Christian Indians, sent to teach them the ways of the English. According to the colonists' plans, the village at Pakachoag was on that day to begin a more formal tutelage. In time, it was to graduate to the status of a full-fledged, English-style "praying town," similar to those Eliot and Gookin had established at seven locations closer to the coast and on the Merrimack River. On this journey, the "apostle to the Indians" and his close friend, the colony's superintendent of Indians, were giving official status to seven new praying towns in the hills of central Massachusetts. Not coincidentally, the region was just beginning to attract English traders and settlers.

The missionary and the superintendent arrived around noon. Horowaninit, welcoming the dignitaries to his large wigwam, offered food and drink. As soon as the other residents could be brought in, Eliot preached a sermon in Algonquian, the language shared, in different dialects, by all of the native peoples of southern New England. James Speen, a praying Indian trained by Eliot, then read from the Bible and "set the tune of a psalm, that was sung affectionately." The religious service closed with prayer.

Gookin's turn had now come. He convened a session of a Massachusetts court, with several Nipmuc leaders sitting with him as judges. Except for a brief interval, Gookin had since 1656 been superintendent or "ruler" of those Indians who had agreed to submit themselves to Massachusetts law. It was his responsibility to appoint Indian judges to hold court on minor matters, as well as Indian constables to enforce the law. When Gookin himself joined the judges, the court was legally equivalent to a Massachusetts county court. All significant matters decided by Indian judges needed Gookin's approval before they could take effect.

On that day, the main business of the court was to establish formal English civil order among the people of Pakachoag. Gookin chose the leaders of the Nipmuc, Horowaninit (Sagamore John) and Woonaskochu (Sagamore Solomon), and constituted them "rulers of this people, and co-ordinate in power, clothed with the authority of the English government." The residents were invited to nominate a constable, and their choice fell upon Matoonas, a leader Gookin could confirm as "a grave and sober Indian."[1]

What the English called "Nipmuc country" included most of interior Massachusetts, from the Merrimack River in the northeast to the Connecticut River in the west. The English used the name "Nipmuc" or "Nipnet"—meaning "fresh water people"—for all inhabitants of the region, though the Indians probably used the term only for the people living in an area stretching from the current city of Worcester southward into northern Connecticut. Also living in the loosely defined "Nipmuc country" were the "River Indians" along the Connecticut, including the Agawam, Waranoke, Nonotuck, Pocumtuck and Squakea. Around Brookfield lived the Quabaug. The Nashaway had their main village near Lancaster.

The inhabitants of the region lived in scattered villages that formed a loose confederation based on kinship. Less centrally organized than the major coastal tribes, the Nipmuc may have paid tribute at various times to the more powerful Wampanoag in Plymouth Colony (now southeastern Massachusetts), the Narragansett of Rhode Island, the Penacook of the Merrimack, the Pequot of the Long Island Sound and the Massachusett of the bay region. They shared the Loup dialect and other cultural and trading ties with their western neighbors on the central Connecticut River, as well as with Indians of southern Vermont and New Hampshire. In what is now Worcester, the Nipmuc lived in three main villages when Eliot and Gookin visited in 1674. In addition to those on Pakachoag (today the site of the College of the Holy Cross) and Tataessit (now the location of the Worcester Regional Airport), a third stood on what is still called Wigwam Hill, on the western shore of Lake Quinsigamond. In all, between two and three hundred people probably lived in the three communities.[2]

A few generations earlier, before Europeans had begun exploring, fishing and trading in North America, there had probably been around 80,000 people living in southern New England, though modern estimates have gone as high as 144,000. Among the Nipmuc and Pocumtucks, there may have been over 15,000. Europeans brought to America diseases against which the Indians had developed no antibodies during forty thousand years of isolation following their ancestors' migration from Asia. As a result of epidemics that began in 1615 and culminated in a great smallpox outbreak in 1633, the native population of southern New England decreased catastrophically. The survivors in all of southern New England in 1674 numbered around 20,000. Of those, 3,000 to 4,000 people lived in Nipmuc country.[3]

By that time, there were also approximately 45,000 English in New England, settled in 110 small towns, most of them along the coast and up the rivers. Massachusetts had an English population of around 17,000. The other colonists lived under the governments of Connecticut, Rhode Island or Plymouth—a separate colony until 1691.[4]

For centuries before the arrival of the English, the Nipmuc had been an agricultural people. However, in contrast to the English farmers who would succeed them on the land, the Nipmuc moved their living quarters from place to place in the course of each year to take advantage of the fluctuating bounty of the seasons. Their wigwams, as Gookin described them, were "built with small poles fixed in the ground, bent and fastened together…on the top." These frames were covered with bark or with mats woven of reeds. When a family or the village moved from one seasonal site to another, the framework could be left behind, while the mats were rolled up and carried to the new site.[5]

English explorers and colonists marveled at the natural abundance of New England's fields, forests and waters. At the same time, they shook their heads at the "poverty" of the Indian peoples who lived in this land of plenty. They placed most of the blame for this on Indian males, whom they regarded as lazy, because they did not normally work in the fields. Indeed, the burden of agricultural labor—as well as the burdens of childbearing, child rearing, food preparation and carrying possessions from site to site—fell on the women. In addition to warfare and diplomacy, men carried on the hunting and much of the fishing. Though these were often arduous and dangerous tasks, they were regarded by the English as leisure activities.[6]

The Indians were "poor" only by English standards. By their own, they lived well and had few economic wants or complaints. The Indians' way of life, however, provided the English with one of their readiest justifications for appropriating Indian lands. Since only a small part of the territory inhabited by the Nipmuc or other Indian peoples was under active cultivation, the English could regard the rest as unused, and therefore morally available to anyone who would "improve" it through the labor of fencing or planting. The hunting, fishing and plant gathering that caused Indians to move throughout large territories gave them no more claim to the land, in the English view, than such activities gave to the wolf or the deer or the bear.[7]

The Massachusett tribe of the bay area and the Pawtucket of the lower Merrimack River numbered only about two hundred by 1630. Beginning that year, they were literally overwhelmed by the great migration of Puritans seeking religious, political and economic autonomy. Around three thousand new settlers had arrived by 1633. The weak Massachusett and Pawtucket, under frequent attack from northern Indians and by Plymouth settlers, looked upon the new colonists as protectors, readily selling them land in exchange for security. The Indians were eager to receive English cloth—in some cases trading their labor for it—as well as iron tools and alcohol. There were soon so many Indians working as servants on English farms that the Court of Assistants asserted its authority to regulate their employment.[8]

In marked contrast to many of their contemporaries, John Eliot and Daniel Gookin saw the Indians less as obstacles to English expansion than as benighted fellow creatures in need of Christian charity and guidance. Nevertheless, the missionary and the superintendent were powerful representatives of an ongoing European invasion. The history that brought the missionary and the superintendent to Pakachoag in 1674 had been a long and costly one for the Indians, a harsh but profitable one for the English.

No one knew this better than the new constable, Matoonas, who had lost a son to the English five years earlier. Accused of murder, the young man had been hanged in Boston. Then his head had been cut off and placed on a pole on the common. Hearing that Matoonas had vowed revenge, the governor's council had ordered him in for a hearing. Matoonas had admitted that "he found his heart so big hot within him" due to his son's execution, but he had nevertheless promised to remain "a faithful friend of the English." Daniel Gookin undoubtedly relied on that promise when he appointed Matoonas to enforce English law at Pakachoag.[9]

As events would soon demonstrate, the superintendent did not know his man, nor did he understand the full dimensions of the crisis confronting Matoonas and his people. Ten months after his appointment, the new constable would lead the first Indian attack ever made on an English settlement in the Colony of Massachusetts Bay. The Nipmuc assault on Mendon, in which five English settlers were killed, would be the opening act of King Philip's War in Nipmuc country. Before that, even as they appeared to welcome the missionary and the superintendent to their village, the Nipmuc were being pulled between two radically different strategies for survival. They would soon have to choose between the submission they displayed before Eliot and Gookin and the violent resistance many Indians were secretly discussing. If they followed the course proposed by the missionary, the Nipmuc would adopt both the English God and the English way of life. They would settle in farming towns, fence their fields, raise livestock, cut their hair, wear English clothes and send their children to English schools. If they opted instead for the strategy advocated by a growing number of New England Indians, they would rise together to defend their sovereignty and their identity against the ever-expanding power of the English. Among colonists and natives alike, rumors about such a scheme were often associated with the name of Metacom, sachem of the Wampanoag on the eastern shore of Narragansett Bay, known to the English as Philip, and to many later generations of storytellers as King Philip.

One of the most significant events in the history of relations between the natives and the colonists had occurred in 1637, during a war between colonists and the

Portrait of King Philip (Metacom) by Paul Revere, illustration from the 1772 edition of Benjamin Church's *The Entertaining History of King Philip's War. Courtesy American Antiquarian Society.*

Pequot, who lived on the lower Thames River and on Long Island Sound. Warfare among Indians in southern New England, though not unusual, had rarely resulted in great loss of life. Although fire would have been effective against the wooden palisades Indians sometimes erected for defense, they considered it too horrible and deadly a weapon to use. The Narragansett were therefore astonished when their English allies in 1637 set fire during the night to a fortified Pequot village on the Mystic River, shooting or burning to death between four and seven hundred people, most of them women, children and old men. As the surviving Pequot were rounded up, many of the men were executed, the women and children sold into slavery and the Pequot nation was declared dissolved.[10]

To justify such wholesale slaughter of noncombatants, the Puritans turned to Biblical accounts of the extermination of heathen peoples. Captain John Mason of Connecticut, who had ordered the massacre, boasted that "God...laughed his enemies and the Enemies of his people to Scorn, making them as a fiery Oven...Thus did the Lord judge among the Heathen, filling the Place with Dead Bodies!"[11]

Following the Pequot War, the English played an equally decisive role in the rivalry between two men who had been their allies against the Pequot: Miantonomi, a leader of the Narragansett, and Uncas, chieftain of the Mohegan. Miantonomi, after receiving assurances that the English would not be offended, went to war in 1643 to avenge Mohegan injuries to some of his allies. He was captured in battle, and his people paid Uncas a forty-pound ransom for his release. Rather than free his enemy, however, Uncas brought him to Hartford and placed the case before the commissioners of the newly organized United Colonies of New England, which had been formed largely to coordinate Indian policy. After consulting church leaders, the commissioners concluded that Miantonomi would be a constant threat to their Mohegan ally if allowed to live, and therefore he could morally be put to death. However, rather than accept responsibility for the execution, the Puritans handed Miantonomi back to Uncas with permission to kill him somewhere outside their jurisdiction. Miantonomi was marched out of Hartford; somewhere between there and Windsor the brother of Uncas stepped behind the prisoner and "clave his head with a hatchet."[12]

While the killing of Miantonomi infuriated the largely autonomous Narragansett, the lesson of English power and its uses was not lost on the less powerful Indians living within the boundaries of the Massachusetts Bay Colony. They began in a few months to make formal submission to the rule and "protection" of English authorities.[13]

Getting to Quinsigamond

The political submission of the Merrimack and coastal Indians coincided with the start of the missionary career of the Reverend John Eliot. He arrived in Boston in 1631 and soon after became pastor of the church in Roxbury, where many of his English friends and relatives had located. In the early 1640s, Eliot began learning the Algonquian language from a Long Island Indian, enslaved during the Pequot War,

Reverend John Eliot, "apostle to the Indians." *Courtesy American Antiquarian Society.*

who had learned to speak and read English. By 1646, the Roxbury pastor felt sufficiently prepared to begin preaching to the Indians closest to Boston who had formally submitted to the English two years earlier.[14]

Eliot succeeded in establishing the first praying town at Natick in 1651. By 1660, six more had been established at Wamesit (Lowell), Okommakamesit (Marlborough), Nashoba (Littleton), Punkapaog (Canton), Magunkaquog (Ashland) and Hassanamesit (Grafton). Land for the praying towns was granted by the General Court, the legislature of Massachusetts. In 1674, Gookin addressed the curious phenomenon of Europeans granting land in America to Native Americans. The English, he said, had gained title to the land both by a grant from their king and "either by purchase or donation from the Indian sachems and sagamores." The praying Indians thus had "to receive the lands by grant from the English, who are a growing and potent people, comparatively to the Indians."[15]

Gookin himself was a major actor in the process by which Indian lands had been passing into the hands of this "growing and potent people" from across the Atlantic. Born in Kent in 1612, he had spent his boyhood among colonizers in Ireland, where his family owned a substantial estate. In the 1630s and 1640s, he had accumulated large estates of his own in Virginia, mostly by claiming headrights of fifty acres for each of the ninety-eight indentured servants and slaves he and his father had brought over to work their lands. When Virginia passed a law in 1643 requiring conformity to the Church of England, Gookin's Puritan sympathies induced him to move first to Maryland, then in 1644 to Massachusetts with his wife and infant daughter.[16]

Though he was quickly admitted to Boston's First Church, Gookin soon moved to Roxbury, where he became a near neighbor and close friend of John Eliot, minister of the Roxbury church. In 1647, he bought a sailing vessel, which he used for trade between the Chesapeake Bay and New England, at least into the 1670s. Gookin also set out to add land in New England to his holdings in Virginia and Maryland.

In 1649, Gookin was made captain of Cambridge's trainband, a militia command he would hold for nearly forty years, even after being elevated to sergeant major of Middlesex County, then major general of Massachusetts. Also in the spring of 1649, Gookin was elected to represent Cambridge as a deputy to the General Court. In 1652, he was chosen as an assistant, one of the body of eighteen who served as a judicial court, as the upper house of the legislature and as executive councilors to the governor. With the exception of one year, he would be reelected to the powerful Board of Assistants annually for thirty-five years.[17] Gookin in 1656 was appointed superintendent of the Indians within the jurisdiction of Massachusetts. He journeyed to England two years later. Following his return, Gookin in 1661 was reappointed "in answer to the petition of Mr. John Eliot on behalf of the Indians." As a reward for "publicke service donne," Gookin in 1657 was granted five hundred acres on the Pequot River. The General Court in 1665 granted him another five hundred acres that, at his request, were laid out between Concord and Lancaster, adjacent to Nashobah, which had been established as a praying town in 1654.[18]

Gookin's account of the 1674 visit to Pakachoag with John Eliot did not mention important trips he had previously made into Nipmuc country. In 1668, he had ridden in as the leader of a committee appointed by the General Court to see whether the area bordering on Quinsigamond Pond might "be capable to make a village" for English settlement. The committee had found the area indeed suitable for settlement, and had recommended a committee "to lay it out, to admit inhabitants and order the affaires of this place." The General Court had promptly appointed Gookin and three others to carry out that task.[19]

For the next few years, the plans of Gookin and the committee had been thwarted by the presence in Quinsigamond of several thousand acres previously granted by the General Court to the church of Malden and to several private individuals. Title to one of these grants had been purchased by Ephraim Curtis of Sudbury, who by 1673 not only had 250 choice acres laid out at the heart of the proposed settlement, but had also begun to put up a trading post. In June 1674, the General Court adjusted the conflicting claims, freeing the committee to pursue its plans. The time had come to dispossess the Nipmuc.[20]

No new praying towns had been established in more than a decade. However, a new burst of missionary activity coincided with the beginnings of the first English settlements in Nipmuc country: Mendon and Brookfield in the late 1660s and Quinsigamond in the 1670s. According to Gookin, Indians in the Nipmuc region had begun "to hearken unto the gospel" around 1671 "or thereabout." In July 1673, Eliot and Gookin had made their first joint visit to the "new praying towns" to "encourage and exhort them to proceed in the ways of God."[21]

A year later, still two months before his ceremonial visit with Eliot, Gookin had met on Pakachoag with Horowaninit (Sagamore John) and with Woonaskochu (Sagamore Solomon). There each of the sagamores had made a mark at the bottom of a deed. For twelve pounds in New England money, they had "bargained, sold, alienated, enfeeoffed, and confirmed" to the committee appointed by the General Court a tract eight miles square, encompassing all of present-day Worcester, as well as Holden and part of Auburn. On behalf of their "kindred and people" the natives gave up "for ever...all and every p[ar]t of our civill or natural right, in all...the broken up land and woodlands, woods, trees, rivers, brooks, ponds, swamps, meadows, mineralls, or any other thing, or things whatsoever, lying and being within that tract of land."[22]

Though he was a party to the transaction, Gookin as a member of the colony's Board of Assistants had signed the instrument, verifiying that the sagamores had acknowledged it in his presence. Four praying Indians, one each from Okommakamesit (Marlborough), Wamesit (Lowell), Chabanakonkomon (Webster) and Pakachoag had made their marks as witnesses.[23] As a down payment valued at twenty-six shillings, Gookin had handed over two coats and four yards of cloth, "made of coarse wool, in that form as our ordinary blankets are made." Had full payment been made in that form, the several hundred Nipmuc of the two villages would have received eighteen coats and thirty-seven yards of cloth in exchange for sixty-four square miles of land.[24]

It was two months after that transaction that Gookin and Eliot arrived to "settle teachers...and to establish civil government among them as in other praying towns." To the missionary and the superintendent, the future of the Quinsigamond Nipmuc seemed settled. Though no land had yet been set aside for a praying town, the hills on which the Indians lived no longer belonged to them. Like the Massachusett Indians near the bay and the Penacook on the Merrimack, the Nipmuc were expected gradually to conform to English civil, economic and religious ways.

As the Nipmuc began what Eliot and Gookin regarded as their slow transformation into Christian and civilized beings, arrangements for the English invasion at Quinsigamond began to move at a faster pace. At the committee's request, in December 1674 the Middlesex County court granted a license to keep an inn and serve "wine and strong watters" at Quinsigamond.[25] In the spring of 1675, land was surveyed, and the General Court's committee began assigning house lots. A fifty-acre lot went to Daniel Gookin, a twenty-five-acre lot to his son Samuel. Captain Daniel Henchman of Boston, also a member of the committee, joined in granting himself a twenty-five-acre house lot. A third member, Captain Thomas Prentice of Boston, received fifty acres. The energetic Ephraim Curtis finished building his trading post, and at least six other grantees put up buildings.[26] They were clustered on the Connecticut Road, now Lincoln Street, to the north of what would later become the central village.[27]

THE NIPMUC CHOOSE WAR

Meanwhile, ominous events were developing to the southeast. There, the colonies of Plymouth and Rhode Island shared borders with one another and with various Indian peoples, most important among them the Wampanoag and the Narragansett. As the English later told the story, Metacom, or King Philip, sagamore of the Wampanoag, had been "plotting with all the Indians round about to make a general Insurrection against the English in all the colonies." Metacom ruled at Pokanoket, where Mount

Hope peninsula extends into Narragansett Bay, the present site of Bristol, Rhode Island. Though he had successfully resisted English efforts to Christianize his people, Metacom had suffered a series of humiliations at the hands of English authorities. In 1671, he had been forced by Massachusetts and Plymouth to sign a document making his people subjects of the government of Plymouth. At the same time, he had to agree to pay a fine for behaving "insolently and proudly" toward colonial authorities, and to refrain from selling lands without Plymouth's approval. By the summer of 1675, he was under pressure from younger men in his own and other tribes to lead them in a violent assault upon the encroaching colonists.[28]

The killing began on June 23 in Swansea, when a young Englishman shot and mortally wounded a Wampanoag he saw running from an English house. King Philip's War had begun. The next day, Metacom's men killed 9 Englishmen and mortally wounded at least 2 others.[29] On June 26, Massachusetts sent two military companies to assist its southern neighbors. One was led by Captain Daniel Henchman and the other by Captain Thomas Prentice, both members with Daniel Gookin of the committee to settle Quinsigamond. Following a series of bloody encounters, the English decided to starve out Metacom and the Wampanoag by sealing off the Mount Hope peninsula. Henchman's company of about 125 soldiers and 17 friendly Indians were given the task of building a fort at Pocasset to keep the enemy from escaping by water.[30]

Meanwhile, Boston continued to gather intelligence about the Nipmuc. Ephraim Curtis of Sudbury, the owner of the trading post at Quinsigamond, rode out from Boston with three Indian volunteers from the praying town at Natick.[31] What he found was clear evidence of trouble in the interior. He learned that his building at Quinsigamond had been robbed. To prove it, Curtis reported, the Indians "showed me some of the goods." Daniel Gookin's constable at Pakachoag, Matoonas, was reported to have been "the leader of them that robbed my house."[32]

Curtis added another praying Indian and two English settlers from Marlborough to his party before proceeding on his mission. After passing several abandoned Indian villages, he found the natives setting up a large encampment at Menameset, on an island in the Ware River, in the present town of New Braintree. A frequenter of the frontier, Curtis quickly recognized around twenty men and "asked their welfare, knowing that many of them could speak good English," but he got no response. Curtis managed to reach the leaders of the gathering communities and deliver the message he had been sent with, that the governor of Massachusetts wanted "to put them in mind of their engagement to the English." When the Indians insisted on their peaceful intentions, Curtis asked why he had encountered such a hostile reception. The sagamores replied that they had heard that the English "had an intent to destroy them all."[33]

Curtis undoubtedly looked for Matoonas, but the plunderer of the Quinsigamond trading post was not around that day. The erstwhile constable of Pakachoag was at Mendon, leading the first organized Indian assault on English settlers in the history of Massachusetts. The raiders killed five settlers, including a woman and a child.[34] To the south, the Narragansett were resisting urgent pleas to join their Wampanoag neighbors. That did not stop rumors of a substantial Narragansett presence in the Massachusetts interior. Told that "the Narragansett Indians are come downe with about 100 armed men into the Nipmuc Country," the governor and council on July 27 ordered a military force into the area. To lead it, they selected another man with property interests to protect. Captain Edward Hutchinson owned "a very considerable farm" in the vicinity of Brookfield and had employed Nipmuc men as laborers. With Captain Thomas Wheeler and "Ephraim Curtis for a gide and sufficient interpreter,"[35] the officers were to tell the Indians that the Massachusetts authorities had been informed "that Matoonas & his Complices who have Robbed and murdered our people about Mendon" were now at the encampment at Menameset. Unless they were turned over, the English would regard the rest of the Indians as "no friends to us, but ayders and abettors." With that peremptory demand, the English practically forced the Nipmuc to take sides, to choose between the demands of their most militant kinsmen and the orders of the colonial authorities.

Accompanied by Curtis and three Christian Indians, Hutchinson, Wheeler and around twenty troops set out from Cambridge on July 28. From Brookfield they sent a message to the Indians a dozen miles north at Menameset, saying they wished to "come to a Treaty of Peace with them." As Wheeler later reported, the messengers witnessed serious divisions among the Indians; the "young men among them were stout in their speeches, and surly in their carriage. But at length some of the chief Sachems promised to meet us on the next morning about 8 of the clock upon a plain within three miles of Brookfield."[36] During the night, the stout young men of the Nipmuc apparently won the argument. The next morning, accompanied by three Brookfield settlers who were confident of the Indians' friendly intentions, Hutchinson led his men into a carefully planned ambush. Eight Englishmen died in the fighting, including the three from Brookfield; five others were wounded, including both Hutchinson and Wheeler. One of the Christian Indians was taken prisoner. Guided by the other two, the survivors struggled back to Brookfield, where they did their best to fortify one of the largest houses as a garrison to hold off the expected Nipmuc attack. The rest of Brookfield's terrified residents, around fifteen families in all, crowded into the house.[37]

When no Indians had appeared after two hours, Hutchinson and Wheeler decided to send Ephraim Curtis and Henry Young of Concord for help. On his third attempt, Curtis succeeded in crawling to freedom. Already exhausted from fighting and from lack of sleep, he managed to walk thirty miles to Marlborough to sound the alarm.[38]

After the Indians lifted the Brookfield siege, Hutchinson's surviving troops brought him to Marlborough. Five days later he died of his wounds. Simon Willard and his men remained at Brookfield for several weeks; by then the danger had become so great that the town was abandoned by settlers and soldiers alike.

While Ephraim Curtis was serving with Hutchinson and Wheeler in Nipmuc country, Captain Daniel Henchman, also a member of the committee to settle Quinsigamond, remained at Mount Hope among the New England forces trying to starve out Metacom and his people. On July 31, Henchman learned, to his dismay, that Metacom and many of the Wampanoag had slipped out of the Pocasset swamp, crossed the Taunton River and set off for Nipmuc country. Henchman pursued the fugitives, inflicting casualties, plundering camps and taking prisoners, but he was unable to prevent the escape of the main body.[39] Within days of the August 5 lifting of the siege of Brookfield, Metacom had reached the Nipmuc camp at Menameset with around forty men, three of them wounded, plus a larger number of women and children. Around thirty of his men carried guns, the rest bows and arrows. When he heard what the Nipmuc had done to Hutchinson's company and to Brookfield, Metacom showed his approval by distributing wampum among the sagamores. Whatever their earlier hesitancy, the Nipmuc were now part of King Philip's War.[40]

Appeals for the Indians

Though the Indians inflicted great punishment on the English in the early stages of the war, they were themselves suffering many casualties, bearing the near-total disruption of their economic lives and losing family members to captivity. Among the colonists, the immediate issue of how to treat the captives raised the more general problem of future policy regarding the native peoples. When the colonists attacked Indian villages, noncombatants who survived were supposed to be taken as prisoners. After Metacom's escape, as English troops searched the surrounding territory, fugitives were either killed or added to the stock of captives. From the start of the war, the English disposed of many of these prisoners by selling them into slavery in the West Indies, Spain and the coasts of the Mediterranean. Following the destruction of Dartmouth in July, Indians who had not taken part in the attack were persuaded to go to Plymouth for their own safety. There the whole group, numbering around 160, was ordered sold to the slavers. Hundreds of others followed them.[41]

In Boston, John Eliot begged the Massachusetts authorities to desist from what was already revealing itself as a policy of Indian extermination. "This useage of them is worse than death," Eliot wrote in a petition to the governor and council on August 13. "The design of Christ in these last dayes is not to extirpate nations, but to gospelize them."[42] What should, perhaps, have been evident to Eliot years earlier was dawning on him now with chilling clarity. Among the settlers themselves, there had never been much support for missionary efforts. Financial assistance had always come, not from New England, but from old England. Now it was becoming evident that neither civil contract nor religious duty would stand in the way of Indian removal. Eliot fought courageously to reverse the tide.[43]

"When we came," he reminded the council, "we declared to the world, & it is recorded, yea we are ingaged by letters patent fro[m] the king[']s Majesty, that the indeavor of the Indians['] conversion, not their extirpation, was one great end of our enterprize, in coming to these ends of the earth." God had granted success to the missionaries, Eliot argued, and though there was now a war underway, the war itself could very well result in new opportunities. "I doubt not but the meaning of Christ is, to open a dore for the free passage of the gospel among them." The Roxbury minister tried to place the issue on the highest plane possible in a Puritan community: would the authorities submit to the will of God? "My humble request," Eliot wrote, "is that you would follow Christ his designe in this matter, to p[ro]mote the free passage of Religion among them, & not to destroy them—to sell soules for money seemeth to me a dangerous merchandize. To sell them away from All meanes of grace w[hic]h Christ hath p[ro]vided…is a way for us to be active in the destroying of their Soules."[44]

Eliot's appeal had no effect on the policy of Massachusetts or of the other colonies toward their captives. Some Indians may have lived or died according to their likely value in the slave market. Daniel Henchman, commanding troops near Quinsigamond, reported taking eleven prisoners, including eight women, a boy, a girl and "an old fellow, brother to a Sachem." The boy, the girl and seven of the women were allowed to live. "Two of the oldest," Henchman reported, "by council we put to Death." The commissary was ordered to convey the rest to Boston.[45]

As the fires of war spread, colonists found it increasingly inconvenient to distinguish between Indians who were part of the fighting and those who had remained peaceful. Once again, the authorities acted to eliminate any middle ground on which the Indians might stand. Responding to public pressure for greater controls, on August 30 the council designated five of the old praying towns as the only permissible locations in Massachusetts for Indians who wished to be regarded as friendly. Once concentrated at Natick, Punkapaog (Canton), Nashoba (Littleton), Wamesit (Lowell) and Hassanamesit (Grafton), they were not to "presume to travel above one mile" from the center of the town "unless in company of some English, or in their service." It would thenceforward be permissible for anyone to seize or kill any Indian found "in any of our towns or woods, contrary to the limits abovenamed."[46] Under the order, the Christian Indians at the old praying towns of Okommakamesit (Marlborough) and Magunkaquog (Ashland) were required to abandon their homes. All who moved into the concentration centers were prevented by the restriction on their movements from hunting, from tending cattle and swine and from working for wages among the English. They could not even harvest their corn unless an Englishman was willing to accompany them to the fields.[47]

Though the pleas of some colonists had been satisfied, those living near the concentration centers continued to demand the removal of Indians from their neighborhoods as well. In late October, the General Court ordered the transfer of the peaceful praying Indians of Natick to Deer Island in Boston Harbor. Captain Thomas Prentice, a Quinsigamond proprietor regarded as friendly to the Christian Indians, was given the task of marching the two hundred Natick people to a spot on the Charles River, where boats would be waiting to transport them to the island. The Indians "quietly and readily submitted." At the riverside, they met John Eliot, who "comforted and encouraged and instructed and prayed with them, and for them; exhorting them to patience in their sufferings." Painfully aware of the English policy of enslaving and selling captives, the Natick people were in "fear that they should never return more to their habitations, but be transported out of the country." At about midnight on October 30, the tide lifted the three vessels, and the Christian Indians were carried to their island exile, where they were under orders, as winter approached, not to cut down any live wood or in any way harm the sheep kept on the island.[48]

Eliot, his friend Gookin and a very few others formed a minority faction among the Puritan leaders in Boston, urging just treatment of the praying Indians and, on occasion, of Indian captives. Although the missionary's efforts on behalf of Indians during the war brought heavy public criticism upon him, his interventions were treated with much greater tolerance than were those of Gookin. Gookin undoubtedly owed his original appointment as superintendent of Indians in part to his prominence as a military man. Now, as hostilities spread, he had crucial responsibilities for fighting Indians, both as a military commander and as a member of the council. Many in Boston were therefore infuriated at his repeated and effective appeals to the council for humane treatment of Indians. The anger of the public was expressed in a particularly blunt way on May 4, 1676, when Gookin was denied reelection as assistant after thirteen years of continuous service.[49]

The council in Boston sent out troops with orders to join forces with Captain Daniel Henchman, who was then on his way to Mendon, to seek out the enemy Indians (reported to be at Pakachoag) and to do their best to destroy them. If, as expected, they found stores of Indian corn at Pakachoag, they could seize it and divide it among themselves as plunder.[50] When the English arrived at Pakachoag, they found no Indians to fight, but plenty of evidence that the Nipmuc had been there recently, including more than one hundred bushels of freshly harvested corn. There was also "a great quantity of corn still standing." Gookin later complained that soldiers disobeyed instructions "not to spoil any thing belonging to the poor Christian Indians, that lived among us, and had deserted their plantations of Hassanam[e]set [Grafton], Manchauge [Sutton], and Chobonakonkon [Webster], three villages that lay next the English, in the Nipmuc country." Against orders, the soldiers chose "to destroy much of the corn, and burn the wigwams, and mats, and other things that they found in those three villages, that belonged to our praying Indians."[51]

Soon after the troops left Pakachoag, on December 2, 1675, Indians burned all of the six or seven abandoned buildings in the fledgling settlement of Quinsigamond.[52]

Winter of Starvation

The decisive events of December 1675, however, were taking place neither on Deer Island nor in Nipmuc country. In November the United Colonies of New England had decided to destroy, at long last, the independence of the Narragansett, which with one thousand warriors was the most powerful of the southern New England tribes. They had not joined the Indian resistance, despite the urgent pleas of the Wampanoag. In fact, they had on June 15, under pressure from the colonists, signed a treaty requiring them to surrender any Wampanoag who came into their territory. Though they had produced a few severed heads, for which the English had paid the promised bounty, the Narragansett had failed to turn over most of their Wampanoag guests.[53]

As a New England army of around one thousand men took positions on the western shore of Narragansett Bay near Wickford, Rhode Island, the Narragansett withdrew with their friends and families into a large, secret village they had fortified on an island in the midst of the Great Swamp, near the present town of West Kingston, Rhode Island. With the help of a Narragansett turncoat, the English found the fortified village and assaulted it on December 19. During a furious fight in which they lost around seventy men, the English set the village afire. Between three hundred and one thousand Narragansett, mostly noncombatants, were burned, shot, bludgeoned or stabbed to death. The scattered survivors faced winter without shelter or supplies. Though fighting continued in the Narragansett region, many of the Narragansett warriors who escaped the Great Swamp fled into Nipmuc country.[54]

Having broken the power of the Narragansett to the south, the commissioners of the United Colonies decided that the time had come to demonstrate who would rule in Nipmuc country. They voted to raise a new army of six hundred men to campaign in the interior. As they were organizing, four hundred Indians converged on Lancaster on February 10, burning, killing and taking captives, among them Mrs. Mary Rowlandson, whose account of her experience would become a classic piece of colonial literature. Six weeks later, Lancaster was abandoned by the English survivors. On February 21, Medfield was attacked and partially burned. Four nights later, on the Atlantic Coast itself, south of Boston, buildings were ablaze at Weymouth. During these weeks, Mary Rowlandson traveled across the breadth of Nipmuc country, which to her was a "vast and desolate Wilderness." From Lancaster she was led along a trail that went through today's Princeton, Rutland and Oakham to the encampment at Menameset (New Braintree). From there she followed her captors north, through what are now Hardwick, Barre, Petersham, New Salem, Athol, Orange, Warwick and Erving, to Squakeag (Northfield). From there she went even farther north, through what are now Vernon and Hinsdale, New Hampshire, to Chesterfield, Vermont. By approximately the same route, she was led back to Mount Wachusett.[55]

Early in April, while Rowlandson was still struggling eastward, Massachusetts authorities sent a Christian Indian to Mount Wachusett to open negotiations concerning the captives. By the middle of the month, Metacom reached the mountain with his Wampanoag, a large group of Nipmuc and several captives, including Mary Rowlandson. After messages had been carried back and forth, principally by Christian Indians, releases began on May 3, when Rowlandson was ransomed and carried to Boston for a reunion with her husband.[56]

THE END OF ONE HUNDRED CENTURIES

Earlier disagreements among experienced sachems and younger warriors were apparently revived in a new form. The more cautious elders favored a strategy of hit-and-run raids against isolated settlements, while the younger men were more eager to engage in pitched battles with English forces, as they had at Sudbury. There were also disagreements about the wisdom of ransoming the captives or of responding to English feelers about peace negotiations. Based on reports from his spies, Daniel Gookin believed the negotiations over prisoners caused a deep rift among the Indians, with Metacom among the leaders "utterly against treating with the English or surrendering the captives." In Gookin's opinion, it was this disagreement that led Metacom, his Wampanoag and the Narragansett to separate from the Nipmuc and head back "into their own country" in June.[57]

During the late summer, the combination of hunger, policy disagreements and declining military capability gradually forced groups of Indians to seek negotiations or simply to surrender. Early in July, the Nipmuc opened communication with the authorities in Boston. In a letter written by a former praying Indian, five of the sachems, including Horowaninit (Sagamore John) of Pakachoag, first asked Governor Leverett and Waban, a leader of the praying Indians, to see to the safety of their wives, some of whom were prisoners of the colonists. They then entreated the English to "consider about the making Peace." To this and to several subsequent pleas, the English answered that those who had begun the war or had engaged in especially bloody deeds could expect nothing but death; those found to have been drawn into the war by others would have their lives spared.[58]

On July 13, Horowaninit visited Boston to arrange the surrender of his people. He told the English he was sorry to have taken up arms against them, and that he had done so only under pressure. In an effort to regain their favor, he said he would soon produce convincing proof of his true allegiance. Two weeks later, the sagamore of Pakachoag returned to Boston, this time with 160 or more starving and terrified people. As evidence of his fidelity, he handed over to the English a coveted prize: Matoonas of Pakachoag, securely bound with ropes. The authorities dealt promptly with the renegade constable whose attack on Mendon had touched off the war in Massachusetts. After a brief trial before the council, Matoonas was led to Boston Common, fastened to a tree and shot to death by Horowaninit and his men, who were eager to gain whatever advantage such a deed might bring them. Matoonas's head was cut off, fastened to a pole and set up on the gallows, facing a skull that had been placed there six years earlier. It was all that remained of Matoonas's son.[59]

Though there was more blood to be shed, the war in Nipmuc country was effectively over. Metacom returned without hope to his land at Pokanoket. There, on August 1, the English captured his wife and son. Although leading members of the Massachusetts clergy thought that the boy could legitimately be put to death, others objected, and the child and his mother were sold into slavery.[60]

On August 12, Metacom fell face down in the mud at Mount Hope after being shot through the heart by an Indian ally of the English. Captain Benjamin Church ordered the body dragged to dry land, later observing that the slain Wampanoag chieftain had the appearance of "a doleful, naked, dirty beast." Church had the body cut into quarters and hung up in trees to rot. Metacom's head and one of his hands were awarded to the man who had killed him, "to show to such gentlemen as would bestow gratuities upon him." The hand, preserved in rum, was thereafter displayed throughout the region. Church led his men back to Plymouth, where they were paid thirty shillings per head for each Indian killed or captured. Metacom's head was fastened to a pole and publicly displayed in Plymouth for at least the next quarter-century.[61]

Throughout the interior of Massachusetts, desperate people were on the move as the ten-thousand-year reign of the Indian came to an end. Many surrendered at the nearest English settlement or at Boston. They faced trials, often followed by execution, enslavement or temporary servitude. Some fled with the remnants of their families to Connecticut, where they found refuge with the Mohegans, or to the lower Hudson. Many of the Nipmuc fled north and east, hoping to be accepted and absorbed by the Penacook and the Abenaki.[62]

Among the colonists, over six hundred men—one of every eleven among those of military age—had died. Thirteen communities had been totally destroyed: on the Connecticut River, Northfield and Deerfield in Massachusetts and Simsbury in Connecticut; at the center of Nipmuc country, Brookfield and Quinsigamond; to the northeast, Lancaster and Groton; to the southeast, Mendon and Wrentham in Massachusetts, Middleborough and Dartmouth in Plymouth Colony; in Rhode Island, Warwick and Wickford. Others, such as Springfield, Westfield, Marlborough, Scituate, Rehoboth and Providence, had suffered extensive damage.[63]

By a conservative estimate, of an Indian population of approximately 20,000, at least 2,000 were killed in battle, and another 625 died later of wounds. More than 3,000 perished from exposure, starvation and disease. Over 2,400 were captured, of whom more than 1,000 were sold into slavery. Another 2,000 became permanent refugees. The political and military power of the native peoples had been destroyed throughout southern New England. All of the colonies placed the surviving Indians under strict control, often assigning them small patches of territory that became, in effect, reservations. Those who had sided with the English, most conspicuously the Mohegans and the praying Indians, were nevertheless consigned to the margins of the new order.[64]

Between August and October 1676, Daniel Gookin presided over a committee assigned by the General Court to place into temporary servitude thirty-two children surrendered by Horowaninit, sagamore of Pakachoag. Some had parents or relatives present to acquiesce in the assignments, though they had little choice if their children were to escape the full burden of slavery. The committee recommended, and the General Court subsequently adopted, a term of service lasting until each child had reached the age of twenty-four. Masters and mistresses were to provide religious education and teach the children to read English. Gookin himself accepted the services of "a Boy named Joshua aged about eight years, son to William Wunuko, late of Magunkoog [Ashland]; his father dead." He also took charge of "a girle aged about six yeares, daughter to the widdow Quinshiske late of Shookanet beyond Mendon."[65]

Less fortunate were the daughters and sons of parents who had been taken by force. Children who had been given or sold to anyone in Massachusetts were left "at the disposal of their masters" or anyone to whom their masters might assign them, for the rest of their lives. The masters were to provide instruction in "civility" and the Christian religion.[66] In 1677, the General Court banished all Indians from the entire territory of Massachusetts, except for the praying towns of Natick, Punkapaog (Canton), Hassanamesit (Grafton) and Wamesit (Lowell). Unable to carry on their traditional economic lives, many became poor tenant farmers, hired laborers or servants among the English.[67]

During these weeks, Gookin took care of a piece of unfinished business. Two years earlier, as a magistrate, he had authenticated the Nipmuc sale of Quinsigamond to him and to the other members of the General Court's committee, certifying that part of the selling price had been paid. Now he apparently conveyed to some of the captives in Boston cash or goods equivalent to the amount still due. No Indian signed or made his mark, but as the destruction of the Nipmuc was nearing completion, Gookin took out the deed and wrote across the bottom, "Full payment rec'd August 20, 1676. D. Gookin."[68]

Nipmuc country was no more.

Chapter 2
UNQUIET SETTLEMENT
(1676–1731)

Some months after the close of King Philip's War, probably in the vicinity of Boston, Daniel Gookin came across Nipmuc who had claims to land in Quinsigamond, but who had not participated in the land transaction of 1674. To reinforce his title, and perhaps out of some sense of fairness, in February 1677 Gookin obtained a new deed and paid again for the eight miles square already sold to him and to the other members of the General Court's committee. The sellers this time were the widow and heirs of a sagamore named Pannasunnet, whose main village had probably been on Wigwam Hill on the western shore of the lake, a Nipmuc center Gookin had not mentioned in his account of his visits to Quinsigamond.[69]

Although the war and the laws had cleared the region around Lake Quinsigamond of most native inhabitants, English settlers would not be able to live there without fear of attack for another fifty years. On their own or as allies of the French, warriors from the west, from the east and from the north resisted the expanding Massachusetts frontier up to the eve of the American Revolution. Though hostile natives last appeared in Worcester itself in the 1720s, Moses Rice, who had moved from Worcester, was killed by Indians in nearby Rutland as late as 1755.[70]

RESETTLING QUINSIGAMOND

The committee's major problem, once the heavy fighting of 1675–76 was over, was to get settlers back into Quinsigamond. In 1678, the three surviving committeemen—Gookin, Thomas Prentice and Daniel Henchman—ordered colonists who had been granted lots before the war to move to Quinsigamond by the end of 1680 or risk forfeiture. The flaw in this approach was evident in the additional requirement that the new and returning settlers "build together as to defend themselves." Not a single family chose to risk their lives in order to save their land.[71] Six years after the death of Metacom, the General Court warned the committee that its entire grant would be forfeited unless it found a way to get the settlement reoccupied soon. By then, the narrative of Mary Rowlandson's captivity had been published, reinforcing the dread that was discouraging people from again venturing onto the frontier.[72]

Under such unpromising circumstances, the committee in 1682 began discussing an extraordinary proposal. Gookin wrote down the details of the new plan on April 24, 1684. It took the form of an agreement between the three surviving members of the committee (Gookin, Henchman and Prentice) on the one hand and Daniel Henchman and several unnamed "undertakers" on the other. Since Gookin later revealed that he was himself one of the undertakers, at least two of the three members of the General Court's committee were making a deal with themselves.[73]

Under the agreement, the whole Quinsigamond plantation was divided into 480 eighteen-acre lots, 200 of them entrusted to the undertakers "to be planted by them and such as they shall procure." These 200 lots would be granted to settlers in the southern half of the tract, the area that is today Worcester. In the northern half, 200 lots—later incorporated as Holden in 1741—were left in the hands of the General Court's committee, to grant in the usual way.

That left eighty lots in the southern part, which would be forever exempt from taxation. The committee and undertakers' plans for those lots reveal a great deal about the nature of community planning in Massachusetts late in the seventeenth century. To establish a successful farming community, more was required than land, seed, farmers, livestock and tools; the eighty lots would be used to provide for those additional needs.

They were to be tax-free because they were viewed as instruments for achieving public purposes. Meanwhile, the men who organized and promoted settlement under public authority expected to be well compensated for their services; that compensation was also to come from the supply of tax-free lots. Under this process, which was never fully implemented, the members of the committee granted to themselves as individuals over 10 percent of the land in what would become Worcester. The rest they turned over to the management of the undertakers, among whom were also at least two of themselves, Gookin and Henchman. At the same time, they had provided means of support for religion, education, milling, manufacturing, military training and burial of the dead.

Besides adding to the assets of the committee members and laying the groundwork for a new community, the agreement effectively substituted Henchman, leader of the undertakers, for Gookin, leader of the committee, as the person most responsible for advancing the settlement. Henchman, who had moved to Quinsigamond in 1683, promptly had the land surveyed and began moving settlers in. Under the agreement, the "first planters," who had by now forfeited lots granted before the war, would be granted the same lots again if they complied with the undertakers' conditions.[74]

Life in the Second Settlement

By April 1684, enough people had begun to settle at Quinsigamond to induce the Middlesex County Court, at the request of the committee, to order them to "constantly meet together on Sabbath days to celebrate the worship of God in the best manner they can at present." The court also authorized Daniel Henchman to enforce its order. At the same time, it granted an innholder's license to his twenty-two-year-old son, Nathaniel Henchman.[75]

It was during these years that the settlement lost its Indian name and acquired an English one. Daniel Gookin had been using Worcester as an "alias" for Quinsigamond since 1668. On September 10, 1684, the General Court finally made the name official by granting the committee's specific request "that their Plantation at Quinsigamond be called Worcester." Though Gookin left no record of the thinking behind his selection, it seems to have been a gesture of Puritan defiance. Gookin was a military man, an associate of Oliver Cromwell, and he may have had his new town named for the 1651 Battle of Worcester, Cromwell's final victory over the Stuart pretender, the future Charles II. Though the reign of the Puritans had ended in 1660, with Charles II restored to the throne and the Church of England again the official church, the Puritans of Massachusetts remained largely unreconciled. Gookin, in fact, returning from England in 1660, had brought with him two of the men responsible for pronouncing the death sentence upon Charles I. Gookin had subsequently helped to shield the regicides from English pursuers.[76] In the name of Worcester, the moment of Puritan triumph in 1651 could be permanently memorialized in Massachusetts.

As was the common practice in new settlements, individuals to whom "house lots" were granted by Henchman became members of a select group known as the proprietors of Worcester. The proprietors alone were entitled to shares in future divisions of the remaining land. Other men might purchase land from individual proprietors, but only the purchase of one of the original house lots would carry with it membership in the propriety and a share in subsequent divisions. The intended difference in status between proprietors and other settlers was displayed in 1669, when the General Court's committee, borrowing the hierarchical terminology of English society, distinguished between the proprietors and the "commons" of Worcester.[77]

In contrast to the lots in the first settlement, the house lots of the restored town were mostly scattered among the hills in the southeastern quarter of Worcester, on Oak Hill and Sagatabscot (later Union or Grafton) Hill. Others were concentrated near the fortified "citadel" established north of what is now Lincoln Square.[78]

The aging Daniel Gookin seemed especially eager to take advantage of the new arrangements. The first four Henchman grants, entered into the proprietors' record book by Gookin, were made to Gookin himself, for more than 200 acres. On the reverse side of the page, he made a personal note, estimating that when the second division of the land was carried out, he would be entitled to another 1,260 acres.[79]

In October 1684, the General Court appointed two new members to the Worcester committee: Adam Winthrop of Boston, grandson of Massachusetts's first governor, and Captain John Wing, a prominent Boston mariner and innholder. Unlike Winthrop, Wing was to become much more than an absentee ruler. Henchman granted him ten eighteen-acre lots in Worcester, including all the tax-free lots reserved for the builders of the first mills. Henchman also granted Wing the exclusive right to use the waters of the stream, already called the Mill Brook, that flowed southerly from North Pond (now Indian Lake) on the border of the future Holden, through the center of settlement.[80] Wing built on the west side of the stream, just north of the citadel and garrison to which settlers were expected to flee in case of alarm.

Wing later claimed that Henchman had promised to grant him, in future divisions, all of the land on the west side of the stream, north to the pond itself. However, Henchman subsequently granted to George Danson, a Boston baker, two hundred acres between Wing's land and the pond. When Danson on three occasions tried to have the land surveyed, his surveying party was interrupted by a group of men, among them John Wing, determined to prevent the building of any dams or mills upstream from his own. Wing's men cut the boundary markers and took away the surveyor's chain. After extended litigation, Danson's title was confirmed, but he was ordered not to "erect any corn mill or saw mill upon the Mill Brook."[81]

During the Wing-Danson controversy, Daniel Henchman stood firmly behind Danson's claims, and Daniel Gookin stood firmly behind Henchman. The people actually settled in Worcester, however, rallied behind Wing, on whose mills they would all soon depend. Ten men, claiming to be a majority of the settled inhabitants, addressed a statement to the judges praising Wing for his investment in the mills and his general helpfulness in public affairs. To support Wing's claim, they testified that Henchman had told some of them that land above Wing's on the west side of the stream was no longer available, because it had been promised to John Wing.[82] The bitterness generated by the dispute was displayed on October 8, 1685, when Daniel Henchman, founder of the second settlement, was carried to his grave by two servants, followed by his wife, his children and only one or two other people.[83]

John Wing had become the effective leader of the Worcester settlers. The "plantation," still too small to govern itself through a town meeting, remained at least nominally under the supervision of the committee appointed by the General Court. In 1686, Wing led the proprietors in petitioning for a new committee to regulate the settlement's affairs. Their motivation is not clear. If Wing hoped to get free of Gookin, or to serve on the new committee as he had on the old, his hopes were disappointed. The authorities appointed Gookin, Thomas Prentice and three other men, stipulating that no committee business could be conducted without Gookin being present.[84] Despite this apparent setback in Boston, the settlers seem to have continued to look to Wing for leadership. Following the death on March 19, 1687, of Daniel Gookin, the settlers apparently chose Wing to succeed the founder as keeper of the town's record book.

While men and women in Worcester were struggling with the land, the elements and one another to begin a new town, dramatic developments in England were again reverberating through the politics of Massachusetts. Ever since the collapse of Puritan government in England and the restoration of the Stuart monarchy in 1660, imperial officials had attempted, with little success, to assert greater control over the Puritan colonies in New England. Massachusetts vigorously defended the virtual autonomy it had enjoyed under the charter of 1629. Following protracted legal proceedings, the charter was revoked by royal authority in 1684, the year Worcester was given its defiantly

Puritan name. In 1687, the colony was placed, along with the rest of New England, New York and New Jersey, under the rule of a new government called the Dominion of New England. The king's appointee, Governor Edmund Andros, ruled with a royally appointed council, and without the elected representative bodies that had become a tradition in self-governing New England. Colonial leaders divided over whether to resist the new regime or to collaborate with it. Meanwhile, in England, a more important opposition was taking shape.

There, opposition reached revolutionary heat in 1688 when James II had his son and heir baptized a Catholic. Leading men of both the Whig and Tory Parties asserted that Stuart political despotism was now openly bound to popish religious tyranny. They offered the crown to James's Protestant daughter, Mary Stuart, and to her Dutch husband, William of Orange. James II fled, clearing the way for William and Mary and the Glorious Revolution that permanently established the dominance of Parliament in the British constitutional system, as well as the principle of Protestant succession to the throne.

In April 1689, Massachusetts leaders proclaimed the reign of William and Mary and arrested the Dominion governor, Sir Edmund Andros. Negotiations with royal officials produced in 1691 a new Massachusetts charter, often seen as a symbol of the province's transition from its Puritan to its Yankee character. Property owners who were not members of a Congregational church would no longer be denied the right to vote for members of the legislature. Under the new arrangements, the governor would be appointed by the king rather than elected by Massachusetts freemen. Otherwise, Massachusetts had recovered its elected assembly, to be called the House of Representatives, and, as events would show, it had also recovered much of the independence it had exercised under the original charter.

After becoming king of England, the Dutch William of Orange continued his policy of leading European resistance to the ambitions of Louis XIV of France. In 1689, England joined other European powers to challenge the Sun King in what became known as the War of the League of Augsburg. The conflict soon burst out across the northern frontiers of New England and New York, where it was called King William's War. Outlying farmers in Worcester were ordered to take shelter in John Wing's garrison at the northern edge of the center of the settlement. Some hesitated, pleading for permission to remain on the eastern hills, where they were building a garrison of their own. Otherwise, they said, they would be ruined. "[We] now live on our growth," they explained, and if forced to abandon the fields, "shall lose all [we] have."[85]

The appeal of those farmers, who preferred the peril of Indian attack to the certainty of economic ruin, is one of the very few documents that survive to shed light on life in Worcester between November 1686 and the day, probably in 1702, when the settlement was once again abandoned, this time by all but one family. The gap in the record may be partially explained by the death in March 1687 of Daniel Gookin, custodian of the proprietors' record book.

The settlement was not abandoned during King William's War, which ended with the Peace of Ryswick in 1697. However, the frontier of English settlement again felt the repercussions of European events following the death in 1700 of Charles II of Spain. In 1702, disagreement over who should inherit the throne led in Europe to the War of the Spanish Succession, in New England to Queen Anne's War and in Worcester to the failure of the second English settlement. Preparing as early as 1699 for the inevitable reopening of hostilities, the General Court prohibited settlers from deserting certain frontier settlements in the event of war. The list included the central Massachusetts towns of Lancaster, Marlborough, Brookfield and Mendon, but not Worcester, which may have been regarded as too weak to defend itself successfully.

Worcester, twice abandoned, apparently remained a ghost town during the decade between 1702 and the close of Queen Anne's War. Following a failed expedition by English and colonial forces against Quebec in 1711, combat in North America at long last ground to a halt. Word spread of peace talks starting up in Europe, and men and women in Massachusetts began thinking once again about reclaiming Worcester. While 1713 is noted in European history for the signing of the Treaty of Utrecht, in Worcester it marks a related event—the beginning of the third and permanent English occupation of the town. For the next thirty years, the European powers would manage to avoid a major war, giving Worcester the time it needed to grow and prosper. When called upon once again to fight both Indians and French, the town would be strong enough to survive what turned out to be more decades of costly warfare.

Launching the Third Settlement

John Wing had died in Boston in 1703. In 1713, as in the aftermath of King Philip's War a quarter-century earlier, men with property interests in Worcester were searching for leaders who could direct the repopulation of the settlement. They appeared in 1713 in the persons of two Marlborough men, Jonas Rice and his brother Gershom. The Rices had, during the previous few years, been purchasing property in Worcester. In a political system dominated by gentlemen of influence on the seacoast, the Rices needed a well-placed patron if they were to get legislative action on a revival of Worcester. They turned to Colonel Adam Winthrop, son and heir of the Boston representative appointed to the General Court's Worcester committee back in 1684, and thus heir to substantial properties in Worcester. With Winthrop as their co-petitioner, the Rices asked the General Court in October 1713 for a new committee to take charge of the settlement of Worcester. The legislature promptly responded with a five-man committee that included Winthrop and other powerful eastern magnates, but not the Rices.[86]

In the settlement itself, nevertheless, early leadership was largely in the hands of the Rice family. In fact, in October 1713, while the petition for a new committee was still before the legislature, forty-year-old Jonas Rice moved his family into a house he had built on Sagatabscot (Grafton) Hill. Jonas and Mary Rice and their children remained the only inhabitants until the spring of 1715, when they were joined by Jonas's brother Gershom, then forty-eight, and his family. The third family to settle was that of

Nathaniel Moore, who was married to Grace Rice, sister of Jonas and Gershom. Many more Rices soon followed them to Worcester.[87] Although tradition places the Jonas Rice family alone in the wilderness from 1713 to 1715, in all likelihood they had guests for part of that time, for on November 7, 1714, Mary gave birth to her fifth child and fourth son, Adonijah Rice. It is highly unlikely that she went through that ordeal without the support of female friends or relatives.[88]

Mary Stone of Sudbury had married Jonas Rice in 1702, when she was twenty-four years old and he was twenty-nine, both four years older than the average New England bride and groom. New England women usually married at or near the age of twenty, to a man around five years older. They gave birth to around eight children before their childbearing years ended twenty or twenty-five years later.[89] Mary Rice's first child, Silence, was born in 1703. A son named Adonijah, born in 1705, died during his infancy. Jonas Rice Jr. was born in 1707, and Absalom in 1709. The two-year cycle of pregnancy, birth, nursing and a new pregnancy was a typical one among New England women. Much less typical was Mary Rice's experience after the birth of Absalom. For whatever reasons, she did not give birth for another five years, and the second Adonijah, born in Worcester when she was thirty-seven, was her last child.

If Mary managed to get enough female help, she would normally have been confined to her room for a week after the birth of Adonijah.[90] In a settled community, the act of giving birth entitled a woman who was not poor to as much as a month of special care and attention. On the frontier, Mary could not have enjoyed the usual train of female visitors who were attracted to the lying-in chamber, and she probably did not observe the customary three-week exclusion of all men, including her husband, from the chamber.[91]

While Mary Rice was bringing Adonijah into the world, the males of the family were helping to oversee the birth of a town. The initiative demonstrated by Jonas and Gershom in getting a new committee appointed by the legislature did not go unrewarded. Most of the lots granted by that committee between 1714 and 1718 went to the Rices, to their relatives or to other men who, like them, had previously lived either in Marlborough or in Marlborough's mother town, Sudbury.[92] Slightly later arrivals, like Benjamin Flagg of Watertown and his brother-in-law, Nathaniel Jones of Boston, did not receive their first grants as proprietors until 1718, when the committee was already in the process of making second-division grants to the others.[93] As the years unfolded, when Jones and the Flaggs sought to exercise influence in the community, they often clashed with the pioneering Rices.

Decisions about locating the new dwellings echoed the choices made by members of both the first and second settlements. As in the first settlement, some dwellings in the third were clustered north of the geographic center, along the Connecticut or Country Road (now Lincoln Street). However, as in the second settlement, farms also sprang up on Sagatabscot and Oak Hills, southeast of the center. Despite this dispersal, or perhaps because of it, the meetinghouse would soon be built in the north-south valley through which the Mill Brook flowed. The site, now occupied by Worcester's City Hall, was on the Connecticut Road, south of one cluster of farms and west of the other. The location of the meetinghouse, where both town and church would gather, established the nucleus of a central village that would, in time, perceive its interests as differing in important ways from those of the outlying farmers.[94]

The Church and the Scotch-Irish

Though the permanent English occupation of Worcester was just getting underway after 1713, nearly a century had elapsed since the beginning of English settlement in New England. Most of the new Worcester settlers, though born in America, preserved from their Puritan heritage the belief that the central institution in any community must be its church. Soon after arriving in their new home, perhaps in 1716, women and men who had been church members in other towns gathered in the home of Gershom and Elizabeth Rice to form a Puritan or Congregational church in Worcester. It was formally recognized by an ecclesiastical council in 1719.[95] All adults in Puritan communities were legally required to attend religious services, but a powerful distinction was drawn between the congregation, made up of all who lived in the community, and the church, made up only of the "visible saints." Membership in the church was accorded only to men and women who convinced those who were already members that they had, through the work of the Holy Spirit, been converted from their sinful ways and reborn into spiritual life. Only these members of God's elect were allowed to participate in the sacrament of the Lord's Supper. Until the Worcester church could call a minister, leadership would of necessity remain in the hands of laymen. The members chose as their deacons Daniel Heywood, formerly of Concord, and Nathaniel Moore, one of the Sudbury men. In 1717, a rough, temporary meetinghouse was erected on the north side of what would later be the intersection of Franklin and Green Streets, a short distance south and east of the Worcester Common.[96]

In 1718, a year after the erection of the first meetinghouse, Worcester had a population of around two hundred. Then a new and very different group of people joined the settlement. From the north of Ireland, Presbyterians of Scottish descent migrated to New England in search of economic opportunity and religious freedom. By one estimate, fifty Scotch-Irish families moved to Worcester immediately after arriving in Boston in the summer of 1718. If true, that would mean the population of the settlement was approximately doubled in a matter of weeks. John Gray, one of the Scotch-Irish leaders, did buy land in Worcester as early as October 1, 1718, but it is difficult to imagine that a group of that size could have procured adequate food and shelter in a frontier settlement before winter set in. The migration probably took a year or more, but the Scotch-Irish soon made up at least a third of the population of Worcester.[97]

Like the original English settlers of New England, the Presbyterians adhered to the teachings of the sixteenth-century reformer John Calvin. They, too, had sought to "purify" the churches of England and Scotland of the vestiges of Catholicism, and thus they, too, had been called "Puritans." They differed from Congregational Puritans principally on matters of church governance. While the Congregationalists asserted the independence of each local church, the Presbyterians believed proper discipline in matters of faith and practice required the supervision of synods, to which each church sent representatives. The Scotch-Irish brought to Worcester one of their own clergymen, the Reverend Edward Fitzgerald, and met for worship in an "old garrison house," perhaps a restored version of the one that had been built decades earlier by John Wing, just north of the town center.[98]

In 1719, the inhabitants of Worcester began to build a larger meetinghouse on the site now occupied by Worcester's City Hall.[99] The expenses associated with it, as well as the salary of the Congregational minister, were the town's responsibility. Thus the Presbyterian taxpayers, besides providing voluntary support to Fitzgerald, were also required to pay for the construction and maintenance of the town meetinghouse and the support of the Congregational minister.

The pastor was, necessarily, one of the most important members of a Puritan community. In deciding who that individual would be, it was the full members of the church, or at least the males among them, who had the principal role. Technically, they alone had the power to select the man who would be the spiritual leader of the community and enjoy its financial support. However, the rest of the men in town also had a say. Under normal practice in Massachusetts towns, the church members notified the town meeting of their selection of a candidate for the pulpit. The town either concurred with the choice or refused to concur. If the town refused, it was up to the church to propose another candidate. When the church in Worcester chose its first minister in 1719, the community had not yet begun holding town meetings, because Worcester was still under the supervision of the committee of the General Court. Since no relevant church or civil records have survived, it is impossible to know whether taxpayers who were not members were fully consulted. In either case, the church in August 1719 ordained as its first pastor, and Worcester's first minister, the Reverend Andrew Gardner, twenty-eight years old, a member of the Harvard College Class of 1712.[100]

Worcester's first pastor was soon in serious trouble. According to tradition, Gardner fell out of favor with his hardworking flock because some of them believed he devoted himself much more ardently to the sport of deer hunting than to the labor of saving souls. Gardner, on the other hand, complained that Worcester was refusing to pay the bonus of sixty pounds it had offered, in addition to his salary, to encourage him to move to the frontier.[101]

CHURCH CONTROVERSY AND THE START OF TOWN GOVERNMENT

In September, a council representing seven other churches tried in vain to work out a solution. In June, the legislature asked the church council to return to Worcester and try once more.[102] The church council was willing to meet, but not in Worcester. It gathered instead in the town of Dedham, because by the summer of 1722 Worcester was once again too dangerous a place to visit.

The young settlement in 1721 had asked to be released from the guidance of the General Court's committee in order to govern itself as an autonomous town. This effort was more successful. On June 14, 1722, the General Court granted Worcester, in the county of Middlesex, the powers and privileges of the other towns in Massachusetts.[103] On guard against Indians and divided against one another, the men of Worcester held their first town meeting on September 28, 1722. The records begun that day reveal that factional lines had divided the new municipality some time before it began to govern itself. One group, led by Jonas Rice, was made up largely of the earliest settlers from Marlborough and Sudbury. The members of this faction, who may have been largely responsible for Andrew Gardner's coming to Worcester, apparently regarded themselves as the principal guardians of the church and its work in Worcester. They wanted a prompt and final monetary settlement with the minister, and they pressed to get the church building, begun in 1719, finished at long last, presumably to help attract a qualified successor to Gardner in the near future.

A second faction was led by three men from Sudbury's mother town, Watertown: Benjamin Flagg, Benjamin Flagg Jr. and Nathaniel Jones, son-in-law of the senior Flagg. They wanted their townsmen to take a hard line against Gardner's financial claims, and they seem to have been in no hurry to have the taxpayers resume the full burden of supporting a resident minister. The Scotch-Irish evidently did not throw their lot in with either faction, perhaps because they were hoping to establish themselves officially under the independent Presbyterian ministry of Edward Fitzgerald.[104]

Things began fairly cautiously. Deacon Daniel Heywood, who sided with the Rice or church faction, was chosen to moderate the first meeting, called to elect town officers on September 28, 1722. The other deacon, Nathaniel Moore, was elected to the board of selectmen, as was his brother-in-law and ally, Jonas Rice. From the other side of the factional divide, both Nathaniel Jones and his father-in-law, Benjamin Flagg, were elected to the board. The fifth member was the leader of the Scotch-Irish, John Gray.[105] The Presbyterian leader may have been chosen to prevent either the Rice or the Flagg faction from controlling the board.

The controversy over paying Gardner and selecting his successor provides an unusual opportunity to observe how Puritan families pursued their rivalries within the institutional boundaries of town and church. Each town meeting, for example, opened with the election of a moderator. When one of the factions was numerous enough to control the meeting, it would choose one of its own leaders to preside. By its choice of moderator, the meeting usually revealed the attitude it would take toward Gardner and toward church spending.

On October 31, 1722, a meeting called specifically to deal with the religious affairs of the town chose Jonas Rice as moderator. The church council meeting at Dedham had recommended that Gardner be dismissed from his connection with the Worcester church, and that he be paid what he was owed. Before proceeding with the dismissal, however, the town meeting pointedly voted to "secure to the Rev. Mr. Andrew Gardner his temporal Interest." If the Rices got their way, Gardner would get his money. The meeting then voted to dismiss Gardner, as recommended by the council.

However, at the next meeting, held five months later for the election of town officers, the anti-Gardner, anti-spending faction assumed a narrow control. Anticipating an extended vacancy in the pulpit, the meeting decided to pay visiting preachers twenty-five shillings per day. A later meeting voted to raise thirty pounds in taxes "for the support of transient preaching [of] the word of God in Worcester."[106] The wording customarily used in such resolutions was "trenchant preaching." The strange deviation recorded by town clerk Benjamin Flagg Jr. captured, perhaps inadvertently, the policy the community, or one faction in the community, was in fact adopting. Not about to settle a new minister, Worcester could plan on hearing "transient" preachers for the near future.

On June 4, 1723, when the anti-Gardner leader, Nathaniel Jones, was chosen moderator, the meeting formally declared that the town's October vote to "secure to the Rev. Mr. Andrew Gardner his temporal interest" had not been intended to include the sixty-pound gratuity supposedly promised him before he moved to Worcester. The question then put before the meeting was, if in October it had not voted to grant the sixty pounds as part of a settlement with Gardner, was it prepared to do so now? The answer, not surprisingly, was "in the negative." These actions precipitated the first formal notice of dissent recorded in the Worcester town books. Twenty-three men went on record as opposing the vote that denied Gardner the sixty pounds. Seventeen of them, including Deacon Nathaniel Moore, had previously lived in Sudbury, Marlborough or both. Ten of them were named Rice. Also on the list of dissenters was the other deacon, Daniel Heywood.

Although the financial dimensions of the Gardner affair had not been settled, Worcester's first minister had been dismissed, and the process of finding a successor had to begin. On June 24, 1723, Jonas Rice was chosen moderator of a meeting at which the church group extended the hand of compromise to its antagonists. The church had appointed a member to join with someone selected by the town to lead the search for a new pastor. To represent the town's interest, as distinct from that of the church, the town meeting—under the control of the Rice group—chose a man who had frequently assumed the role of taxpayers' champion on his own: Benjamin Flagg Jr. Perhaps because of this compromising spirit, the town was able on January 6, 1724, to concur with the church's selection of the Reverend Shearjashub Bourne as Worcester's next minister. Bourne, however, prolonged the process by turning Worcester's invitation down.[107]

The contentious settlers may have been spurred toward greater cooperation during the spring of 1724 by the suddenly increased danger of Indian attack. In May, the selectmen described Worcester as a place "very much exposed to the Indian rebels in the present war," and they pleaded for soldiers to guard the town and scout the surrounding forests.[108] On June 21, Selectman Gershom Rice addressed a similar, but more urgent, request to Colonel John Chandler of the Middlesex County militia. Indians had been sighted in Worcester, Rice wrote, and the town was so exposed that "a small number of Indians…might overcome the whole place." On behalf of his neighbors, Rice called upon Chandler "to be a father to us, and we hope the country [Massachusetts] will not see us stand here waiting to be a prey to our enemies." If Worcester did not get enough protection to permit a successful harvest, the selectman wrote, it would "be starved out of necessity."[109]

By late summer, nineteen Massachusetts soldiers were posted at Worcester. Cultivation and harvesting were disrupted, as alarms were sounded and families fled from the fields to the protection of the garrisons. During August, Indians were again seen in the town, but neither side was eager for combat. During the night of August 7, the Indians deprived the badly frightened settlers of sleep by howling like wolves and beating triumphantly on the sides of an abandoned house. The soldiers remained in Worcester until October, when, it was hoped, the Indians had returned for the winter to their northern homes.[110]

Despite this threat, the Worcester settlers seemed to be making progress in the task of choosing a new minister. In September 1724, a meeting was called to see whether the town would concur with the church's desire to call the Reverend Thomas White. However, no vote was taken on concurrence. Instead, the town appointed one leader from each side, Benjamin Flagg and Gershom Rice, to carry on further discussions with White. When those negotiations proved unavailing, the town appointed another factionally balanced committee to treat with the Reverend Isaac Burr about preaching in Worcester for a term.

On February 10, 1725, nearly two and a half years after the dismissal of Andrew Gardner, the town concurred with the church in calling Isaac Burr, twenty-eight years old and, a 1717 graduate of Yale College. There is no evidence of serious resistance to the decision. However, even as the community made plans for the ordination of its second pastor in the fall of 1725, the possibility arose that, by fall, there might not be any Worcester left to welcome the new pastor. The town might, for the third time in its turbulent history, have to be abandoned.

In April, the selectmen informed Lieutenant Governor William Dummer that they had just received news of "two companies of Indians…between us and Wachusett." During the previous year, they wrote, farming had been so disrupted that it had been "very difficult to subsist ourselves and our families." Unless they received military assistance, they feared "that the corn cannot be planted, the earth tilled, the harvests gathered, or food provided, and that the settlements in the town will be entirely broken up." Provincial authorities responded, but the division in the new town led to an unusual recommendation from a Middlesex officer. He had led soldiers from the eastern towns to Worcester, where he thought they should be left under the command of someone who knew the local geography and had the trust of the local population. After making careful inquiries, he recommended that, in accordance with "the mind of the town," Colonel Chandler appoint "Moses Rice and Benjamin Flagg to be the officer over them alternately, when one comes in, the other to go out, to have but one man's pay; which will be likely to have the duty better performed, and is the mind of the town." Chandler complied with the request. Thus, in military command, as so often in the town's first few years of political life, when Rice came in, Flagg went out; when Flagg came in, Rice went out.

Throughout the spring and summer of 1725, reports made their way to Boston of Indians moving in and around Worcester.[111] The winter of 1725–26 brought relief when Massachusetts authorities reached a treaty with the northern Indians. Fifty years after King Philip's War, Worcester's settlers had reason to hope that, at long last, the surviving natives would cease to disturb their labor and their slumber. The prospects of peace within the community had also been enhanced by the ordination, on October 13, 1725, of Isaac Burr as second minister of the Worcester church. Burr's wife, Mary Eliot, coincidentally, was a great-granddaughter of both John Eliot and Daniel Gookin.[112]

HARBINGERS OF COMMERCE

During the next several years, new alignments evolved as new issues arose and new men came into prominence. The political influence of the Scotch-Irish declined following Burr's ordination in 1725. Their leaders were no longer included on the board of selectmen, perhaps because they had lost their value as a counterweight between opposing factions. Their minister, Edward Fitzgerald, seems to have left Worcester around 1725, and for a time afterward the Scotch-Irish worshipped with their Congregational neighbors. However, sometime during the first decade of Isaac Burr's ministry, they stopped attending the town church and began meeting on their own once again, this time under the ministrations of another of their countrymen, the Reverend William Johnston.[113] This division in the Worcester community would not heal easily. Tensions between the Scotch-Irish and the Anglo-Americans continued to build.

For years there was, in effect, a Rice seat on the board of selectmen, held most frequently by Jonas, less often by Gershom. James, Zephaniah and Gershom Jr. also took their turns. Then, as if their time had passed, in the early 1740s the Rices stopped getting elected to the board, except for a one-year return by Gershom in 1746. The Rice family may usefully be regarded as representatives of a type. The very first permanent Worcester settlers, they were ambitious yet traditional farmers who strongly supported the church as the center of community life. As the decades passed, influence would slip very gradually from the hands of such men into those of more secular, market-oriented settlers, often men and families who had arrived in Worcester somewhat later. Though in 1713 the Rices had made the crucial Boston connections necessary to get the Worcester settlement revived, the newer men tended to have more constant contact with the political, social and economic powers of the metropolis.

Among the Rices' earliest rivals, Nathaniel Jones can be most clearly categorized as a man seeking his fortune in pursuits other than farming. In 1717 Jones, then of Boston, was granted a thirty-acre plot east of Pakachoag Hill on which to build and operate a gristmill. He soon became one of the most extensive land speculators in the early history of Worcester. The settlers' awareness of Jones's useful Boston connections may have played some role in his election as Worcester's first member of the Massachusetts House of Representatives in 1727.[114]

Another harbinger of change was William Jennison, who at the age of fifty moved to Worcester from Sudbury in 1726. Probably due to his notable wealth, he was elected both selectman and assessor in 1727. In 1728, Jennison succeeded Nathaniel Jones as representative in the General Court and was reelected each of the next three years. He also served as selectman nine more times before his death in 1741.[115]

Jennison was a man of ambition, and among the ideas he promoted was one that would have a decisive impact on Worcester's future. During his first year in Boston, Jennison petitioned for the creation of a new county in the west, with Worcester as the shire town or county seat.[116] Jennison's wife, Elizabeth, was the sister of Palmer Goulding, who also rose in prominence during the late 1720s. Goulding, too, bought and sold a great deal of land. Just north of the common land on which the meetinghouse stood, Goulding built his house and the shops in which he engaged in such varied occupations as tanner, shoemaker, maltser and curer of meats. Beginning in 1727, Goulding frequently served as assessor, selectman or both, and he would in the 1740s take a turn as representative in Boston.

In April 1731, the General Court made a decision that changed the course of Worcester's life forever. Granting the petition of William Jennison and others, it organized the westerly towns of Middlesex and Suffolk into the county of Worcester, effective July 10, 1731. Although four towns in the new county were larger than Worcester, none was as centrally located. When Lancaster's representative objected to making his town a half-shire with Worcester, on the grounds that court days would corrupt the morals of his neighbors, the General Court followed Samuel Jennison's other suggestion and designated Worcester as the lone shire town, in effect the capital of the county.[117]

Court meetings would bring crowds to the streets of Worcester every few months. They would stimulate local businesses by attracting judges, lawyers, clerks, litigants, traders, speculators and spectators of all sorts, all of whom would begin to think of Worcester as a center for conducting business. Only six years after it had come under Indian attack, the small settlement not only had a county named after it, but also as shire town had been officially elevated above its agricultural neighbors. Perhaps more than any other factor in Worcester's history, those acts of the provincial government set the town on the road to its future as an important commercial and industrial center.

Chapter 3

SHIRE TOWN (1731–1765)

O nce the provincial government had declared Worcester the judicial and administrative capital of a new county, the opportunity opened up to make the town something more than a struggling agricultural community on the edge of English settlement. To this task of transformation a number of important leaders devoted considerable energy over the next decades, none with more determination than the Chandler family of Woodstock, upon whom the royal governor and council in 1731 bestowed the most prestigious and lucrative county offices.

THE CHANDLER FAMILY

John Chandler was appointed chief justice of the Court of Common Pleas, judge of probate and colonel of the county regiment of militia. His son, also named John, was appointed justice of the peace, clerk of the Court of Common Pleas, register of deeds and register of probate.[118]

The Chandlers' ties to Worcester can be traced back through Woodstock to Roxbury, or even back to Nanzing in Essex, the English home of the Reverend John Eliot. A considerable number of Nanzing residents had followed Eliot to Roxbury in the 1630s, including the Ruggles and Chandler families, whose descendants would play important roles in Worcester's history. During their 1674 visit to the new praying towns, when Eliot and Daniel Gookin appointed Nipmuc religious and civil officers at Quinsigamond, they did the same thing at Maanexit and Quantisset, in what later became Woodstock. After King Philip's War, the General Court granted the Woodstock area to the town of Roxbury, which sent out settlers to occupy New Roxbury in 1686. John Chandler, father of the man later appointed to head the Worcester courts, was a leader among the settlers from Roxbury, serving as both deacon and selectman before his death in 1703.[119]

John Chandler's son, the future judge referred to here as John Chandler of Woodstock, served as Woodstock's town clerk, selectman and representative in the

John Chandler of Worcester, patriarch. *Courtesy American Antiquarian Society.*

General Court. He also rose to the rank of colonel in the Middlesex militia, the capacity in which he had responded to the desperate pleas for help from Worcester in the 1720s.[120] In 1727, he had been chosen by his colleagues in the General Court to serve as a member of the council—the upper house of the legislature and advisory body to the governor—and he was in that position the following year when Representative William Jennison of Worcester presented his petition for the creation of a new county.

John Chandler of Woodstock did not transfer his residence to Worcester, but his thirty-eight-year-old son, the clerk of courts, did. John Chandler of Worcester was promptly elected to represent his new town in the House, a post he held, except for one year, from 1732 until he succeeded his father on the council in 1743.[121] He was also chosen virtually every year as both a selectman and an assessor. Although the practice of "plural office-holding" was not unusual in Massachusetts, the concentration of offices in the Chandler family eventually reached extraordinary proportions. The phenomenon was made even more remarkable by the family's unusual structure. Following the death of his first wife, John Chandler of Worcester in 1740 married Sarah Clark Paine, a widow from Bristol, Rhode Island. A year later, his son, John, married his stepsister Dorothy Paine. Eight years after that, Chandler's daughter, Sarah, married her stepbrother and brother-in-law, Timothy Paine.[122]

DEFERENCE AND RESISTANCE

John Chandler and his relatives did not accumulate all of their offices without the active support of many of their fellow citizens. All of the town offices they held were elective, as were the town's seat in the House of Representatives and the county offices of treasurer and register of deeds. In eighteenth-century Massachusetts, it was broadly assumed that social, economic and political prominence should be joined in an elite of ruling families. The right to vote may have been more widely distributed in Massachusetts than anywhere else in the British world, but the right to choose leaders had not replaced traditional assumptions of hierarchy or traditional deference to the established elite.

Timothy Paine and Sarah Chandler Paine, his sister-in-law and his wife. *Courtesy American Antiquarian Society*.

Nevertheless, the townsmen sometimes took small steps to keep the price to the elite of their own predominance as high as possible. In 1733, John Chandler of Worcester, in his role as community patron, offered the town eight pounds to help with the painting and the varnishing of the meetinghouse. The town gratefully acknowledged this gesture, then immediately tried to squeeze a bit more out of the new county aristocracy. Hearing a rumor that the new sheriff, Daniel Gookin (grandson of the founder), had let slip a remark about making a similar contribution, the town promptly appointed a two-man committee to visit Gookin and find out "what he will give toward said coloring and varnishing."[123]

Even when the new justices began to meet as a court of law, they quickly discovered that at least some of the inhabitants of the region were not prepared to accord them the respect they considered their due. The first person to answer charges before the Court of General Sessions of the Peace was Solomon Johnson of Shrewsbury. Charged with breach of the peace by striking a man in the face, Johnson behaved in what the court found to be "a very insolent, rude and unbecoming manner both to the Court and officers thereof." For striking his accuser in the face, Johnson was fined twenty shillings; for his "rude and insulting behaviour" toward the new officials, he was fined twice as much.[124]

Although justices of the peace had full authority to adjudicate minor charges, their decisions could be appealed to a jury trial when the justices sat together as the Court of General Sessions of the Peace. In 1734, the first five men who appealed from the justices to the jury in Worcester paid a heavy price.

Samuel Terry of Mendon was originally found guilty of drunkenness and ordered to pay a fine of five shilling, plus costs and fees. When he appealed, the jury found him not guilty. The court responded by setting Terry's costs and fees at seven pounds, nearly thirty times the original fine. Ebenezer Albee of Mendon, appealing a conviction and fine of ten shillings, was found not guilty by the jury and then taxed fourteen pounds, eight shillings in costs and fees. Three other men paid a similar penalty for appealing and being found not guilty. Thomas Newell of Dudley suffered the greatest penalty, more than forty times his original fine. The punishment may have been especially severe because in this case, the jury had overturned a guilty finding made by Justice of the Peace John Chandler of Worcester.[125] People who resented the authority of the new court could not have been appeased by the justices' practice of dividing among themselves in open session the money they imposed as court costs.[126]

PUBLIC BUILDINGS, PUBLIC SCHOOLS

Although the first sessions of the courts were held in the town's meetinghouse,[127] the judges, not the town meeting, were in control. At least one early session was in the home of Judge William Jennison. On that occasion, September 21, 1731, the Court of General Sessions ordered the construction of a prison on land north of property given to the county by Jennison. Until the prison was built, the court accepted Jennison's offer of the use of his house, provided a "suitable cage" be built in the back section, adjoining a well-fenced prison yard.[128]

In 1732, the court ordered that a courthouse be constructed on the land Jennison had offered, at the north end of the principal street in the village center, the Connecticut or Country Road. With this decision the center of Worcester was fixed between the meetinghouse on the south end of the main street and the courthouse on the north. The location of the courthouse also would greatly enhance the value of Samuel Jennison's adjacent lands. The judges knew very well that the creation of a county, like the creation of a town, promised financial rewards to large property owners. The court therefore sought contributions for the new building from landowners, especially absentees who had "an interest in lands in the county, and especially in the town of Worcester, which, by that town's being made the shire town, are greatly advanced."[129]

Another item on the agenda of Worcester's new leaders was the provision of respectable public schools. That required action by the town meeting, and it was in this arena more than in any other that the traditional farmers put up a spirited resistance to the innovators.

Although all Massachusetts towns were required to provide basic instruction in reading and writing, the Worcester town meeting did not take up the question of schooling at all during its first three years as a self-governing town. In April 1726, after the ordination of the second minister, the town had for the first time directed the selectmen to "provide a sufficient school." "Sufficient" meant good enough to meet the demands of the law. In truth, the town was that day, with some reluctance, dealing with two of its neglected obligations, under the threat of fines in both instances. The second issue was the provision of a public stock of ammunition, which the town voted to purchase "as the law directs." The selectmen, made up principally of members of the Rice faction, immediately after the school vote contracted with Jonas Rice to teach whatever children were sent him to read and write.

Under the agreement, parents would ostensibly send children to Rice's home on Sagatabscot (Grafton) Hill, southeast of the village, where he would teach such as came to him during the next eight months. Naming him as schoolmaster in his own house may, in fact, have been a stratagem for getting around the law. What the town would pay the schoolmaster was not stipulated in the agreement, nor is there any record of money being raised for school purposes or paid to Rice for teaching.

On December 19, 1726, four days after the expiration of Rice's term as schoolmaster, the town dug in its heels and reversed both actions that had been taken the previous March. It voted not to have a school and not to provide a town stock of ammunition. Both March votes had required spending town money to meet demands made by outsiders, and both December votes expressed defiance of those same authorities. During 1727, the town again made nothing more than a gesture in the direction of education, and it was later fined by the county court for failing to keep a proper school.[130] The town in September 1731 voted to maintain a "free school" for the ensuing year, but required that it be a moving school. A schoolmaster would spend a few months in one section of the town, then move on to another. Just as the new courts and their associated dignitaries were preparing to move into the shire town center, the town meeting was voting to keep the school out of the center for most of the year.

Although Worcester by 1732 finally had a real schoolmaster and regular schooling, it still lacked three things the leaders of any self-respecting shire town thought their central village should have: a proper schoolhouse, a continuous writing (or "English") school and a grammar school, in which the sons of leading families could learn enough Latin to gain admission to Harvard or Yale College.

In May 1733, with John Chandler of Worcester in his already customary role as moderator, the town voted at last to build a schoolhouse as close as possible to the center of the town, and it appointed Chandler as surveyor to determine precisely where the center was. Due in part to delays in determining the location, it was not until June 1738 that the town was able to order the school built between the courthouse and "the bridge below the fulling mill."

After six years of effort by Chandler and his supporters, probably backed by Benjamin Flagg and his, the shire town got its schoolhouse. During many more decades, school finances in Worcester would divide the residents of the town center from the farmers who lived miles away from them in all directions. The influential people in the center wanted a schoolmaster for the full year, rather than the three months normally allowed them under the moving school system. They also wanted the grammar school Worcester was required by law to maintain. The inhabitants of the outskirts, on the other hand, wanted a moving school, which allowed them two or three months of schooling in their districts. They sometimes had to settle for a system in which their share of the school taxes would be made available to them to cover the costs of such schooling as they could provide in their own districts. The outlying farmers also wanted no part of the cost of maintaining a grammar school for the benefit of the town's aristocracy.

THE FLIGHT OF THE SCOTCH-IRISH

The role of the Chandler family is more difficult to discern in the controversy that flared in the 1730s over the continuing desire of the Scotch-Irish Presbyterians to establish an independent ministry. All that is clear is that leaders of the Scotch-Irish eventually formed a close working relationship with John Chandler of Worcester.

After more than a decade in Worcester, the Presbyterians by 1730 had not achieved what they considered an acceptable place in the community. Soon after the establishment of the county in 1731, they stopped attending Aaron Burr's sermons. In 1734, four prominent Worcester men presented the county court with a list of twenty men, all Scotch-Irish, who had been absenting themselves from "the public worship of God on Lord's days at the usual place of meeting."[131] The Presbyterians had secured the services of a second minister, the Reverend William Johnston, had ordained him as their pastor and were holding separate meetings.[132] Scotch-Irish settlers living in Rutland and Shrewsbury were fined for traveling to Worcester on the Sabbath, even though they argued that travel was necessary to reach what Matthew Barber of Shrewsbury described as "a place of public worship in Worcester where he found by experience 'twas most for his spiritual advantage to attend." Three Rutland men who refused to pay fines and court costs for traveling on the Sabbath spent eight days in jail before changing their minds.[133]

Such harassment did not deter the Scotch-Irish from maintaining their own ministry. They even sought the approval of the town, petitioning in late 1736 or early 1737 for relief from the taxes they were paying to support the ministry of Aaron Burr. In turning them down, the town meeting questioned the Presbyterians' claims to "principles of conscience" and suggested that their withdrawal was due more to "some irregular views and motives which would be unworthy for us to countenance." The town admitted that it was worried about the increased burden Burr's salary would place on the remaining taxpayers should the Presbyterians be allowed to withdraw their support, but it finally rested its denial on the contention that having two ministers would tend "to breed and cherish divisions and parties greatly destructive to our civil and religious interests, [and] the peace, tranquility and happiness of the town."[134]

The Presbyterians were no more successful in an appeal to the legislature for exemption from taxation for the Congregational ministry. Although Quakers in 1737 were granted such a waiver, the House in June and again in December dismissed petitions from "the committee of the Presbyterian Inhabitants of the Town of Worcester."[135]

Meanwhile, the Presbyterians proceeded with plans to build a meetinghouse of their own, north of the village center. Some of their Congregational neighbors decided to make their opposition forcefully and emphatically evident. One night, while most of the community slept, they demolished the half-built house of worship and carried the materials off into the darkness.[136]

For many of the Scotch-Irish immigrants, life in Worcester had, after nearly two decades, become intolerable. John Clark, the leading petitioner to the legislature in 1737, became in February 1738 one of the first proprietors of the Scotch-Irish community of Colrain, fifty miles to the northwest of Worcester. In October, with John Chandler of Worcester as their clerk, two of the remaining Scotch-Irish—Robert Peables and James Thornton—agreed to buy from Jonathan Stoddard of Northampton the tract of land in Hampshire County that later became the town of Pelham. Peables and Thornton would each be responsible for raising half the sale price by selling shares in the enterprise, and each contracted to settle twenty families on the land within three years.[137]

There could be no doubt about the character of the migration from Worcester. Peables and Thornton were to recruit "such as were Inhabitants of the Kingdom of Ireland or their descendants, being Protestants, and none to be admitted but such as bring good and undeniable credentials or certificates of their being persons of good conversation and of the Presbyterian persuasion as used in the Church of Scotland and conform to the discipline thereof." Pelham was to be a Presbyterian refuge.[138]

The meetings continued to be held in Worcester until August 6, 1740, when the proprietors gathered at their new settlement and chose James Thornton as moderator and William Gray as clerk. Free at last, they began immediately to make arrangements for building their long-coveted meetinghouse.[139]

At least one-third of the Worcester Scotch-Irish, probably more, joined the flight to Colrain, Pelham and other settlements.[140] Their countrymen who remained in Worcester were slowly absorbed into the town church and into the Anglo-American population. In 1746, when the fifty male members of the church in Worcester signed a new covenant, only one, Robert Barber, was Scotch-Irish. In the community at large, however, inter-ethnic mixing proceeded more rapidly. A careful student of Worcester's early families has estimated that by the American Revolution, about half the residents of the town were at least partly of Scotch-Irish descent.[141]

THE GREAT AWAKENING AND TURMOIL IN THE WORCESTER CHURCH

The Great Awakening was a powerful revival of religious consciousness and sensibility that swept over many parts of the British world in the middle years of the eighteenth century. To its adherents, known as "New Lights," this great surge in piety was dramatic evidence of a special work of the Holy Spirit, stirring up stagnant souls, depriving men and women of the complacency with which they customarily regarded—or disregarded—the ultimate fates of their souls. To its opponents, the revival was hardly a work of the Spirit; it was, rather, the misguided enterprise of dangerous men. "Old Lights" acknowledged that these forceful evangelical preachers, many of them roaming from town to town, knew how to send their listeners into temporary fits of religious fervor. However, the Old Lights complained, the revivalists lacked a decent respect for the religious institutions earlier generations had carefully established to sustain the community's spiritual life over the long run.

The most famous preacher of the Awakening was George Whitefield, an Anglican clergyman who rode into Worcester in the company of Governor Jonathan Belcher

Leading Great Awakening evangelist George Whitefield preached at Worcester in 1740. *Courtesy American Antiquarian Society.*

during the evening of October 14, 1740. The twenty-five-year-old evangelist and the governor, like all dignitaries who visited Worcester, stayed at the home of John Chandler, where, according to Whitefield, they were "kindly entertained." The next day the great evangelist preached outside the meetinghouse on the Worcester Common, where he was heard by thousands.[142]

For several years, the conduct of Worcester's Reverend Isaac Burr had been a matter of growing complaint. How much his problems had to do with the Great Awakening is open to question. One witness to the tensions and divisions caused by the Awakening was David Hall, the New Light minister of Sutton, who preached in Worcester in January 1743. Hall noted in his diary that Burr, though he had given his permission, "seemed not pleased at my coming, as I am informed." By the next month, the Worcester pastor was refusing "urgent requests" that Hall be invited back to preach. The Sutton pastor bemoaned "the prejudice of Mr. B. who is, I fear, too much a stranger to the power of godliness, or otherwise, surely, he would rejoice in having his people in concern about their souls, and in the help of such ministers as wish their salvation."[143]

The precise sources of Isaac Burr's problems in Worcester are impossible to determine. A majority of church members in 1744 wrote out their complaints against the pastor, but the list does not survive. Disagreements over visiting preachers undoubtedly played some role early in the dispute, but the subsequent behavior of the town and church suggest that Burr's lack of enthusiasm for the Awakening was not the only, or even the central, issue behind his parishioners' discontent.[144]

After failing to resolve matters privately, Burr faced a council of churches.[145] The surviving records do not reveal in detail what transpired next, but the pastor may have helped resolve matters by asking for dismission. In any case, the council concluded by advising that Burr be dismissed, and the church took that step in November 1744, effective the following March. The records do not show that the church divided into Old Lights and New Lights in the Burr controversy. Nevertheless, the search for Burr's successor was inevitably influenced by the two most important issues separating most of the Whitefield followers in New England from their opponents. One was simply their approval or disapproval of the emotional preaching and itinerant habits of the revivalists. The second was a question of theology. As expressed by Whitefield, and more definitively by Jonathan Edwards of Northampton, the revival was a reinvigoration not only of religious feeling, but also of orthodox Calvinist theology.

The Calvinist creed, carried to New England by the Puritans, included the doctrines of election and predestination, holding that humans had no ability to affect the ultimate destiny of their souls. The belief that humans could achieve salvation through moral living, or the performance of good works—a notion increasingly popular, even among the clergy—was denounced by most New Lights as the doctrine of "Arminianism," named after a Dutch anti-Calvinist, Jacob Arminius. Although Isaac Burr's troubles seem to some extent to have involved New Light demands for a more energetic style of preaching in Worcester, the search for his replacement was not dominated by New Light revivalists. In fact, the town meeting—as distinct from the church—was led by the Chandlers and by Benjamin Flagg Jr. It repeatedly expressed a preference for candidates who were Arminian in their theology and Old Light in their criticism of the revival. Meanwhile the church, under the continued leadership of the Rice family, insisted upon Calvinist orthodoxy. During more than two years of controversy, the strong Calvinist faction in the church managed to hold off attempts to settle an Arminian pastor, while the town meeting prevented the settlement of an orthodox minister.[146]

After a protracted series of church and town meetings, by the fall of 1746 the community was considering two principal candidates, Thaddeus Maccarty of Boston and Jonathan Mayhew of Martha's Vineyard. Maccarty was not a partisan of the Old Lights or of the New Lights. He took a public position against itinerancy, and he was

Thaddeus Maccarty, Worcester pastor.
Courtesy American Antiquarian Society.

Calvinist in theology. Despite these Old Light attitudes, he was interested in the ideas and techniques of George Whitefield. Ordained pastor of a deeply Old Light church in Kingston in 1742, he had been dismissed in November 1745, largely due to his open-mindedness toward the revival.

A year after that dismissal, Maccarty was in Worcester for four trial Sabbaths, and his preaching seems to have made a very favorable impression. The extreme Arminianism of Jonathan Mayhew, his chief rival, may have helped to make Maccarty's own tolerant orthodoxy more acceptable to a community that had seemed bent on hiring an Arminian. When the church met on January 19, 1747, forty-two votes were cast for Thaddeus Maccarty and only two for other candidates. Perhaps unexpectedly, the church had reached a consensus. It asked the selectmen to assemble the town.[147]

By the time the town met on January 27, 1747, stories about Maccarty's troubles in Kingston had begun to raise doubts. The meeting appointed John Chandler and two other church members to ask the candidate for details about what had happened in Kingston. On February 9, 1747, the long search for a pastor came to an end. After hearing Chandler's report and before proceeding to a vote, the town meeting took official notice, not only of documents brought from Kingston, but also of "a paper signed this day" by the candidate. The paper Maccarty was required to sign must have addressed a crucial issue still causing some of the townsmen to hesitate. It may very well have been a pledge not to tolerate itineracy. Whatever Maccarty signed, the gesture achieved its purpose. When the question of concurrence was finally put before the town, it passed with only three negative votes.

On June 10, 1747, thirty-one months after the decision to dismiss Isaac Burr, Thaddeus Maccarty was installed as the third pastor of the church in Worcester. He would serve as the community's only resident clergyman until his death in 1784.[148]

"Constant Schooling" and John Adams in Worcester

On the school front, the would-be reshapers of a new Worcester continued to make incremental progress, though they faced frequent setbacks. The arrangement reached in 1740, whereby the residents of the center would by private contributions meet the costs of a grammar school, was apparently allowed to lapse.

In 1745, in the midst of its search for a new minister, the town had again been threatened with fines for failure to keep a grammar school. In response, a new arrangement was made, both to provide a grammar school and to free the outlying farmers from the costs of schooling in the center. The town decided that people living in four outlying quarters would have their school tax money returned to them, to be used for the education of their children, under the supervision of a committee. The inhabitants of the center were to use their share of the school tax for a writing school, and also pay enough to keep a grammar school at the schoolhouse. The extra money was to be provided "by a Subscription or Some other method."[149]

The outlying families, deprived of the moving school, probably found little consolation in the permission granted them to send any of their children for instruction at the grammar school without paying anything for the privilege. Few, if any, of their sons were destined for liberal educations. For the time being at least, the ambitious families in the town center would continue to bear the costs of the grammar school on behalf of the whole community. In return, the taxpayers of the center were freed from the moving school and could use the taxes they paid to provide schooling in their vicinity throughout the year.

In May 1747, just a month before the installation of Thaddeus Maccarty, a motion to restore the moving school was narrowly defeated, but in 1748 educational itineracy was restored, leaving the center with only three months of instruction. In 1751, again after "considerable debate," the town meeting refused to grant money for the repair of the center schoolhouse or for construction of a new one. In 1752, the center got control of its own schooling again, when the school taxes of everyone living within a mile and a half of the schoolhouse were turned over to the center, provided the residents of the area also keep a grammar school for the town.[150]

This time, the advocates of "constant" schooling in the town center managed to hold off the moving school for a full seven years. During three of those years the schoolmaster was John Adams of Braintree. In 1755, Worcester's pastor, Thaddeus Maccarty, attended the Harvard commencement in Cambridge and talked the nineteen-

John Adams, schoolmaster and law student. *Courtesy American Antiquarian Society.*

year-old graduate into moving to Worcester to serve as master of the grammar school.[151]

Adams was debating with himself which of the learned professions—medicine, law or the church—would be most suited to his talents and ambitions. After a year in Worcester, he resolved to become a lawyer. James Putnam, who had opened a law practice in the town in 1749, agreed to become Adams's mentor, and the young schoolmaster moved in with Putnam and his wife Elizabeth, a daughter of John Chandler. Adams continued keeping the town school while boarding with the Putnams and studying law for the next two years.[152]

One of the sons of Thaddeus Maccarty, many years later, recalled that John Adams had not been "one of the best of schoolmasters." Adams allegedly spent most of his classroom time sitting at his desk, writing. When not writing, he seemed "absorbed in profound thought, and abstracted from any thing about him." Schooling went on only because the young master assigned his students to teach one another.[153]

Adams's social life brought him into regular association with the political, social and economic elite living near the center of the village. He was in Worcester while the second generation of the Chandlers was coming into its inheritance, and Adams moved constantly in their social circle. As the Chandlers flourished, other traditional centers of local influence were fading. Jonas Rice served his last term as selectman in 1740, the year Gershom Rice and others in the Pakachoag neighborhood first petitioned to be set aside as part of a new town, an effort that resulted during the 1770s in the creation of the town of Ward, later renamed Auburn. Though they occasionally served as selectmen, the younger Rices did not achieve the prominence the founding brothers had once held in the community.[154]

Constant Warfare

The Chandler family's virtual monopoly on high militia commands added greatly to the family's prestige in an age of almost constant warfare in North America. While

Worcester church members were taking steps to remove their pastor in 1744, France and Britain were entering the War of the Austrian Succession, known to the American colonists as King George's War. Worcester was soon swept up in the excitement aroused by Governor William Shirley's bold decision in 1745 to send a colonial force to seize, with the help of the British navy, the French fortress of Louisbourg. Command of the fort, located on Cape Breton Island at the mouth of the St. Lawrence River, would give the British full control over the North Atlantic fisheries as well as a chance to choke off supplies and reinforcements bound for New France.[155]

Both New Light revivalists and Old Light traditionalists joined George Whitefield in encouraging the Louisbourg expedition as part of the ongoing, universal battle against popery and the antichrist. Among the three thousand men who volunteered for the Louisbourg expedition was Adonijah Rice, the first child born among the permanent English settlers of Worcester. He served in a company of rangers and survived; Benjamin Gleason lost his life outside the walls of Louisbourg during the siege that led to a French surrender on June 17, 1745.[156]

Massachusetts males between sixteen and sixty were required to belong to local militia units. Except in the most extreme emergency, it was not practical to march those units off in a body, leaving the community with weak defenses and insufficient manpower to sustain its economic life. During times of war, Massachusetts would raise special armies, usually once a year. Authorized by a gubernatorial commission, a commanding general and his subordinate officers would have to begin by recruiting their forces. In each town, the militia train bands would be mustered, and voluntarily or through conscription the town's quota of men would be enlisted. Those conscripted were allowed to find a substitute or to pay a fee to be released from their obligation.[157] In August 1746, while Worcester was still inching its way toward a ministerial settlement, Fort Massachusetts, on the upper Hoosick River, twenty-five miles east of Albany, fell to a combined force of French and Indians. Before a relief party could be sent west, the appearance of a French fleet off the Massachusetts coast threw Boston into a panic. When Worcester men assembled for a regular town meeting on September 23, they took only enough time to direct the selectmen to supply the pulpit for the time being. The meeting then broke up hurriedly so the militia could respond to Governor Shirley's call for men to resist a rumored French invasion.[158]

In 1748, Great Britain and France signed the Treaty of Aix-la-Chapelle, returning Louisbourg to the French, to the consternation of Americans, and especially of New Englanders. Though Louisbourg was now clearly a French possession, the line between British and French territories was in dispute over much of the rest of eastern North America. By 1754, Anglo-American encounters with the French and their native allies were setting off the Seven Years' War, declared in 1756 and concluded with the Treaty of Paris in 1763.

In 1757, a powerful French force under the marquis de Montcalm laid siege to Fort William Henry at the southern end of Lake George. The British garrison, which included eight hundred Massachusetts men, held out for only six days.[159] The shocking news traveled overland, reaching Worcester on its way to Boston. When a messenger arrived, looking for Colonel John Chandler at the law office of James Putnam, just south of the meetinghouse, law student John Adams became one of the first in town to learn what had happened. He led the courier to the Chandler farm, northeast of the village center at Chandler Hill, later called Bell Hill or Belmont Hill.

Residents of the center poured out of their houses and shops as the dramatic news spread, setting off panic and despair. As Adams recalled it, people screamed that the country had been "betrayed by the English—they had sold us to the French—we were undone." The consequences of being taken by the French would be horrible: "They would make Catholics of us all." Colonel Chandler, a member of the council, forwarded the report immediately to the governor, along with his recommendation that ten thousand men be called out in Massachusetts and set on the march.[160]

In this emergency, officers did not muster the militia to recruit individuals into a special army. This time, men of the town marched westward in their own local companies, in a military organization that reflected the social structure of the community. Colonel John Chandler Jr. led one company, as well as the whole regiment. James Goodwin, an extensive landholder who would serve as selectman in 1759, was captain in the company under Chandler. Noah Jones, forty-five-year-old son-in-law of Deacon Daniel Heywood, was lieutenant; David Bancroft, forty-one, was ensign. Another company of fifty-four marched under John Chandler's brother, Major Gardiner Chandler. Their captain was John Curtis, forty-nine, selectman in 1754, 1755 and 1760. The lieutenant was Luke Brown, forty-six, an innholder at the north end of the village center. The company's ensign was Asa Flagg, twenty-seven, son of Benjamin Flagg Jr. The townsmen in arms traveled over one hundred miles to Sheffield before word came that Montcalm had decided not to advance farther. Except for a few men detached to garrison duty in Stockbridge, the infantrymen were released from service on August 8.[161]

Late in September, Lord Loudoun, the British commander, ordered Colonel Chandler to raise 150 men from the Worcester county regiment to reinforce his army. Once again, town milita companies marched in a body, along with men mobilized by other communities. This time they were under the command of Colonel Chandler's son-in-law and John Adams's legal mentor, Major James Putnam. The county force of 300 reached Westfield, where it waited to rendezvous with men from Hampshire County. While there, word came that the latest alarm had passed, and the troops once again returned home.[162]

The rank and importance of the elite families were reinforced in another unmistakable way during the war. Only they were in a social position to entertain British officers when the opportunity arose. During the 1758 campaign, forces under General Jeffrey Amherst succeeded in taking Louisbourg, as the New Englanders had done thirteen years earlier. Following the conquest, Amherst landed his army at Boston and marched to Albany, stopping for several days in Worcester with an army of 4,500 men, whom he encamped on a hill west of the courthouse. As Adams remembered it, "The officers were very social, spent their evenings and took their suppers with such of the Inhabitants as were able to invite, and entertained us with their music and their dances. Many of them were Scotchmen in their plaids and their music was delightful;

even the bagpipe was not disagreeable." General Amherst, inevitably, lodged with Colonel John Chandler.[163]

In 1759, Amherst's forces recaptured both Ticonderoga and Crown Point on Lake Champlain. Brigadier General James Wolfe, meanwhile, sailed up the St. Lawrence to Quebec, landed troops on the Plains of Abraham and, while losing his life, won a spectacular victory. A year later, the governor general of New France surrendered Montreal, ending the war in Canada and on most of the northern colonial front after six years of fighting. By the Treaty of Paris in 1763, Quebec became a possession of Great Britain.

ARISTOCRACY ATTACKED

Throughout the long war, Worcester had mustered its troops and sent them into service, had mourned British losses and celebrated British triumphs and had coped with both the costs and the profits of accommodating large numbers of troops. On the surface, the Chandler family continued to reign, though in ways hardly anticipated, things had begun to change. Just before and during the war, new men had been coming to town with new ideas that could be used to revive the tradition of opposition and redirect it. For some of them, opposition to the Chandlers became a political way of life.

In 1756, Gardiner Chandler notified the selectmen that he had taken into his home the family of Nathan Baldwin of Medford. A saddler by trade, Baldwin was staying temporarily with Chandler while getting himself established in Worcester. He was a self-educated man with strong opinions, remembered by John Adams as a voracious reader of "deistical books." Deists, inspired by the progress of modern science, were part of the eighteenth-century rationalist movement, known as the Enlightenment. They believed in a supreme being, but not in the mysteries of the Christian faith. They accepted the existence of a rational creator, who had endowed the natural universe with laws that could be discovered by the careful use of human reason. They rejected such central Christian beliefs as the fall of humanity through the sin of Adam and Eve and its redemption through the sacrificial death of Jesus.[164]

Though he had not had the advantages of a college education, Baldwin, thirty-six years old in 1756, loved to discuss religious and political ideas. He was soon serving the town in such minor offices as tithing man, warden and surveyor of wheat and flour. As tithing man, it was his duty to inspect houses licensed to sell liquor, as well as to prevent unnecessary travel on the Sabbath. Worcester created the office of warden in 1761 "to see the Lord's Day duly kept agreeable to law." While the outspoken deist probably had little enthusiasm for some of his official responsibilities, he could use his posts of trust to extend his range of local acquaintances while thinking about how his intellectual and political talents might be more fully engaged, and more adequately recognized.[165]

Ephraim Doolittle, born in 1725, apparently came to Worcester from Palmer soon after his marriage in 1750 and set himself up as a hatter in the village center.[166] He also developed a close relationship with Nathan Baldwin. Like Baldwin, Doolittle was a deist, and the men had other traits in common. Both lived and carried on small businesses in the center of Worcester; neither could realistically aspire to the honor or to the income of the higher political offices. Since they lacked access to the governor and his circle, patronage appointments were quite beyond their reach, and the elective offices that provided an income, such as county treasurer and register of deeds, were as fully controlled by the Chandler clan as were the appointive positions.[167]

During John Adams's stay in the town, Doolittle and Baldwin frequently sought him out for intellectual conversations, perhaps measuring their self-taught learning against that of the college-trained schoolmaster and law student. As readers of Enlightenment literature, the two tradesmen had absorbed a great deal of theory about the natural equality of all men and about the equal rights they could claim by the mere fact that they were human. Adams found them both "great sticklers for equality as well as deism."[168]

When they looked around Worcester, Baldwin and Doolittle saw not equality, but the domination of the community by a privileged aristocracy. In true Enlightenment spirit, they set out to reform their society. The crucial means they settled upon was the power of the vote. Although virtually all adult males in Worcester owned enough property to vote, they exercised that right over and over again to elect Chandlers and their kin to major offices. This tradition of deference gave a form of democratic blessing to what Doolittle and Baldwin regarded as an unnatural hierarchy.

Part of their early strategy was to select a person who, while not a member of the Chandler clan, might attract the support of voters due to his evident qualifications for office. As they sized up potential candidates, the budding political managers set their sights on the promising young student of the law, John Adams. In 1758, as Adams was completing his apprenticeship in James Putnam's office, Baldwin and Doolittle paid one of their frequent visits. At first, they merely encouraged him to consider settling in Worcester, where there would be plenty of legal business for him, and where his "character was fair and well esteemed by all sorts of people in the town and through the county." Finally, they came to the point. They wished, in Adams's words, "to get me chosen at the next election which was very near, Register of Deeds."

The proposition was at the very least audacious. The sitting register, who had held the office for twenty-seven years, was no less a personage than John Chandler of Worcester, the sixty-five-year-old patriarch of the clan, member of the governor's council, judge of the Court of Common Pleas, judge of probate and commander of the county militia.

Of course, Chandler's formidable public profile was for Baldwin and Doolittle precisely the point. It was, they told Adams, because "the Chandler family has engrossed almost all the public offices and employment in the town and county" that "they wished to select some person qualified to share with them in these honors and emoluments."

Adams, no stickler for equality, declined the offer. He went further, and rejected the premises on which it had been made. The Chandlers, he said, were worthy of the offices they held and were carrying out their duties responsibly. He did not envy them their good fortune, nor did he wish to set himself up in opposition to them, especially given his personal relationship with James Putnam and his wife, the daughter of the very register of deeds Baldwin and Doolittle were seeking to depose.[169] Though Adams went back to Braintree, and on to a political career beyond even his imagining, his would-be campaign managers in Worcester did not abandon their aspirations.

Before long, the demands and opportunities of war provided Ephraim Doolittle an avenue to leadership and to greater respectability. He received a captain's commission and served with Amherst in the 1759 campaign that opened the Champlain Valley and set the stage for the fall of Montreal. After returning to Worcester, Doolittle began his public service in 1761 at a fairly prestigious level, serving with John Chandler Jr. on a committee to settle accounts with the town treasurer, Timothy Paine. In 1762, he again served on a committee with John Chandler Jr., this time to "renew and ascertain the bounds of public lands."[170] Meanwhile, the concentration of offices in the Chandler family was reaching new extremes. In 1761, thirty years after the establishment of the county, whenever John Chandler of Worcester met with his stepson Timothy Paine and his sons John Jr. and Gardiner, the public officials present included a member of the Massachusetts Council, the town's representative in the General Court, the chief justice of the Court of Common Pleas, the clerk of the court, the judge of probate, the register of probate, the register of deeds, the county sheriff, the county treasurer, the moderators of the town meeting, two of the town's selectmen, two of the assessors, the town clerk, the town treasurer and three colonels of the county militia. That did not discourage Ephraim Doolittle. In fact, it inspired him. In 1763, he took an important step forward, joining John Chandler Jr., Timothy Paine and two others as a member of the board of selectmen. He also served as surveyor of boards, shingles, hoops and staves. Though he was returned to the board of selectmen in 1764 and 1765, Doolittle did not shun the lower offices that brought him into contact with ordinary people in the daily course of business in the village center. He continued to serve as surveyor of boards, shingles, hoops and staves and also took on the responsibilities of clerk of the market. His friend and ally, the saddler Nathan Baldwin, served regularly as sealer of leather as well as surveyor of wheat and flour.

In 1765, something happened that must have been puzzling to those who paid only cursory attention to Worcester politics. Ephraim Doolittle was elected to what had been the Chandler-Paine seat in the House of Representatives. It happened in stages. After representing Worcester in Boston since 1752, John Chandler Jr. in 1755 had been succeeded as representative by his stepbrother, Timothy Paine. In 1763, following the death of the patriarch, John Chandler of Worcester, the legislature "elevated" the town's representative, Timothy Paine, to the council to succeed his stepfather. John Chandler Jr. was then elected by Worcester voters to the House. Three years later, the family's fortunes reached new heights as John Chandler Jr. joined Paine on the council. For the first time, two members of the clan served together at the peak of the provincial political system.

The legislature then asked Worcester whether it wished to fill the vacancy in the House created by Chandler's elevation to the council. The town did so wish, and in September 1765, in accordance with the vote of his townsmen, Ephraim Doolittle took over the Worcester seat in the House of Representatives. He promptly abandoned the conservative political course Paine and the Chandlers had charted. Where Worcester's first family had been loyal supporters of the royal governors in their political battles with the House, Doolittle joined such popular leaders as Samuel Adams, James Otis Jr., Joseph Hawley and John Hancock in resisting measures designed to tighten British control over the province and the empire.[171]

Having sent a new man to the House, Worcester in October 1765 instructed him not to join in any measure that might indicate support of the Stamp Act, by which Parliament was seeking to raise from the colonies some of the costs of maintaining British troops in North America. Doolittle and his followers, imitating Samuel Adams in the Boston town meeting, had begun a process that would turn the Worcester meeting into an arena for political agitation over matters far beyond the authority of the town.

The representatives of the old order still had their supporters. When Worcester chose its board of selectmen for 1766, it included Chandler and Paine, as well as Doolittle. It also elected two new selectmen with roots deep in Worcester's past, but with current ties to the dissident Ephraim Doolittle. One was the third Benjamin Flagg, who at the age of forty-two had not previously broken through the wall of Chandlers to succeed his father as sheriff, representative or selectman. The other was thirty-five-year-old Samuel Curtis, great-grandson of Joseph Curtis, whose brother Ephraim a century earlier had been the first Englishman to put up a building in the proposed plantation of Quinsigamond. Samuel's only previous service to the town had been in the offices of fence viewer, hogreeve and tithing man.[172]

In May, the anti-Chandler forces dramatically escalated their attack. After reelecting Doolittle as representative, the town meeting appointed Nathan Baldwin, Benjamin Flagg and Jonathan Stone to prepare instructions for him. The committee based their work on a set of model instructions that had been published in Boston. However, the instructions Worcester adopted make it clear that in 1766 the primary target of the local insurgency was not imperial taxation, but instead the system of patronage and privilege that allowed a small circle of men to rule over their neighbors in provincial Massachusetts. The instructions also make clear that in attacking the system, Worcester townsmen were attacking their leading family.[173]

Doolittle was instructed first to do what he could to prevent the election to the council of any person holding a judicial or military office under the governor. The only examples of such officials cited by the Boston Sons of Liberty were "judges of the superior court, secretary, etc." Worcester also specified judges of probate, registers of probate, secretaries or clerks of the courts and sheriffs. In adopting this revised list, the town was not only urging the General Court to exclude from the council the two sitting members from Worcester—John Chandler Jr. and Timothy Paine—it was also going out of its way to proclaim the unsuitability of two of Chandler's sons: Clark, who had succeeded Paine as register of probate, and Gardiner, who had succeeded his father as sheriff.

The town's second instruction to Doolittle echoed the Boston Sons of Liberty in calling for the opening of the legislature to public scrutiny, the lowering of fees paid to public officials and an end to "monopolizing of public offices." However, Worcester added a provision calling for the dismissal from the legislature of any representative who received a commission from the governor, unless and until he had been reelected by his constituents. The town also added an instruction that took dead aim at the institution that had annoyed common people in the town for decades. The instruction called for the repeal of the law requiring towns to maintain grammar schools, and proposed that there be only one grammar school required in each county. Finally, Worcester added an instruction calling for a law to prevent bribery and corruption in the election of representatives.

The instructions were strikingly republican in spirit, reflecting the assumption that there was an inherent conflict between the holders of power and the people they ruled. The protection of the people's rights, the townsmen believed, required new laws exposing legislative deliberations to public observation and preventing men who received gubernatorial appointments from continuing to claim that they represented the people.

If Timothy Paine, John Chandler and their allies thought they were being accused of self-aggrandizement at the expense of their neighbors, they were hearing correctly. Thirty-five years after the establishment of the county, the ruling circle was facing open revolt in the shire town.

Chapter 4

REVOLUTION (1765–1777)

Despite the appearance of local opponents, the Chandler family continued to be entrusted with major elective offices in the years after 1765. They continued to be respected and trusted as influential men who could advocate for Worcester at the highest levels of provincial power. Timothy Paine was elected register of deeds every year until 1775. John Chandler Jr. (known as John Chandler following his father's death in 1762) also was chosen as moderator of every town meeting, and the two stepbrothers continued to be selectmen. Each year two or three selectmen who shared the political leanings of Doolittle and Baldwin served with them, but the Chandlers were considered the first family of the county as well as the town.

WORCESTER POLITICS AND IMPERIAL POLITICS

Leaders of the Worcester insurgency increasingly linked their homegrown disputes to the developing controversy between Great Britain and the American Colonies. The antiaristocratic instructions of 1766 had been focused on the internal workings of the Massachusetts political system. Those adopted by the town in May 1767 began to address issues involving American relations with Britain. Joshua Bigelow was to encourage "harmony and good will between Great Britain and this province" by maintaining "a steady and firm attachment to English liberty and the charter rights of this province."

"Liberty" was fast becoming the central and dynamic idea of the struggle. It was impossible to predict how this would affect colonial thinking, as was dramatically displayed in Bigelow's second instruction. Worcester directed its representative "to put an end to that unchristian and impolitic practice of making slaves of the human species in this province." A 1770 tax list shows there were eight slaves in Worcester, three of them owned by John Chandler and two by Timothy Paine.[174] The town told Bigelow to oppose the election to the council of any persons who would resist a law abolishing slavery, or who had not "distinguished themselves in the defence of our liberty."

The instructions also forged a triumphal link between the struggle for liberty in the empire and the long struggle of Worcester taxpayers to be free of the grammar school. Bigelow was ordered to try to "relieve the people of this province from the great burden of supporting so many Latin grammar schools," because spending tax money on those schools rather than on the English writing schools prevented young people "from attaining such a degree of English learning as is necessary to retain the freedom of any state." Joshua Bigelow was an effective successor to Doolittle as a leader of the opposition movement in Worcester. He would serve as the representative for the next decade, and as selectman from 1768 through 1775, with the exception of one year. He had two considerably younger first cousins living in Worcester: David Bigelow, a carpenter and innkeeper born in 1730, and David's brother Timothy, a blacksmith born in 1739. One after the other, the Bigelows would play major roles in the upheaval of the next two decades.[175]

In March 1768, Joshua Bigelow brought before the town meeting a proposal to resist the Townshend Duties—revenue measures adopted by Parliament following the repeal of the Stamp Act—by boycotting British manufactured goods. Though the wording of the official town record is ambiguous, the meeting seems to have endorsed the boycott. Worcester men were soon going from door to door gathering signatures on an agreement to follow the lead of the Boston merchants who were managing the nonconsumption movement. The signers promised not to buy any European goods "but what is absolutely necessary," to boycott anyone who bought or sold such goods and to regard anyone breaking the agreement as "dishonored, an enemy to the liberties of his country, and infamous."[176]

Once again, taking sides with the colonial opposition to British taxation served the more limited purposes of the men opposed to the preeminence of the Chandler family in Worcester. The town's principal importer of British goods, and its principal merchant, was John Chandler, whose son Clark managed the general store while his father was engaged in public business. The Chandlers' chief commercial rival was Stephen Salisbury, who at the age of twenty-one had arrived in Worcester from Boston in 1767. Salisbury had opened a branch of his family's hardware stores at the north end of the village, near the courthouse and the jail. Like all merchants, Chandler and Salisbury had to calculate both the politics and the economics of the boycott. As a member of the patronage elite, Chandler was disdainful of colonial resistance to British measures and eager to sell items that boycotting merchants would be unable to provide for their customers. On the other side, Stephen Salisbury's brother, Samuel Salisbury, was working closely in Boston with the Committee of Merchants enforcing nonconsumption and nonimportation. Stephen in Worcester had to worry about the impact on his business of refusing to carry items that John Chandler was quite willing to sell. That willingness was one reason the House of Representatives in 1768 refused to reelect Chandler to the council seat he had held since 1765. Timothy Paine, who was always more popular than Chandler, was reelected to the council.

Late in 1769, Chandler returned from a trip to Boston claiming that the boycott against the Townshend Duties was falling apart, and that for the right price contraband goods were easily available there, even from such leaders of the protest movement as John

Hancock. Stephen Salisbury then learned that Chandler had brought to Worcester British goods, which were supposedly being held in storage until the boycott ended. Salisbury sent an urgent letter to his brother in Boston, insisting that the boycott organizers force Chandler to return those goods to the capital. If not, Stephen declared, he would regard himself as "entirely free of any engagement concerning nonimportation." After pressure mounted in both Boston and Worcester, the Committee of Merchants summoned the individual who had sold the contraband goods to the Chandlers and convinced him that it would be in his best interest to bring them all back to Boston.[177]

On March 5, 1770, the day harassed British troops fired on a crowd in Boston, the opposition in Worcester succeeded in elevating to the board of selectmen the man who, along with Ephraim Doolittle, had tried twelve years earlier to persuade John Adams to launch a challenge to the Chandler hegemony in Worcester. The saddle-making deist, Nathan Baldwin, joined two other members of the opposition, Joshua Bigelow and Benjamin Flagg, on a board that also included, as usual, John Chandler and Timothy Paine.

In 1770, the repeal of the Townshend Duties—except for a symbolic tax on tea—quieted the crisis that had been developing between the colonies and the mother country. While provincial life seemed to be returning to normal, Samuel Adams and other Bostonians did not cease to express alarm at British attempts to enforce British law in Massachusetts, or to organize a resistance movement. On November 2, 1772, on Adams's motion the town of Boston created a Committee of Correspondence to assert colonial rights, to alert the province and the world to violations of them and to request from each Massachusetts town "a free communication of their sentiments on this subject."[178] In Worcester, forty-one men petitioned for the town meeting to consider "the pamphlet drawn up by the Town of Boston containing the grievances this province labors under."[179] When it spoke out in May 1773, the majority of the Worcester town meeting demonstrated once again its sympathy with the Boston radicals.

The meeting opened with a broad philosophical consideration of the origins of natural rights, especially the rights to life, liberty and property. As articulated in the 1690s by John Locke, the theory had become familiar throughout the British world. Locke's insistence on the principle that governments existed to preserve individual rights was particularly useful to the colonists as they attempted to ward off what they regarded as invasions of those rights.

To its philosophical statement, Worcester added an idealized version of New England history, a narrative of heroism and success. It traced the ancestors' acquisition of land titles by purchase from the natives (rather than conquest), and it declared that after all that sacrifice, current threats to the colonists' natural and civil rights were "too great a grievance for us silently to bear." The meeting established a local Committee of Correspondence.

While Worcester was considering the Boston pamphlet, Parliament was passing the Tea Act. The legislation, which grew out of the need of the East India Company to dispose of surplus tea, allowed the company to send tea directly to selected colonial merchants under conditions that would permit them to sell at prices below those that other merchants were charging. The duty on tea, left over from the Townshend Duties, would continue, as a matter of Parliamentary principle. In June, the Boston Whigs received from Benjamin Franklin in London private letters written by Governor Thomas Hutchinson and Lieutenant Governor Andrew Oliver to political friends in England. In them, Hutchinson had unguardedly argued that the empire could not be preserved without "a diminution of what are called English liberties" in Massachusetts.[180] Samuel Adams and his colleagues now had powerful new evidence to show that corrupt Massachusetts officials were part of a dreaded ministerial conspiracy against constitutional liberty. In Worcester, opponents of the Chandlers also had new support for their contention that members of the local patronage elite pursued their own welfare at the expense of the liberty and property of their neighbors.

Resistance to the Tea Act in Boston reached its climax when a band of determined men tossed East India Company tea into the harbor during the night of December 16, 1773. Eleven days after the Boston Tea Party, a group of equally determined men met in Worcester to form the American Political Society, a secret body that was also the first voluntary association in the town's history. For the first time, some Worcester men were separating themselves into a distinct body with a limited, voluntary membership. Although their stated purpose was "to take under our consideration and debate upon such matters and things as concerns our rights and liberties," the society would soon take upon itself the direction of the resistance movement in Worcester, selecting candidates for public offices, issuing orders to public authorities and plotting strategies to control town meetings. A private organization with a public purpose, the American Political Society inadvertently set in motion a process of fragmentation and confusion in the institutional life of the community that would persist well beyond the struggle for American independence.[181]

The leaders of the colonial resistance frequently called themselves Whigs, to associate their cause with that of the Glorious Revolution of 1688, when British Whigs had overthrown James II in the name of constitutional liberty. It was the Whigs of Worcester—and the longstanding opponents of the Chandlers—who were organizing themselves as the American Political Society late in 1773. When they met again on January 4, 1774, thirty-one men signed the covenant of the society, much as they would have done for the founding of a new church.

First to inscribe their names were the three Whig members of the board of selectmen. Next came the three members of the Committee of Correspondence: William Young, Timothy Bigelow and John Smith. The members then signed the document roughly in the order of their wealth. In terms of economic condition, the Whig leadership was widely distributed, though nearly three-quarters of the founding members were men of substantial property. However, wealth did not determine leadership. Both John Smith of the Committee of Correspondence and Nathan Baldwin, who helped draft the covenant, were in the lowest quarter of property holders.[182]

The covenant declared that Massachusetts, "and with respect to some particular circumstances the Town of Worcester in particular," suffered under "many impositions and burdens grievous to be borne" that would never have occurred if the people had presented a united opposition to "the machinations of some designing persons in this province, who are grasping at power and the property of their neighbors." The members promised to meet at least once a month to consider "the proper methods to be pursued by each of us respecting our common rights and liberties, civil and religious."[183]

The Loyalist Counteroffensive

At its meeting on February 7, 1774, the American Political Society mapped strategy for the annual town meeting in March. The records do not reveal what the plan was, so it is not possible to say that the society was responsible for the fact that John Chandler, who was present at the March meeting, was not chosen to moderate and also was not chosen as a selectman for 1774. Perhaps the local Whigs, striking a moderate stance, endorsed the election of Timothy Paine rather than Chandler as moderator, and also endorsed Paine's reelection as selectman.

Another part of the meeting clearly fell within the "plan of procedure" adopted by the Whigs two weeks earlier. The town agreed to consider the Tea Act, and it appointed a committee of American Political Society members to draft a statement. In two hours, the Whig committee was back with a long and carefully drafted report. It recapitulated the list of grievances that were convincing more and more Americans that the alleged ministerial conspiracy really did exist: taxes; the multiplication of customs officers; the vice admiralty courts with no juries; the presence of troops in Boston; the British plan to free Massachusetts's highest judges from local control by granting them royal salaries; and now the attempt to slip huge amounts of taxed tea into the colonies by lowering its cost. The town resolved not to buy tea of any kind and to break off all relations with anyone violating the boycott.

Another portion of the town meeting clearly did not conform to the plan adopted by the American Political Society. After the Whig resolutions had been adopted and the town clerk, Clark Chandler, had been explicitly ordered to record them in the official book of records, a group of twenty-six men stepped forward to enter their "dissent and protest" against the proceedings. For the first time, the Chandlers and their supporters were formally placing themselves on record against the rising tide of opposition that had surfaced with the election of Ephraim Doolittle as representative nine years earlier. First to sign the protest was the county's leading lawyer, James Putnam, brother-in-law of Judge John Chandler. Then came Chandler himself, followed by the venerable Daniel Ward, seventy-five, a town founder who had served as selectman in the middle 1740s and again in the early 1760s. Putnam, who probably drafted the protest, seems to have made a point of collecting the signatures of older men before those of younger ones. In local property holding, most of the protestors were not strikingly different from the Whigs. There was, however, a noteworthy difference in age between them. Half the protestors were over fifty years of age, as compared to 28 percent of the founders of the American Political Society. Of the Loyalist protestors, 35 percent were between thirty and fifty years old; among the Whigs, 68 percent fell into that category.[184] That difference in age may have been part of what James Putnam was trying to emphasize when he collected the signatures. Older leaders were taking a stand against the dangerous political deviations into which the community was being led by inexperienced younger men.

While the Loyalist protestors were beginning to gather their strength, the better-organized American Political Society had largely succeeded in gaining control over the town meeting. The Whigs began to address themselves to matters affecting Worcester County. Treating the town's Committee of Correspondence as if it were the society's own creature, it ordered it on April 14, 1774, to send out circular letters alerting all county towns to the recent failure of the Court of General Sessions to count the votes for county treasurer and warning that this omission might set the stage for "fraud, or deception." The society then resolved to share the fines or charges that the Superior Court might impose on Joshua and Timothy Bigelow when, as grand jurors for Worcester, they would refuse to be impaneled, in order to protest the presence on the bench of Massachusetts Chief Justice Peter Oliver. Oliver had been impeached by the House of Representatives for accepting a salary from the Crown, rather than from the provincial legislature.

Five days later, a majority of the grand jurors chosen by the county towns—including Ephraim Doolittle of Petersham—handed the judges of the Superior Court a remonstrance attacking Oliver and refusing to cooperate with the court if he sat. Only when the judges had assured them that Oliver would not be in attendance did the jurors agree to be sworn. With its allies from other towns, the American Political Society, only four months old, had come very close to preventing the operation of the province's highest court. [185]

In response to the destruction of East India Company tea in Boston, Parliament had adopted the first of the Coercive Acts, quickly labeled the Intolerable Acts by American Whigs. Boston Harbor was to be closed to all shipping until someone had paid for the tea. To enforce the blockade, British regiments would be stationed in the city and British frigates would patrol the harbor. When the town of Worcester met on May 16, Joshua Bigelow was reelected, and six members of the American Political Society, along with Stephen Salisbury, were designated to prepare instructions. On May 20, the town adopted the committee's report, condemning "unconstitutional stretches of power" and declaring that Massachusetts had reached "the most difficult period that hath ever yet commenced since the first arrival of our worthy ancestors." Once again following the lead of the Boston Whigs, the Worcester meeting for the first time extended its concern for liberty to the other British colonies. It declared the Port Act "a blow aimed through Boston at the whole of American liberties" and urged Joshua Bigelow to work for "a strict union of the colonies" through intercolonial committees of correspondence and by the formation of a general congress of deputies from the various colonies. Bigelow was also ordered to oppose any attempt to have the destroyed East India Company tea paid for by the taxpayers of Massachusetts. [186]

Although the town had officially taken its stand once again with the Whigs, there were important men (and no doubt women) in Worcester who still believed that the tide of protest and resistance had reached its crest. Sober people everywhere had reacted with shock to the lawlessness and destructiveness of the Boston Tea Party. Besides that, the vote on the Whig resolutions at the March meeting in Worcester had been close. The Worcester men still loyal to the Crown and Parliament decided the time had come to recapture the initiative from the troublemakers.

On May 14, the selectmen published a warrant for a special meeting, to be held on June 20, because a "great number of the Freeholders, inhabitants, and voters" of Worcester were seeking an opportunity to "bear their public testimony against all riots, unlawful assemblies, acts of violence, oppression, and robbery." The petitioners wished especially to "manifest their utter detestation and abhorrence of that unparalleled act of violence, the destruction of the teas, the last winter in Boston." The men asking for the meeting also hoped to restore the reputation of Worcester, where, they asserted, the votes of the March meeting had been passed "against the express will and opinion of the respectable inhabitants of the town then assembled."

The petitioners believed that if the same matters were to come up again, the outcome would be very different. At the very least, they believed, the Loyalist voters would include "the owners and proprietors of by far the largest share of Interest and property of the whole town."

The Loyalist petitioners, despite the fact that they were competing in the quite democratic arena of the town meeting, were making an unmistakable association between property ownership and political legitimacy. They portrayed themselves as the "respectable inhabitants," the "sober, judicious" people, the real "owners and proprietors" of the town. They did not hesitate to assert their superiority over most of the others who voted in the meeting, especially people whose intellectual capacity was largely limited to "copying" inflammatory rhetoric turned out by Boston agitators.

One flaw in this argument based on property was the fact that there were men of considerable wealth among the most active Whigs. The Loyalists, to reach the conclusion that they were collectively the dominant property interest in Worcester, had to rely on the fact that the very richest among them, the Chandlers and the Paines, owned more property than most of the leading Whigs combined.[187]

The openly elitist tone of the petition could not have been better calculated to infuriate many of the men who had organized to oppose the Chandlers and the Paines. The petitioners were either blind to the antiaristocratic origins of the local revolt or, more likely, were unwilling to compromise with it by adopting a more egalitarian tone as they tried to bring Worcester into the Loyalist fold. They made another serious strategic error by suggesting that the Committee of Correspondence was a self-appointed body acting independently of the town. The charge might have been made with some justice against the American Political Society, had the Loyalists known of its existence, but not against the Committee of Correspondence. That mistake reinforces the impression that the petitioners were fatally underestimating the extent to which the Whig argument had taken hold in Worcester. The Committee of Correspondence had been quite deliberately established by the town because a great many people believed that every possible precaution had to be taken to ward off a conspiracy against their liberty and property. To those people, the Committee of Correspondence was not a pernicious threat; it was the first line of defense.

On June 20, the town met, and the Whigs were more than ready for the Loyalist challenge. A motion was made "to see if the Town will proceed and act on any of the matters and things contained in said warrant, and it passed in the negative." It was then voted "that this meeting be dissolved."

So much for reversing the tide. The Loyalists had not even succeeded in being heard by the town meeting. Rather than face the terrifying possibility that most of their neighbors had been detached from their traditional allegiances, the Worcester Loyalists told one another that, through "irregular and arbitrary proceedings" in the town meeting, they had been cheated out of their opportunity to take a public stand. They would find other means of taking an even more public stand.

On June 21, the day after the town meeting's refusal to hear the Loyalist case, John Chandler, Timothy Paine and the other justices of the county courts signed an address welcoming General Thomas Gage to his new office. Gage was replacing Thomas Hutchinson as royal governor, which was further evidence of the British ministry's determination to bring Massachusetts back into submission. The commander in chief of the troops would now be the chief civil magistrate of Massachusetts. The Worcester judges took the occasion to bear personal testimony "against all riots, routs, combinations, and unwarrantable resolves, which we apprehend have been the unhappy occasion of many of our troubles."[188]

In their determination to be heard, the Loyalists also prepared for publication an impassioned protest against the brief town proceedings of June 20, and against the whole resistance movement. Then, unbeknownst to the Whigs, they had the town clerk, Clark Chandler, copy it into the official town record book. Having thus given some official status to their protest, they boldly sent copies to the capital, where it was published, with fifty-two signatures, in the *Boston News Letter* on June 30 and in the *Massachusetts Gazette* on July 4, 1774.[189]

If Worcester's Whigs needed any more evidence of the aristocratic pretensions of their local families of privilege, the Loyalist letter provided all that could have been desired. Like the Whigs, the Loyalists had become convinced that there was a conspiracy afoot, but where the Whigs saw corrupt ministers and venal colonial officials grasping for wealth and power, the Loyalists saw "evil-minded and ill-disposed persons…under the disguise of patriotism…falsely styling themselves the friends of liberty." In true aristocratic fashion, the Loyalists sneered at men who got hopelessly out of their appropriate place, such as the Whig leaders in Worcester, who were "neglecting their own proper business and occupation, in which they ought to be employed for the support of their families, spending their time in discoursing of matters they do not understand." In Worcester, so many had been "led aside by strange opinions" that the town had refused to dismiss "the persons styling themselves the Committee of Correspondence" or to investigate "their past dark and pernicious proceedings." The committees in Worcester and throughout the province were "contrived by a junto to serve particular designs and purposes of their own."

The Revolution of 1774

Like the Worcester Loyalists, the leaders of Parliament had come to see the Massachusetts town meeting as a dangerously democratic institution that could be manipulated by a small band of conspirators to the detriment of all legal authority. They had reached a similar conclusion about the Massachusetts Council. Unlike all other colonies with a royally appointed governor, Massachusetts did not have a royally appointed council. Under its charter, a new council was annually chosen by a joint vote of the incoming House of Representatives and the outgoing council. Since the Stamp Act troubles, Loyalists like John Chandler and Timothy Paine had been losing their seats, and the council, far from bolstering the governor's authority, had become another instrument of Whig resistance. While Worcester was meeting in 1774 to condemn the Boston Port Act, Parliament was passing the Massachusetts Government Act to help bring the Bay Colony back under control. The second of the Intolerable Acts, the new law banned town meetings, except for the annual spring gathering held to elect town officers and make decisions about local taxes and spending. Furthermore, the members of the council would in the future be appointed and removed by the Crown.

During 1774, the most momentous year in its history, Worcester did not hold a town meeting between May 20 and August 22, but that was not because the town was obeying the Massachusetts Government Act. The mounting crisis had brought into play new institutions, like the American Political Society and the Committee of Correspondence, which were gradually providing alternatives to the town meeting as the focal point of local politics. The new institutions were also adding to confusion over where legitimate authority lay.

The town meeting, for example, had no role in initiating a new nonconsumption agreement, a Worcester version of the Solemn League and Covenant sent out on June 8, 1774, by the Boston Committee of Correspondence. Though the covenant had been sent to Worcester's Committee of Correspondence, a town agency, it was the self-created American Political Society, meeting in secret, that voted on June 10 to "sign a solemn agreement and covenant" not to buy any English goods after August 31 and to boycott anyone who refused to sign the covenant. On July 4, it voted to draw up a similar covenant "for all the women, of an adult age, of said town to sign." Not until August 22 did the town itself appoint a committee of Whigs to "offer" people who had not signed the covenant "an opportunity to sign."[190]

An unprecedented body called the Worcester County Convention was responsible for many of the most dramatic events of the revolutionary summer and fall of 1774. Fifty-two delegates from the towns of Worcester County, many of them members of Committees of Correspondence, assembled at the public house operated by Mary Stearns in Worcester on August 9. Worcester's delegation was presumably chosen by the American Political Society, though neither its records nor those of the town show any authorization of delegates. Worcester's representatives were Joshua Bigelow, selectman and member of the House of Representatives, and the three members of the town's Committee of Correspondence: William Young, Timothy Bigelow and John Smith.[191]

Timothy Bigelow was quickly made chair of a committee to draw up resolutions. One after another, British decisions had been interpreted by Whig leaders as evidence of a conspiracy to destroy constitutional liberty. Each item added to the list convinced more Americans that the conspiracy was real, and not just a figment of overwrought political imaginations. To the county convention delegates, the point had come "when it no longer remains a doubt, that the acts annihilating our once free constitution, are actually come authenticated, attended by three more transports and a ship of war, and the Council, appointed by His Majesty, are about to take the oaths required for that office." At the next meeting of the convention, they hoped "the united wisdom and aid of the whole" would be present "to oppose the torrent of tyranny rushing upon us."

The delegates could take a clear stand on the unconstitutionality of the acts of Parliament, but they had little idea what to do next to resist the "torrent of tyranny." The convention managed only to urge united action "in every virtuous opposition that can be devised," to endorse nonconsumption of British goods and to urge all towns in the county and the province to adopt "some wise, prudent, and spirited measures." As disaffection spread through the Massachusetts countryside, the Boston Whigs were losing their role as the main source of provincial resistance, but the Worcester Convention was not yet ready to set the future course of opposition in the county.

It was the town of Worcester that took the next major step toward revolution. While the convention was in recess, the town rose up in righteous fury over the publication in Boston of the Loyalist manifesto. Worcester Whigs began a formal process of repudiation and humiliation of the Loyalists. On August 22, for the first time in sixteen years, it chose a moderator other than John Chandler of Worcester, John Chandler Jr. or Timothy Paine. Four days earlier, the American Political Society had decided that the meeting should be moderated by Nathan Perry, a fifty-six-year-old weaver who would later become deacon of the church.[192]

The town meeting appointed a committee of Whigs, led by Joshua Bigelow, to draft resolutions concerning the published Loyalist protest and report back in two days. On August 24, the town performed a ritual of degradation that would soon be imitated by mobilized citizens and by the County Convention. The drama had been carefully prepared. During the previous weeks, Whigs had been paying hostile visits to the signers of the Loyalist protest.[193] In the August 24 town meeting, the Bigelow committee reported that all but five of the fifty-two signers of the protest had "made satisfaction for their offense to the acceptance of the town."[194] The meeting then ordered that Clark Chandler, the town clerk, "in the presence of the town obliterate, erase, or otherwise deface the said recorded protest and all the names thereto subscribed, so that it may become utterly illegible and unintelligible."

Though it must have taken the young storekeeper many minutes of scratching in the town record book to carry out his laborious punishment, feelings were still running high when he finished. As Chandler put down his pen, one further humiliation awaited: his fingers were plunged into the inkwell and rubbed over the page, leaving in the official book of the town a permanent record of the clerk's political and physical abasement.[195]

Town record book as it looks today, smeared under duress by the Loyalist town clerk in 1774. *Courtesy Worcester City Clerk David J. Rushford.*

The next day, riders set out for the neighboring towns, summoning men to Worcester for a special event planned for August 26. The king, by writ of mandamus, had named Timothy Paine to the new council, a singular honor in ordinary times, but a dangerous mark of favor when angry men were denouncing the "Mandamus Council" as a tyrannical substitute for the old elective body. Paine had added to his problems by courageously accepting the post and taking the oath of office on August 16.[196] The Whigs had decided that he would resign that office on August 26.

By nine in the morning, more than two thousand men had paraded onto the Worcester Common, most of them in militia companies under the command of their officers. A committee, including Joshua Bigelow, went to Paine's house north of the village[197] to demand his resignation, warning that they could not be responsible for the consequences if he refused. After some argument, Paine signed a document promising not to sit on the council unless it were brought into conformity with the old charter; in effect, this was a resignation from the Mandamus Council. As in the case of Clark Chandler two days before, Paine's ordeal did not end when he might have expected it to. The committee insisted that the people would not be satisfied unless Paine accompanied them to the body assembled on the common. Then began an extraordinary procession, as one of the town's most illustrious citizens, effectively a prisoner, was escorted to the common and a rendezvous with "the people." Paine found the men drawn up "in the form of a hollow square," into which he was marched and ordered to read his resignation. When he had done so, the much-honored justice of the peace, register of probate, selectman, register of deeds, former councilor and former representative was required to remove his hat before passing through the ranks of the militia on his way home. The grand officeholder was being taught a political lesson: that the people would now rule, and they would expect proper deference from their servants.[198]

That same day, the next stage in the escalating revolution was being agreed upon in Boston. Acting on the suggestion of the Worcester Convention, delegates from Worcester, Boston, Middlesex County, Salem and Marblehead met in Faneuil Hall. They resolved to regard as unconstitutional all judges acting under the Massachusetts Government Act, called for resistance to the sitting of such courts and urged the establishment of a temporary government of Massachusetts, to be called the Provincial Congress.[199]

Artemas Ward of Shrewsbury, judge, soldier, legislator and congressman. *Courtesy American Antiquarian Society.*

When the Worcester County Convention resumed its work four days later (August 30), 130 members of Committees of Correspondence were present, as well as other delegates. The convention was about to play its most dramatic role in that season of deadly serious political theater. The proceedings began with an appropriately symbolic act: adjourning from the inn of the Widow Stearns to the more spacious surroundings of the county courthouse. Until that day, the courthouse had been the domain of the Chandlers, Paines, Putnams and others who expected to exercise power over the people of the county by warrant of distant authorities. Now the Committees of Correspondence, appointed by anxious towns to protect them against the encroachment of what they regarded as illegitimate power, were taking control of the courthouse, a central symbol of the rule of law in the county. They may have gained physical access through the authority of Judge Artemas Ward of Shrewsbury, who in the summer of 1774 may have been the only man in Massachusetts serving as both a judge of His Majesty's Court of Common Pleas and a delegate to a Whig County Convention.

On August 31, demonstrating that the Faneuil Hall meeting had provided a sense of tactical direction, the convention resolved to prevent the courts from meeting. It summoned men to Worcester on September 6, when the next session of the inferior courts was to be held. It also urged the towns to send delegates to the Provincial Congress, scheduled to meet in Concord in October if the House of Representatives and council were not allowed to meet under the old charter. Citizens were urged to pay their just debts while the courts were suspended, and to do everything possible to prevent disorder in the towns.

Suddenly, the issue before the convention was war.

A delegate moved that the men of the county be asked to come to Worcester on September 6 "properly armed" if, as expected, General Gage sent troops to support the court. After discussion, the motion was withdrawn, and a new one substituted, removing the possibly inflammatory reference to September 6, but taking no less defiant a stand. The convention resolved that any town in danger of invasion by British troops should alert the Committees of Correspondence in adjoining towns, who would notify their neighboring committees "that they all [must] come properly armed and accoutred to protect and defend the place invaded."

As the men of Worcester correctly believed, General Gage had his eye on them. He was expecting with his soldiers to accompany the impeached Chief Justice Peter Oliver to the next Superior Court session in Worcester, and he was expecting a fight. "In Worcester," Gage wrote to his London superiors on August 27, "they keep no terms, openly threatening resistance by arms; have been purchasing arms, preparing them, casting balls, and providing powder, and threaten to attack any troops who dare to oppose them…I apprehend that I shall soon be obliged to march a body of troops into that township, and perhaps into others, as occasion happens, to preserve the peace."[200] The fact that Gage did not march to Worcester may have been partially due to the advice of Timothy Paine. On the very day the governor and commander in chief was reporting to the Earl of Dartmouth, Paine was reporting to Gage the details of his humiliation and forced resignation from the council. Acts of Parliament had been openly defied, Paine told the general, but "I dread the consequences of enforcing them by a Military Power; people's spirits are so raised they seem determined to risk their lives and everything dear to them in the opposition, and prevent any person from executing any commission they receive under the present administration."[201]

The horrors of civil war were also on the minds of Paine's Worcester antagonists. The day before the scheduled disruption of the county courts, the American Political Society voted "not to bring our firearms into town the 6 day of Sept."[202] Though it indicated a desire to avoid violence, the decision not to carry firearms also reflected confidence that General Gage had changed his mind and his troops would not be making an appearance.[203] The judges in Worcester would receive no protection from the British army. On September 6, the County Convention listened to a prayer from their chaplain and promptly voted "as the opinion of this Convention, that the court should not sit on any terms." Six thousand men, organized as town militia companies, were waiting on the common to enforce the will of the convention.[204]

The delegates invited a committee, made up of one man from each company, to notify the judges that the "body of the people" did not want the courts to sit. Mere submission, once again, would not be enough. The committee was also to order the judges to walk deferentially through the ranks as a sign of their subordination to the people. Hours went by as the committee got chosen and organized, got the justices to sign a promise not to open the courts and assembled the jurists for their forced procession through the ranks. While waiting, the convention sent a committee of its own to notify the judge of probate, John Chandler, as well as the others who had signed the infamous protest published in the Boston newspapers, that they would be required to follow the judges of the court of common pleas "through the ranges of the body of the people; that they go immediately after the judges, and read their recantations." Considering the time that would be needed, the convention later resolved that four of the principals would read the recantation on behalf of the protestors, though all would still have to march.

Finally, the ritual unfolded. The judges, the other protestors, Sheriff Gardiner Chandler and other officers of the court were marched "through the ranges of the people," stopping repeatedly to read their recantations and promises. How long the ceremony lasted, no record reveals. Thousands of men had spent a long day to make sure that the submission of the court to the people happened precisely according to their demands. In doing so, they had compelled fellow citizens to deny their own opinions and made them beg to be restored to the community's favor. When it was over, the convention recommended to the militia officers that their companies "march quietly home."[205] Without violence, power had shifted from appointed officials to elected representatives of the people.

The County Convention moved back into the courthouse and took responsibility for replacing royal government on an emergency basis in Worcester County. Despite the press of organizational business, it continued to place a high priority on the ritual abasement of the old aristocracy, punishing men like John Chandler and Timothy Paine over and over again. They had already been denounced in the town meeting for signing the protest, Paine had been mobbed as a Mandamus Councilor and both had been marched through the ranks on September 6. Nevertheless, the convention voted on September 7 to "take notice" of them and the other county judges who had gone out of their way to insult the Committees of Correspondence in their June 21 address welcoming Governor Gage to office. The offending judges were forced, "in the presence of the convention," to "frankly declare that they precipitately entered into the measure; they are sorry for it; and they disclaim an intention to injure the character of any; and were the same measure again proposed, they should reject it."[206]

Sheriff Gardiner Chandler, who had presented the justices' address to Gage, was summoned on September 21 and required to sign a declaration "that he is sorry for it, and disclaims an intention to do anything against the minds of the inhabitants of this county, and, had he known it would give offence, he would not have presented said address." Samuel Paine, son of Timothy and clerk of the courts, was twice summoned for the offense of issuing, under the orders of the court, venires to constables requiring

Finely trimmed waistcoat worn by Gardiner Chandler, longtime sheriff who became a Loyalist refugee in 1775. *From the collections of the Worcester Historical Museum, Worcester, Massachusetts.*

their obedience to the Massachusetts Government Act. When Paine failed to grovel to the satisfaction of the convention, a committee declared that the issue was "of too small importance" for further consideration, pointedly described the twenty-year-old Paine as "a young man who, by his connections, has lately started into the office of clerk" and urged that he be treated "with all neglect."[207]

When it was not humbling the Loyalists, the convention was taking momentous steps in the direction of revolution. One was to coordinate Worcester County's participation in the creation of the Massachusetts Provincial Congress. Governor Gage had called for the election of a House of Representatives to meet in Salem in October. The County Convention urged the towns to instruct their representatives to refuse to take office unless the charter was restored. If prevented from meeting under the charter, they were to go to Concord, where the emergency Provincial Congress would meet to consider how "to extricate this colony out of the present unhappy circumstances."[208] The convention also reorganized the county militia and established the minutemen. It divided the militia into seven new regiments, recommended that the towns choose their own officers, called upon the officers to enlist one-third of the men in special companies "to be ready to act at a minute's warning" and scheduled a meeting in Worcester on October 17 for the organization of distinct regiments of minutemen. Other Massachusetts communities were beginning to organize minutemen at around the same time.[209]

The Whigs were acting together effectively, but they were continuing to blur the boundaries between institutions. When the town met on September 26, Joshua Bigelow was reelected representative to the General Court, but no action was taken with respect to the instructions recommended by the County Convention. A week later, the American Political Society, not the town, examined and approved instructions for the representative, but also a set of instructions for his cousin, Timothy Bigelow, "as a delegate for a Provincial Congress." Although the town had taken no action with respect to a Provincial Congress, the society had made a selection and prepared instructions. The next day, more than a week after electing him, the town voted to instruct Representative Joshua Bigelow. Then it voted also to instruct Timothy Bigelow, described as "the delegate chosen by the town to represent us at the Provincial Congress," though there is no record of the town electing Timothy or anyone else to that post. A committee appointed to prepare instructions for both the representative and the delegate returned in two hours, presumably with the instructions approved the previous day by the American Political Society.[210] It may have appeared to some that plural officeholding was being revived and exercised by, of all people, the Bigelow family.

The instructions to Timothy Bigelow mark a decisive turning point in the thinking of Whigs and in the formal positions adopted by the town. After overthrowing the local aristocracy in both town and county, after concluding that the only legitimate rulers were those elected by the people, Worcester was ready for a declaration of independence.

As Thomas Jefferson would later borrow the ideas of John Locke for the national declaration, Worcester drew upon the English philosopher's theory that civil society is based upon a compact under which people leave a "state of nature" and enter a "state of civil society" in order to protect their individual rights to life, liberty and property. Should rulers violate those rights, the people have a right to consider the compact dissolved. Having returned to the state of nature, the people could then establish a new compact. In its fifth instruction, Worcester told Timothy Bigelow,

> *If all infractions on our right by acts of the British Parliament be not redressed, and we restored to the full enjoyment of all our privileges contained in the charter of this province, granted by their late Majesties King William and Queen Mary, to a punctillio, before the day of your meeting, that then and in that case you are to consider the people of this province as absolved on their part from the obligation therein contained and to all intents and purposes reduced to a state of nature, and you are to exert yourself in devising ways and means to raise from the dissolution of the old constitution, as from the ashes of the Phoenix, a new form wherein all officers shall be dependent on the suffrages of the people for their existence as such. Whatever unfavorable constructions our enemies may put upon such a procedure, the exigency of our public affairs leaves us no other alternative from a state of anarchy or slavery.*

When Governor Gage, as expected, refused to convene the General Court under the terms of the abrogated charter, representatives and delegates assembled, according to plan, in Concord to begin governing Massachusetts as the Provincial Congress. Though it would take nearly two more years for the thirteen colonies to agree to declare independence, an elected government independent of British authority now ruled Massachusetts in the name of its people.

As the Whigs consolidated their hold on the countryside, life became dangerous for leading Massachusetts Loyalists. John Chandler later testified that during those tumultuous weeks he had been "exposed…in a peculiar degree to the outrage and persecution of the disaffected and licentious" and forced to sign "a very treasonable League and Covenant…to save himself from imminent death." In October or November he, too, fled Worcester for the protection of the king's troops in Boston, leaving his second wife, Mary Church Chandler, with nine relatives ranging in age from twenty-two to four. John Chandler, too, had had his last look at the town and county over which his family had presided for more than four decades.[211] Several of Chandler's older sons joined the refugees in the next few months, as did the son of James Putnam.[212] Timothy Paine managed to remain in Worcester, except for a brief period in 1775, when he and his wife took refuge in Malden. His sons, Samuel and William, joined the British forces, Samuel as a lieutenant with the volunteer Associated Loyalists and William as an apothecary, then as a physician in the regular British army.[213] When the town of Worcester met in March 1775, the political purge of the Chandler family was finally completed. The last Loyalist selectman, Timothy Paine, was not reelected. Town Treasurer John Chandler was replaced by the weaver and orthodox church leader Nathan Perry. Town Clerk Clark Chandler was replaced by the deistic saddler, Nathan Baldwin.

On April 19, General Gage at last sent his troops out from Boston to seize ammunition and powder stored under the authority of the Provincial Congress. They might have marched toward Worcester, which was also an ammunition depot. Gage had, in fact, sent military spies during the winter to study and sketch the geography of the town.[214] When the time came to march, however, he selected an objective closer to his headquarters: the provincial stores in Concord. His troops were met with gunfire at Lexington, then at Concord, and were pursued during the whole course of their retreat to Boston. Fifteen months before the Declaration of Independence, the war that would split the empire had begun. When riders reached Worcester with news of the shooting at Lexington, the church bell rang out, cannons were fired, messengers were dispatched and from all parts of town the minutemen rushed with their weapons to the common. After a prayer from Thaddeus Maccarty, seventy-eight men under Captain Timothy Bigelow set off toward Concord to meet the Regulars. Thirty more, members of the town's militia train band, set out soon after, under the command of Captain Benjamin Flagg.

Within days, as armed men by the thousands continued to gather on the outskirts of Boston, the Provincial Congress ordered the organization of a Massachusetts army—in membership truly a New England army—and placed it under the command of General Artemas Ward of Shrewsbury. Timothy Bigelow was appointed a major in one of the regiments. His minuteman lieutenant, Jonas Hubbard, joined as a captain, bringing with him a company of two additional officers and fifty-nine enlisted men, all from Worcester. Seventeen from the town enlisted in other units, including an infantry regiment commanded by the former Worcester hatter and political organizer, now Colonel Ephraim Doolittle of Petersham.[215]

In this emergency, at the meeting of the Continental Congress in Philadelphia, a former Worcester resident was devoting his energies to binding the colonies together in solidarity with Massachusetts. John Adams first got the Congress to take over the Massachusetts army. Then, to further cement the union, Adams proposed as commander of the new Continental army a tall delegate who had repeatedly appeared in the Congress in the uniform of a Virginia militia colonel. By mid-June, George Washington was commander in chief. He had to travel overland from Philadelphia to assume command in Cambridge, as Boston Harbor was under the control of British warships. In early July, Washington passed through Worcester on his journey to immortality.[216]

Worcester Whigs: "Divided into Parties"

The military struggle that would bring independence to the United States over the next eight years placed enormous demands on the people and the resources of local communities. As Worcester entered the most trying years in its history, it was also faced with a crisis of leadership. In overthrowing the Chandler family, the Whigs had done more than eliminate individual men from office. They had also removed the underpinnings of the political system that had provided much of the community's leadership during the last forty years. There had always been some resistance to the pretensions of the ruling elite, but the legitimacy of their leadership was broadly assumed, readily accepted and habitually depended upon by their neighbors. By the spring of 1775, it was no longer obvious who should be in charge. The town meeting had its traditional claims, as did the selectmen, but authority was also being exercised by a bewildering assortment of previously unknown bodies, including the Committee of Correspondence, the County Convention, elected militia officers, the American Political Society, the Provincial Congress, the Continental Congress and a new Committee of Inspection established to enforce the boycott of British goods that had been adopted by the Continental Congress.

Some of the new leaders may have been what John Adams called "sticklers for equality" when they were attacking the pretensions of the aristocrats, but what principle of authority could be found in equality? Who would defer to whom? As early as December 1774, the society had been interrupted by Jonathan Gleason's formal complaint that he had been "ill-treated" by a fellow member, Robert Smith. Following its rules, the society allowed each man to pick an arbitrator, after which they mutually chose Nathan Baldwin to serve in the same role. Smith and Gleason, however, were not about to be permanently reconciled; their controversy was an early symptom of a deep and persistent fracture within the Whig leadership.[217]

When the Whigs took control of all town offices in March 1775, there were not enough places to go around. The board of selectmen was increased from five to seven men, apparently to accommodate the needs of two incipient factions, based on allegiance to different political leaders. Joshua and Timothy Bigelow, who had played such prominent roles in the final overthrow of the aristocracy, were coming under political challenge, especially after Timothy had gone off to war. Their antagonists were rallying behind the third Benjamin Flagg. While the Bigelows continued to enjoy considerable support among the members of the American Political Society, the Flagg faction was showing considerable strength in the town meeting.

Following Jonathan Gleason's complaint, the American Political Society continued to meet, but it took little action other than admitting new members, rejecting motions to dissolve the society and voting to adjourn to a later date. On February 26, 1776, while Americans everywhere were discussing *Common Sense*, Thomas Paine's rousing call for republican liberty and American independence, the society in Worcester formally acknowledged "that there is an unhappy difference subsisting in this town and the town is divided into parties."[218]

The Flagg faction had been clearly in the driver's seat since the annual election of 1775, and they had gained an important ally in the person of Levi Lincoln, a twenty-six-year-old native of Hingham, a Harvard graduate and a lawyer. Lincoln had studied under a prominent Whig, Joseph Hawley, in Northampton, and had been admitted to the bar in Hampshire County in 1775. He immediately moved to Worcester, where only two practicing lawyers had survived the purge of the Loyalists, and where new judicial appointments would soon be available under the revived General Court of

Massachusetts. In December 1775, Lincoln was appointed to Timothy Paine's old position as clerk of the county courts.[219] Patronage had been reborn, and Benjamin Flagg was not far behind Lincoln in benefiting from good connections in Boston. On February 2, 1776, the council agreed with the House in appointing him lieutenant colonel of the First Regiment of the Worcester County militia.[220] The March 1776 town meeting, controlled by the Flagg faction, dismissed the members of what was then called the Committee of Correspondence and Inspection. Among those removed were the absent Timothy Bigelow, his brother Joshua and their ally, John Smith. In their place, the town chose a set of Flagg loyalists, including the town's newest professional man, Levi Lincoln. The American Political Society died a quiet death two months later. On May 20, after the defeat of yet another motion to dissolve, the society debated whether an investigating committee that had been appointed in February to look into members' "grievances" with one another should make its report "together or separate." The decision was "separate, at our next meeting." The surviving records of the society show an agreement to meet on June 5 to hear those separate reports, but no further activity is recorded.[221]

WORCESTER LOYALISTS: EXILE AND CONFISCATION

While the Worcester Whigs were jousting with one another, their countrymen besieging Boston were executing a decisive military maneuver. Under cover of darkness, on the nights of March 4 and 5, 1776, they carried out General Washington's orders to haul prefabricated fortifications and artillery onto Dorchester Heights, from which they could fire at will into the British forces on land and sea below. General William Howe, who had taken over from Thomas Gage as British commander the previous fall, recognized the hopeless situation his forces had been placed in, and accelerated the evacuation of Boston he and Gage had long been planning. With the army, nine hundred civilian refugees set sail, most of them for Halifax, Nova Scotia. Among them were many members of what had been the intermarried patronage elite of Worcester County.

When the state legislature passed a Banishment Act in 1778 it listed, among others, John, Rufus and William Chandler, James Putnam, William Paine and several members of the Ruggles, Murray and Willard families.[222] In 1779, the legislature adopted a Confiscation Act aimed at the property of the men who had been last to hold office as royal officials. Included on the list of alleged conspirators were Timothy Ruggles, John Murray and Abijah Willard.[223] Another act passed on the same day provided for the confiscation of the estates of "persons commonly called absentees."[224] Under its provisions, John Chandler would lose a huge estate, though his wife would be allowed to retain one-third of it, as if she had been his widow. Chandler's children would eventually inherit that portion of the estate.[225] The estates of Rufus Chandler and James Putnam were confiscated and sold.[226]

William Paine, son of Timothy and Sarah, served in the British army during the War for Independence. He returned to Worcester in 1795, where he practiced medicine and ranked at the top of Worcester society until his death in 1833. He was the first vice-president of the American Antiquarian Society. *Courtesy American Antiquarian Society.*

BEARING THE BURDENS OF WAR

For the politically divided town of Worcester, the major challenges of the years ahead would be providing military recruits and finding ways to pay the financial costs of the war. Both raised the issue of equity, an especially difficult issue to manage when the legitimacy of all claims to authority was open to question.

In January 1776, when they were asked to send one-fourth of all able-bodied Worcester men to reinforce the Continental army outside Boston, the officials responsible for raising troops in Worcester settled on a plan for drafting men if they could not get enough volunteers. The draft would begin at the top of the tax list. The man with the most taxable property, if he had not already served in the war, would be drafted and required to enlist, pay a fine or hire a substitute. Then the second man would be called, and so on down the list. A major problem soon surfaced. Wealth was traditionally measured by household; men with sons over sixteen but under twenty-one were assessed a poll tax on each of those human economic assets, as well as on any servants or propertyless workers attached to their households. When these propertied men were drafted, many sent their younger sons or servants as substitutes. Having done so, they felt that their taxable estates had done their share for the cause. In the winter of 1776–77, however, some of the propertied men found themselves again at the top of the draft list, while others below them had not yet served, and they objected that "the rule of drafting was unjust." There were frequent complaints that men were being drafted before their turns, and some were even jailed for refusing to serve or pay the fine.[227]

The system clearly placed a financial burden on the men with largest estates. They would remain at the top of every draft list, and would thus be faced with the cost of a fine or a substitute each time a draft was conducted. On the other hand, the burden of actual service fell most heavily on the men who could not afford either the fine or the cost of a substitute. On March 18, 1777, with the Flagg faction solidly in control, the town meeting took a step that would relieve the large property holders. It created a committee to determine what each inhabitant had so far contributed toward the support of the war, including military service, and to "determine how much those who are deficient ought to contribute to make them equal with those who have paid or done their full proportion." In the ordinary conduct of town business, it had never been expected that each taxpayer would bear an equal share of the public costs; taxes were proportioned to the value of one's estate. Under Worcester's new rule, all the taxes the town had collected to support the war were to be included in the committee's calculation. They were to divide that total by the number of taxpayers in the comunity to arrive at an average, which would be applied to each taxpayer. On April 7, the size of the bill that would have to be paid grew considerably, as the town voted to raise £1,656 to defray its unpaid expenses since the beginning of the war.

As this process was unfolding, two events in the life of Captain Ebenezer Lovell set off an explosive battle over war service, war taxes, recruitment and political power in Worcester. When militia companies were mustered on May 15, Benjamin Flagg drafted at least ten men from Lovell's company without the captain's consent and over his vigorous objection that his company had already sent its "full proportion" into the Continental service.[228] Four days later, Lovell was elected to represent Worcester in an expanded House of Representatives,[229] the first step in what turned out to be a stunning reversal of fortunes for the Flagg faction and a revival for the Bigelow supporters.

The new alignment in town politics was undoubtedly influenced by the fact that Timothy Bigelow had come back temporarily from the war. He had been a prisoner of the French for nearly eight months following a failed attack on Quebec. Paroled and then exchanged, he was in Worcester to recruit troops as colonel of the new Fifteenth Massachusetts Regiment of the Continental army.[230] In early July, General John Burgoyne's British troops were moving down from Canada. In this emergency, Ebenezer Lovell initially refused to muster his men. He finally called them together after being threatened with arrest by Lieutenant Colonel Flagg. It was said by some that Lovell discouraged rather than encouraged enlistment.[231] Levi Lincoln, with the help of retired General Artemas Ward on the council, instigated an investigation by the House of Representatives. Lovell was ordered to answer the complaint "that his conduct has been inimical to his country."

A petition signed by 105 Worcester men testified to their confidence in Lovell. Any doubts about the political character of the Worcester dispute were probably removed when the petitioners beseeched the House not only to exonerate Lovell, but also "to dismiss Col. Flagg from the office of Lt. Col. of Col. Denny's regiment, he being in our opinion a person totally unqualified for it, and it being the most likely step your petitioners can conceive of, of bringing the town into a state of harmony and peace."[232] On October 21, the House resolved that although Lovell had been "culpable" in not immediately obeying his orders, he had finally filled his quota and was therefore not guilty of the charges brought against him.[233] Four days earlier, General Burgoyne's army of 5,800 men had surrendered at Saratoga.

Lovell and his supporters had not waited for the authorities in Boston to rescue them from Flagg and his supporters. On October 3, Lovell had surprised the Flagg forces in the town meeting by initiating the repeal of the appropriation of £1,656 made in April to cover costs of the war.[234] Eliminating the appropriation would prevent implementation of the system under which each taxpayer would bear an equal share of the expense after calculation of an average cost. More than two years after the Declaration of Independence, the warring Whigs of Worcester had no plan for meeting the demands of the struggle they had done so much to create, and the attack on the Flagg-controlled board of selectmen was just beginning. The town voted to set aside the assessments made according to the averaging system, and set up a committee to investigate what had happened to all the money the selectmen and Committees of Correspondence had collected "by fines and other payments." Then the members of the committee were selected: Joshua Bigelow, Ebenezer Lovell, Dr. John Green, Captain Edward Crafts and William Stearns. Bigelow and Green had been elected representatives with Lovell as the anti-Flagg revolt had gotten underway the previous May. Crafts had signed the pro-Lovell petition to the House. Green had stood firmly with the Bigelows in the American Political Society. Once the members of the investigating committee had been named, their powers and responsibilities were expanded. They were to extend their inquiry over the last three years; they were empowered to question anyone claiming to have paid or received money collected by the selectmen and Committee of Correspondence; they were to ask the selectmen what they had done with the salt ration allocated to Worcester by the state; and they were to inquire into the state of the town's powder supply and dispose of it.

Three years after overthrowing the Loyalists, Worcester's Whigs were, more bitterly than ever, "divided into parties."

Chapter 5

REORDERING (1778–1790)

Although peace and independence were still five years away, the tide of war had shifted with Burgoyne's defeat. The American victory at Saratoga led in 1778 to an alliance with France, decisively altering the military balance in favor of the United States. A great deal of fighting was still ahead, but the violence took place largely in the Southern states. In Worcester, the political contention between Whig factions had reached a new crisis in 1778, and all signs pointed to nastier struggles ahead. Yet the opposite happened.

The fires of political rivalry were suddenly dampened, if they did not actually go out. The change may have been related to the sudden transfer of the community's attention from political charges to criminal charges, stemming from a sensational murder. When the trials and executions were over, the political energies of the Worcester factions also seemed largely spent. In the aftermath, the long-embattled farmers and artisans who had seized power in the decade after 1765 seem to have concentrated on getting themselves and their families through the remaining years of a seemingly endless war. Meanwhile, new men stepped forward with claims to social, economic and political preeminence in Worcester, claims reminiscent of those put forward by the pre-Revolutionary aristocracy.

THE POLITICAL AND CRIMINAL CHARGES OF 1778

The wheel of political fortune completed its latest revolution in Worcester with the March 1778 town election. The Flagg selectmen were replaced by Joshua Bigelow, Ebenezer Lovell and three of their allies. The report of the town committee investigating the former selectmen was put off until April 13, when two of its five paragraphs were rejected by the town meeting and not recorded by the clerk. The findings that were accepted, nevertheless, reflected very badly on the Flagg selectmen and on Nathan Perry, who had served as both selectman and treasurer. Though it found that the

Committee of Correspondence had turned over to the treasurer all the money received since November 1776, the investigating committee could not vouch for the disposition of that or any other money paid to the selectmen or treasurer, because those men would not respond to repeated requests for an accounting.

The town meeting accepted the investigating committee's finding that those former officials "deem themselves not accountable to your committee or to the town." Though it could get no information directly, the committee concluded that "a considerable quantity of money" was still in the hands of the former selectmen and treasurer, while at least sixteen of the town's soldiers in the Continental army had yet to be paid their bonus money. The findings with respect to the salt allowance were at least as damning.

The town accepted the committee's finding that "the selectmen engrossed to themselves the business of transporting said salt from Boston, and have charged such sums per bushel as must amount to nearly 130 dollars above the original cost." The meeting also officially declared that the distribution had been very unequal, and that people living beyond the town's borders received large supplies of salt while some Worcester residents got none.

Remarkably, the surviving town records show no further reference to these serious charges of dereliction, if not outright corruption. One important effect of the controversy seems to have been the temporary withdrawal or exile of Benjamin Flagg from the political life of the community. He would never again serve as selectman, though after a few years he could once again be found serving on significant town committees.

The feelings aroused by the censure of the former selectmen may have faded quickly into the past because the most engrossing murder trial in Worcester's history got underway only eight days later. On April 21, a grand jury indicted thirty-two-year-old Bathsheba Ruggles Spooner of Brookfield for the March 1 murder of her husband, Joshua Spooner, five years her senior. Also charged were two British soldiers who had surrendered at Saratoga with Burgoyne, and a former American soldier who had become Mrs. Spooner's lover.[235]

The judicial proceedings may have contributed to the calming of Worcester's political waters by sorting its leaders into relationships that clearly transcended their normal political alignments. The attorney appointed to defend the accused was Levi Lincoln, a staunch leader of the Flagg faction. One of Lincoln's clients, Bathsheba Spooner, was the sister-in-law of Dr. John Green, who was a member of the Bigelow-Lovell faction that normally lined up against Lincoln. Looking out at Lincoln from the jury were two of his political antagonists, Ebenezer Lovell and David Bigelow. Seated beside them, however, was Benjamin Stowell, a member of the Flagg-led board of selectmen that had been unseated and then investigated by the Lovell-Bigelow forces during the previous few months.[236]

The tale of Joshua Spooner's demise was shocking in itself, but the matter was made all the more scandalous by the gender and the social station of the alleged instigator of his murder. Bathsheba Spooner was the daughter of Timothy Ruggles of Hardwick, one of Worcester County's most respected pre-Revolutionary citizens, who was then a Loyalist in exile in Nova Scotia. The timing of Bathsheba's 1766 marriage to Joshua Spooner, a Brookfield merchant, may have been related to Ruggles's political problems and his desire to secure his daughter's future before the impending storm broke. Bathsheba would later claim that the match was "not agreeable" to her, and the Reverend Thaddeus Maccarty, who got to know her during the final weeks of her life, believed that "she was unhappy...in her first setting out in the world."[237]

All three of the accused men were allegedly involved when Joshua Spooner was beaten, strangled and tossed head first down his well.[238] Bathsheba Spooner, who reportedly "seemed vastly confused" at the scene, gave the killers money and some of her husband's clothing.[239] Unhappily for the conspirators, one of the British soldiers soon appeared drunk in a Worcester tavern, sporting shoes with silver buckles that bore the initials of Joshua Spooner, whose body had just been discovered. The three killers were quickly rounded up, and Mrs. Spooner was also brought to the Worcester jail.[240]

To accommodate as much of the anticipated crowd as possible, the trial of the four was conducted in the town's meetinghouse rather than the county courthouse. Testimony and argument took up sixteen continuous hours, from eight in the morning until midnight.[241] The next morning, the jury found all four guilty, and the court sentenced them to die by hanging on June 4.[242]

Bathsheba Spooner then added an emotional new dimension to the case: she revealed to Worcester's minister that she was expecting a child. Maccarty immediately asked the Massachusetts Council for a delay on behalf of all of the condemned, to give them more time to prepare spiritually for death and to save the life of Mrs. Spooner's child. The council ordered a one-month stay. A jury consisting of two "men midwives" and twelve "matrons" was summoned to examine Spooner. Following their verdict that she was not "quick with child,"[243] Mrs. Spooner petitioned the council directly. The council turned down repeated requests to extend the stay, and the execution remained scheduled for July 2.[244] On that day, before a crowd of thousands, the four murderers were "launched into eternity." A fifth life was also lost. That evening, at her request, the body of Bathsheba Spooner was cut open, and according to Maccarty, "a perfect male fetus of the growth of five months, or near it, in the judgment of the operators, was taken from her."[245]

For whatever reasons, political behavior in Worcester was different following the excitement and the tragedy of the Spooner affair. Perhaps the chief antagonists in the local battles looked at each other with new eyes after they had crossed factional lines to play out their roles in the investigation, trial and execution. Perhaps they felt a new weariness and a new longing for peace as their attention turned from the swinging corpses of the widow and the soldiers to focus once again on the war and its demands. Although Ebenezer Lovell and his allies controlled the board of selectmen from March 1778 to March 1781, the old factional lines were often blurred as Worcester struggled to cope with the burdens of the protracted military and economic crisis.

CONTINUING TOLLS OF WAR

Because people had no confidence in the paper money issued by the state or by the Continental Congress, the prices of goods rose at a phenomenal rate. In 1779, the Reverend Thaddeus Maccarty protested to the town that the £1,200 he was being paid was worth much less than the £80 he had been receiving before the war. The town agreed, and raised his salary to £2,560, probably knowing that the new amount would hardly be sufficient by the time taxes had been collected and the proceeds had been handed over to the pastor. None of these efforts had the slightest effect on prices. Money came so close to being worthless that by June 1780, the town was offering to pay military recruits their bounties in grain, which was valued at 1774 prices.[246]

As paper accumulated in the coastal towns that dominated the General Court, Massachusetts began making provisions for redeeming the bills. To collect the gold and silver it wanted, the General Court insisted that taxes—mostly levied on farmers' lands—be paid in specie, in effect refusing to honor its own paper or Continental paper. Worcester followed suit, refusing in 1781 to accept as payment for taxes the promissory notes it had issued to its own soldiers,[247] insisting instead on "solid money."[248] While the soldiers waited for the town to pay them, they were expected to pay the town.

Although the averaging system for paying the costs of the war had been thwarted, the town also rejected a return to the system of using property taxes to raise bounty money. Faced with the prospect of having no money at all for raising soldiers, Worcester finally returned to the recourse of borrowing money for the bounties and then voting a tax to pay for the borrowing.[249]

In February 1781, Worcester adopted a new system known as "classing," which had been authorized by the General Court two months earlier. Each time a call for recruits arrived, town officials could divide the taxpayers into a number of groups or classes equal to the number of Continental soldiers the town was required to raise. The membership of the classes was to be determined by "intermixing the poor with the rich, so as to make the several classes [groups] as nearly equal in property and in number of polls [individuals] as may be with convenience." Each class was responsible for finding and paying its own recruit. If the class failed to produce its man, the town could hire a recruit and tax the class members a sum up to twice the amount paid the new soldier.

The system did not involve a real shift in the financial burden, since the tax list was still used to decide the proportion each individual in a class would be required to pay. However, by making each class, and each taxpayer in it, subject to penalties if its recruit was not found, the system vastly expanded the number of men and women with a financial stake in the success of the recruitment effort.

In Worcester, as in most American communities after 1776, service in the Continental army was being left largely to the poor, the young and the black. Classing succeeded in raising men, but Worcester's recruits were drawn largely from outside the town and from the economic margins of society. In one group of twenty-one Worcester recruits hired under the classing system, there were apparently no Worcester residents.[250] Soldiers were being hired wherever they could be found, sometimes becoming objects of commerce, like slaves or indentured servants. Joseph Barber of Worcester, for example, traveled to Stockbridge to hire John Spring of that town, had him mustered in at Great Barrington "for the town of Worcester" and then for ninety pounds in silver money "assigned him over" to the Worcester class led by Samuel Salisbury.[251] In effect, the Salisbury class bought its man from Barber. Indeed, some of the men willing to enter the service probably were slaves. One recruit "for the town of Worcester" was listed as "Jupiter— negro," and another simply as "Cato."[252]

The Massachusetts Constitution and Slavery

As political tensions began to ease in Worcester in 1778, Levi Lincoln and his successor as clerk of courts, Joseph Allen, were frequently chosen as moderators of town meetings. In August 1779 they were elected, along with David Bigelow, to serve as Worcester's delegates to one of the most significant gatherings in Western political history: the convention to draft a constitution for the state of Massachusetts.[253] Though most Americans subscribed to the theory that legitimate governments had to derive their authority from the people, no one had ever worked out the mechanism by which such a grant of authority might initially be established. The Massachusetts legislature, the General Court, was still meeting as an emergency body under the forms of the royal charter of 1691. The court was under considerable pressure, especially from the western counties of Hampshire and Berkshire, for a constitution derived from the people. In 1778, the legislature drafted a constitution and sent it out to the towns for their approval. The proposal was widely rejected, partly on the ground that the General Court, a legislative body, had no authorization to draft a constitution.

It was then that the town of Concord came up with the idea that has since become the touchstone of constitutional legitimacy in republics around the world: A special convention, consisting of delegates directly elected by the people, should draft a constitution and submit it to their constituents. Only after the people themselves had approved a constitution could a legitimate government take power under its provisions.[254] At the 1780 constitutional convention, Lincoln, Allen and Bigelow worked with the former Worcester schoolmaster, John Adams, who is often regarded as the father of the Massachusetts constitution. When the convention's work was submitted to the towns, it faced strenuous criticism, but the convention counted the votes and declared the constitution ratified.

Unlike the future Constitution of the United States, the Massachusetts constitution, in its Declaration of Rights, stated that "all men are created free and equal," a provision frequently cited as the basis for the abolition of slavery in Massachusetts. Though there is no doubt that the long-established institution became illegal in the state in the aftermath of the Revolution, authorities differ on precisely how the process took place. Slavery succumbed to a combination of African American activism, changing public opinion, an increase in the number of formal and informal emancipations and a number of court decisions.[255] The best-known judicial proceedings were associated with a Worcester County man named Quock Walker, who in 1754 had been purchased, along with his slave parents, by Nathaniel Jennison of Barre. In 1781, perhaps relying on a promise made by his previous owner, Quock Walker considered himself a free adult and sued Jennison for beating him up and imprisoning him in a futile effort to force his submission. The jury agreed with Walker's claim that he was free.

The dispute spawned further litigation, stemming in part from Jennison's belief that a pair of his Barre neighbors, brothers John and Seth Caldwell, had enticed Walker to leave his supposed master. It was in this case that Levi Lincoln, attorney for the Caldwells, made what became a famous argument against the legality of slavery, based not on the constitution of Massachusetts but on "the law of reason and revelation."

Lincoln asked the jury,

> *Is it not a law of nature that all men are equal & free? Is not the law of nature the law of God—Is not the law of God then against slavery—If there is no law of men establishing of it there is no difficulty—If there is then the great difficulty is to determine which law you ought to obey—and if you should have the same Ideas as I have of resent & future things you will obey the former—For the worst that can happen to you for disobeying the former is the destruction of the body[;] for the last that of your own souls.*[256]

The jury found for the Caldwells. Following a series of appeals, at a 1783 session in Worcester, Chief Justice William Cushing, citing the state constitution's guarantee of freedom, liberty and protection for life and property, declared that the constitution's guarantees were "wholly incompatible and repugnant" to slavery and that "perpetual servitude can no longer be tolerated in our government."[257]

THE NEW ARISTOCRACY

To an outsider, the Worcester of 1783 might have looked much like the Worcester of 1775. The population was growing, but not rapidly. From around 1,900 people in 1775, it would rise to 2,095 for the first United States census in 1790.[258] The overall composition of the town's population had also remained remarkably constant; most of the new names appearing on tax lists up to 1783 seem to have belonged to young Worcester men coming of age.[259] The number of commercial establishments and professional men in town was also fairly stable.[260]

However, in the center of town the makeup of the population was also changing significantly. This phenomenon was in many ways reminiscent of an earlier phase of Worcester's history, when the opening of the county courts in 1731 brought to town a new elite of appointed officeholders. They came mostly from the South, led by the Chandlers of Woodstock. During the Revolutionary period, there were again outsiders moving into Worcester—ambitious men who would quite rapidly merge with remnants of the old aristocracy to form a new local elite. This time the pretenders to social and economic prominence rode into Worcester mostly from the east, and in those eastern origins lay much of their significance as new members of the Worcester community.

Levi Lincoln won a seat in Congress in 1800 and rose to the cabinet of Thomas Jefferson as attorney general, but soon returned to Massachusetts, where his career included service as acting governor. *Courtesy American Antiquarian Society.*

Some of the newcomers were, like the Chandlers of the 1730s, beneficiaries of a political patronage system based in Boston. One of the most important was Levi Lincoln of Hingham, the 1772 Harvard graduate who had arrived in 1775 to take up Timothy Paine's old post as clerk of courts and was soon serving as judge of probate. In 1779, Lincoln was also designated a special prosecutor in the confiscation proceedings against the estate of the absent Loyalist John Chandler. Two years later, Lincoln resigned from the bench to concentrate on his lucrative legal practice.[261]

Lincoln's successor as clerk was Joseph Allen, born and raised in a mercantile family in Boston. Allen had moved to Leicester in 1770, and then to Worcester in 1776 to take up his new position in the courthouse.[262] Joseph Wheeler, a 1757 graduate of Harvard, was appointed register of probate in 1775 and moved to a home near the courthouse in 1781.[263]

As they rose to the pinnacle of a gradually reconstituted hierarchy in Worcester, the members of the emerging new patronage elite were joined by new businessmen. The four who had been the greatest property owners in 1770—John and Gardiner Chandler, James Putnam and Nathaniel Adams, all Loyalists—were gone by 1778. Their places had been taken by men like storekeepers Stephen and Samuel Salisbury, whose joint holdings placed them at the top of the list of 1778 taxpayers. Just behind them was another merchant who had moved to Worcester during the war: John Nazro.

The trend evident in 1778 was even more pronounced by 1783. Levi Lincoln, after prosecuting the case against John Chandler's estate, had purchased a portion of the confiscated property[264] and in 1783 ranked just behind the Salisbury brothers in taxable wealth. Timothy Paine, in fifty-sixth place on the 1778 tax list, had been managing his many properties carefully, and by 1783 was the eighth wealthiest taxpayer in Worcester. The entrepreneurial Palmer Goulding, who had been roughed up a decade earlier for his Loyalist sympathies, had risen from twentieth place in 1778 to fifth in 1783. In sixth place was another entrepreneur from Boston, Daniel Waldo, who had moved to Worcester in 1782 and opened a store selling hardware and West Indies goods at the north end of the town's main street.[265]

Not all of the wealthy families of Worcester were newcomers or former Loyalists. Some Whig leaders were still among the most prosperous men of Worcester. Dr. John Green, with a mansion on what is still known as Green Hill, had risen to ninth place on the tax list in 1783; Joshua Bigelow, Robert Smith and Samuel Brooks remained in the top twenty, where they had been in 1770. Despite these survivals, what had happened at the top of the wealth structure was unmistakable. The Chandler and Paine fortunes had survived, vigorous if not entirely intact. Beside the old aristocrats now stood new men whose wealth, like that of their predecessors, was based largely on appointive positions at the courthouse, on commerce or on the practice of law.

Perhaps the most remarkable indicator of the new mood in Worcester following the cathartic summer of 1778 was the political rehabilitation of Timothy Paine. On October 6, he was appointed by the town meeting to serve on a committee to examine accounts[266]—the first position of public trust accorded him since his humiliation by the "body of the people" in 1774 and his exclusion from local office in 1775. Over the next five years, Paine would serve in a succession of increasingly important committee posts. His return to a place of honor in the community was certified in July 1783, when Paine, Joseph Allen and Joseph Wheeler were assigned the task of seeking candidates for the Worcester pulpit. The sixty-two-year-old Thaddeus Maccarty was seriously ill, and the town was looking for a second clergyman to serve as Maccarty's colleague, and presumably to succeed him after his death.[267]

The Second Church

The political reconciliation that prevailed among town leaders during the final years of the war did not eliminate unresolved disagreements over who could and should exercise legitimate authority in the community. The search for a new pastor soon brought some of those disagreements again into the open. During the renewed religious controversy, the traditional, and increasingly democratic, majority of Worcester voters—most of them farmers—would use their control of the town meeting to do battle against the new patronage elite, especially the judges, clerks and lawyers who had partially replaced, and partially merged with, the old aristocracy. At the center of the conflict stood Timothy Paine.

When the town entrusted to Paine, Allen and Wheeler the task of recruiting candidates for the ministry, it was presumably trying to take advantage of their connections to Boston and to Harvard, which was still the training ground for most Congregational ministers. Paine and Wheeler were Harvard graduates, and Allen had been born and raised in Boston. However, the first candidate the committee brought to Worcester came as a shock to many of the town's more traditional residents. Aaron Bancroft was a 1778 Harvard graduate who, with the permission of Massachusetts authorities,[268] had spent the last years of the war, from 1780 to 1783, behind British lines in Nova Scotia. Even more disturbing than the candidate's sojourn among the Loyalists was his decidedly Arminian theology.

Reverend Aaron Bancroft, founding pastor of the Second Parish and founder of Unitarianism in the United States. Married Lucretia Chandler, daughter of John Chandler of Worcester. *Courtesy American Antiquarian Society.*

In 1747, disagreements between orthodox Calvinists and liberal Arminians had been officially papered over in Worcester by the selection of the orthodox but tolerant Thaddeus Maccarty. Differences of theological opinion, nevertheless, had continued to be held and expressed. People who had lived in Boston or studied at Harvard were much more likely than inland farmers to have tasted and approved of the confident

Arminian belief that upright living would be rewarded with eternal salvation. They regarded the Calvinist doctrines of predestination and election as hangovers from an age of superstition, and hardly appropriate for a more enlightened era.

Neither the town nor the church took any action before the pastor died on July 10, 1784. The orthodox Calvinist majority in the town meeting then took steps to protect itself against the Arminian bias it had discovered among the members of the pulpit committee. It gave the committee two new members, both of whom were deacons of the church. When the town voted in December to hear yet more candidates, Paine and the other original members of the pulpit committee resigned.[269]

The original committee members had heard more than enough to reach a conclusion about whose preaching they wanted to hear in the future, but they also knew that many of their neighbors were of a different mind. On March 1, 1785, Paine and fifty-three other men proposed to the town that Aaron Bancroft be hired as Worcester's new minister, along with a colleague who would be chosen by those not satisfied with Bancroft's views. The town promptly rejected the notion that theological diversity should be institutionalized within Worcester's only church. The Bancroft men then proposed that religious diversity be institutionalized within the town, if not within the church. They asked the town to consent to their formation of a new religious society. To this the town meeting gave the same negative reply it had given the Scotch-Irish Presbyterians a half-century before.[270] A number of the petitioners then adjourned to a nearby tavern and voted to form a new religious society. As their moderator, they chose the pre-Revolutionary clerk of courts, Timothy Paine, and as their recorder the current clerk, Joseph Allen.[271]

For the next five years, the town majority was pitted against a minority of influential men who were associated, before, during and after the Revolution, with the courthouse. The three most influential leaders of the society that gathered around Aaron Bancroft were the three clerks of court: Paine, his successor Lincoln and Lincoln's successor, Allen. The links between the new courthouse elite and the old became more and more evident as the controversy unfolded. Of the sixty-three men eventually named as incorporators of the Second Parish, eight had been Loyalists a decade earlier.[272] With their sons, brothers and cousins they made up nearly 30 percent of the Bancroft incorporators. Just as every college graduate and every lawyer in Worcester had been a Loyalist during the 1770s, every college graduate and every lawyer in the 1780s joined the Bancroft society.[273] The links to the Chandler family were also conspicuous. In addition to Timothy Paine and two of his sons, the Bancroft men included three sons, a son-in-law and another nephew of the exiled John Chandler. Among the founding members of the new church were two of Chandler's daughters, one of whom, Lucretia Chandler, became the Reverend Aaron Bancroft's wife on October 24, 1786.

The town majority demonstrated what it may have learned from its Revolutionary experience about the power of the vote. Less than a week after the Bancroft men had claimed secession from the town church, Worcester chose its town officers for 1785. The two selectmen who had emerged as supporters of Bancroft were turned out of office. Deacon Nathan Perry of the orthodox town church was elected to head a board of selectmen that did not include a single member of the Bancroft group. The Bancroft men would, in fact, be almost completely excluded from major town offices for the next five years. With the meetinghouse under the control of the town majority, the Bancroft men turned to the justices of the peace and immediately secured permission to use the courthouse for their religious meetings, which began without delay in March 1785.

For the next two years, the Bancroft men functioned as a "poll parish," supporting their society through voluntary giving rather than by taxation. They did not seek from the legislature the act of incorporation that would have legally freed them from taxation for the support of the town church. The lawyerly Arminians were looking for an agreement by which the majority would accept the separation and and settle financial claims. Each time they approached the town meeting for an agreement, their proposals were rejected.[274]

Church Divisions and Shays' Rebellion

The crisis in Worcester's social and church relationships soon became linked to a more famous crisis in the politics of Massachusetts and the infant United States. At the close of the War for Independence, the perennial shortage of gold and silver coin had gotten much worse. Americans rushed to buy British goods they had longed for during decades of boycotts and war. Merchants on both sides of the Atlantic were happy to extend credit to cash-poor customers, creating a chain of debt that reached from British ports to the American hinterland. Meanwhile, American exports and the carrying trade were hindered by the exclusion of United States ships from most of the British empire. At the same time, the government of Massachusetts was determined to fill the financial requisitions coming from the Continental Congress and also to pay off the debt the state itself had incurred during the struggle for independence.

Most of that debt was held by speculators in the eastern, commercial towns. Controlled by legislators from those same towns, the legislature in the mid-1780s levied unusually high taxes and demanded gold or silver in payment. Farmers with substantial holdings in land, buildings and livestock, but no ready cash, were soon being hauled before the courts, confined to debtors' prisons and stripped of their real estate.[275]

Worcester had seen some of these difficulties coming, and it had tried to fend them off. In 1781 and 1782, the town sent delegates to self-created county conventions to protest the financial policies of the state government. In 1784, the town adopted county convention resolutions complaining that the inadequate supply of money was producing the bondage of "one part of the people" to the "other part."[276] In August and September of 1786, the conflict between those two parts of the people in Worcester intensified. The county convention movement was being revived, raising memories of how such protest meetings had assumed Revolutionary authority in 1774. The town meeting on August 10, 1786, rejected a motion to send delegates to a new protest convention that was scheduled to be held in Leicester. Nineteen men then signed a petition claiming that Worcester's refusal to remain in the convention movement "must have been because the notice was somewhat short," which presumably would allow residents of the center to attend more easily than farmers living a greater distance from the meetinghouse. Since the opportunity to attend the Leicester meeting had passed, the petitioners asked for a new meeting to send delegates to the next session of the convention, set for September 26 in Paxton.[277]

The town met to consider this request on September 25, but by then the political climate in Massachusetts had changed radically. The series of events known to history as Shays' Rebellion had begun to unfold. Beginning August 29 in Northampton, armed men calling themselves Regulators had in fact resumed the tactics of 1774, obstructing the civil and criminal courts in five counties. Efforts to raise the militia to protect the courts were useless, because among the citizen soldiers there was widespread sympathy for the farmers/Regulators and their cause, which was to paralyze the courts until a new General Court could be elected and provide legislative relief. In Worcester, on September 5 and 6, several hundred armed men had formed ranks and prevented the judges from entering the courthouse.[278]

Following the outbreak of court closings, critics condemned the county conventions as seedbeds of sedition. Supporters defended them as traditional and legitimate outlets for the expression of popular grievances, as well as an indispensable means of avoiding further armed action by desperate farmers (yeomen).[279] In this atmosphere of crisis, by a narrow margin the town of Worcester on September 25 took its stand once again with the agrarian protest. By a vote of forty-seven to thirty-nine it sent David Bigelow and an important new leader, Daniel Baird, to the Paxton convention.[280] The same scenario was played out in October. A meeting on October 2 dismissed the convention

All licenced and permitted Perſons, and thoſe who have any Duty to pay on Carriages, are requeſted to attend and make Payment, or they may depend on being put to Coſt; and thoſe Aſſeſſors who have neglected to make return of the Carriages in their reſpective towns are requeſted to do it ſpeedily.
April 22d, 1786.   CALEB AMMIDOWN, Collector.

ALL Perſons indebted to the Subſcriber are requeſted to make immediate payment, to prevent being ſued without further notice.
                       CLARK CHANDLER.
Worceſter, April 21, 1786.

WE the Subſcribers being appointed Commiſſioners by the Hon. JOSEPH DORR, Eſq; Judge of Probate for the County of Worceſter, to receive and examine the claims of the ſeveral creditors to the eſtate of BENJAMIN SADLER, late of UPTON, in ſaid county, yeoman, deceaſed, repreſented inſolvent, hereby give notice to the ſeveral creditors to ſaid eſtate that we will attend the buſineſs at the houſe of Mr. *Thomas Bicknall,* innholder in *Grafton,* on the firſt Monday in April next, and the firſt Monday in the five following months from nine to fix o'clock on each of ſaid days.
                          JOSEPH WOOD,   } Commiſſi-
March 18th, 1786.   THOMAS BICKNALL, } oners.

A series of notices from 1786 attesting to the credit problems that crippled Worcester's economy in the aftermath of the Revolutionary War. *Courtesy American Antiquarian Society.*

delegates; a citizens' petition demanded a new meeting; a meeting on October 16 reappointed Baird and Bigelow by a vote of sixty-two to fifty-three.[281]

The close votes in a succession of town meetings reflected Worcester's intermediate position between well-developed market towns, where the Regulators got little sympathy, and rural farming communities, where many understood the suffering of the yeomen all too well. The town's intermediate position was also reflected in the fact that although the town meeting narrowly sided with the extralegal county conventions, there seem to have been few or no Worcester men who took up arms with the Regulators.

In Worcester, the agrarian turmoil was closely related to the conflict over religious affairs. Men who wanted to preserve the undivided orthodox town church tended also to sympathize with the farmers' protests, while men who wanted to establish a separate Arminian church tended to oppose the conventions and court closings. Of the forty-six men who signed petitions for town meetings to choose convention delegates, only three ever appeared as Bancroft supporters, and all three abandoned the Arminians before the new society's incorporation.[282] The only firm Bancroft man who can be identified as a supporter of the conventions was David Bigelow, brother of Timothy and a longtime Whig leader, who was repeatedly chosen as a convention delegate. Bigelow differed in another way from the leaders and many of the members of the Arminian group: he did not live in the village center. Like his fellow convention delegate, Daniel Baird, Bigelow was an innkeeper in an outlying agricultural district.[283]

The Worcester courts, closed by the Regulators in September, were again forcibly disrupted in November. In December, up to two thousand men, some of them under the direct command of Daniel Shays of Pelham, gathered in the town and again blocked the courts. Their leaders sent a petition to Governor James Bowdoin and the council, expressing dismay at "the suspension of the privilege of the writ of Habeas Corpus" and the arrest of several Regulators. They asked for the release of the prisoners and the suspension of the courts until the May election of a new legislature. Recalling their Revolutionary service, the Regulators proclaimed that they also did not fear "the uncertainty of war, the injuries of hunger, cold, nakedness, or the infamous name of rebel; as under all these disadvantages they once before engaged, and through the blessings of God have come off victorious."[284]

"The infamous name of rebel," however, was precisely the term applied to the Regulators by state leaders in Boston. A special state army was organized to march to Worcester and protect the courts during their next session. Under General Benjamin Lincoln, the troops reached the shire town in January 1787. No opposing force gathered, and the courts were able to open without incident. While he was in Worcester, General Lincoln reported to Governor James Bowdoin that "Several Persons of the first character here" were recommending the arrest of Daniel Baird.[285] Farmer, innkeeper and town selectman, Baird had been conspicuous not only as a convention man, but also as a critic of the Arminian separation. Just a week before the arrival of Lincoln's army, after months of hearing the conventions denounced as unconstitutional and inflammatory, Baird had thrown the rhetoric back in the teeth of the Bancroft supporters. At a tumultuous town meeting, he denounced the ecclesiastical proceedings of the lawyerly

Arminians as "irregular, unconstitutional, and of a dangerous tendency."[286] "Persons of the first character" had more than one reason to want Daniel Baird removed from the Worcester scene.

A warrant was promptly issued for Baird's arrest under an emergency statute authorizing the incarceration of anyone suspected of being a threat to "the safety of the Commonwealth." Baird may have gone into hiding; five weeks went by before he was arrested and delivered to jail in Boston on March 5.[287] Baird was eventually released on bond, and was apparently never charged with a crime.[288]

General Lincoln's orders, once he had ensured the safety of the courts meeting in Worcester, were to pursue and capture or disperse the Regulators. Daniel Shays and his men were west of Worcester, heading for the federal arsenal in Springfield to collect supplies and arms to defend themselves. As they approached the arsenal on January 25, 1787, they were met with cannon fire from members of the Hampshire County militia. Four of the Regulators were killed, twenty more were wounded and the rest ran for their lives. Still in Worcester when word of the Springfield shooting reached him, Lincoln set off in pursuit of the insurgent forces. The remnants of the Regulators were overtaken and scattered in Petersham on February 3.[289]

Like the agrarian protest, the parochial struggle in Worcester was ultimately settled by the power of the state. Soon after the Lincoln expedition had crushed the Regulators, the Bancroft men submitted to the legislature their petition for incorporation as Worcester's Second Parish. The town majority continued its vigorous resistance, voting in May 1787 to oppose the petition and sending three selectmen to Boston to convey the town's objections. Nevertheless, the General Court granted the Arminian petition in November. For the first time, Worcester had two officially recognized churches and parishes.

Benjamin Lincoln, as commander of the army sent to protect Worcester from Shays' Rebellion, found himself at the center of one of post–Revolutionary War America's most significant populist uprisings. *Courtesy American Antiquarian Society.*

At the polls, the orthodox, agrarian majority continued to fight back. Whatever "persons of the first character" may have thought of him, voters reelected the former convention delegate, Daniel Baird, to the board of selectmen nine days after his arrest.[290] In December 1787, when Worcester chose delegates to the Massachusetts convention called to consider the proposed Constitution of the United States, one of the two selected was the other convention man, David Bigelow.[291]

The so-called rebellion associated with the name of Daniel Shays had given considerable momentum to a different movement that was already well underway. Its purpose was to give the new nation a stronger central government, one that could pay its debts and properly supervise the supposedly unruly people of the states. Many men who had served in the Continental Congress or as officers in the Continental army believed that under the Articles of Confederation, the states were becoming too democratic, their governments falling into the hands of factions led by irresponsible demagogues. From that point of view, Shays' Rebellion could be interpreted as evidence that the people refused to be governed properly. That interpretation provided the nationalists with a fresh rallying point. In fact, the government of Massachusetts had proven itself more than capable of quelling the disturbances it faced. Nevertheless, many men of property and influence throughout the nation were convinced that the infant republic was menaced by anarchy, or by its close relative, democracy.

The movement to strengthen the national government raised correspondingly grave suspicions among farmers who, as Americans, had just concluded a long struggle to defend the exclusive right of their local legislatures, not Parliament, to tax them. Now a coalition of prominent nationalists, calling themselves "Federalists," were proposing a Constitution that would give a distant Congress the power not only to tax, but also to prohibit the states from issuing paper money. Also alarming to many was the fact that the proposed Constitution, unlike most state constitutions, did not include a bill of rights. That omission helped the opponents of the Constitution, labeled "Antifederalists," to raise once again the specter of tyrannical government.

In the Massachusetts ratification convention, the Federalists narrowly prevailed, after months of debate. The vote to ratify the Constitution of the United States was 187 to 168. The Federalists prevailed only by going along with a proposal put forth by the state's popular governor, John Hancock. Hancock urged the convention both to support ratification of the Constitution and, at the same time, to call for amendments that would specify the rights of citizens and place more explicit limits on the power of the federal government—a promise that eventually led to the national Bill of Rights. One of Worcester's delegates, Samuel Curtis, was apparently not present for the vote by which Massachusetts ratified the Constitution. David Bigelow, however, was present, and he demonstrated once again that his political and economic views coincided with those of the farmers of central and western Massachusetts. When the roll was called on the creation of a powerful and distant government with taxing authority and extensive powers of appointment, Bigelow, like 85 percent of the delegates from Worcester County, voted "Nay."[292]

TIMOTHY PAINE AND THE NEW ARISTOCRACY

Although the Arminians had been incorporated as the Second Parish in 1787, the First Parish was still without a minister and still not reconciled to the separation, however legal. When town officers were chosen for 1788, the orthodox deacon, Nathan Perry, and the anti-Bancroft men again took all seats on the board of selectmen. However, at the May election of a state representative, the agrarian, orthodox majority suffered a setback, and the political rehabilitation of Timothy Paine took a dramatic leap forward. Perhaps because of a small turnout, the man who had last served as Worcester's representative in 1762 was chosen to represent the town in the state House of Representatives for 1788.

In June, the Constitution of the United States, though opposed by David Bigelow and probably by a majority of Worcester residents, was ratified. That meant that Worcester County had the task of electing a representative to serve in the first Congress of the United States. The dynamics of the election show that while the town was being reordered following two decades of political upheaval, Timothy Paine had become a symbol of reconciliation between members of the old aristocracy and many members of the new.

The first voting for Congress on December 18 placed the former Loyalist in the lead, but with less than the required majority. His principal opponents were Jonathan Grout of Petersham and Artemas Ward of Shrewsbury. Both of them had been members of the Worcester County Convention that had helped orchestrate the humiliation of Timothy Paine in 1774. That moment of Revolutionary solidarity, however, had long passed. In the struggle between agrarian and commercial interests still agitating the state, Grout and Ward were in distinctly different camps. Grout had been an active supporter of the agrarian protest movement during the last two years and, like David Bigelow, had voted in the state convention against ratification of the national Constitution.[293] Ward, as chief judge of the county courts in 1786, had faced the bayonets of the Regulators on the steps of the Worcester courthouse.[294]

With a former Loyalist (Paine) running first, followed by an Antifederalist (Grout) and a conservative Federalist (Ward), Worcester County prepared for a second congressional vote on January 29, 1789. Most observers who wrote letters to Isaiah Thomas's *Massachusetts Spy* believed that the contest was effectively between Paine and Grout,[295] and they framed the contest in terms of the conflict between commercial and agricultural interests. Paine's supporters portrayed him as a landowner, and thus an appropriate representative for a district of farmers. Conceding Grout's devotion to the interests of the yeomen, supporters argued that Paine could represent farmers as well as Grout could, while also bringing to the national legislature the wider vision he had gained through education and experience in public affairs.[296]

In the second round of balloting, Paine received around one thousand votes, Grout around nine hundred and Ward only around three hundred. Since Paine's vote was still short of a majority, the district would have to vote a third time. This time Paine's record during the Revolution became a subject of debate. He was attacked as a monarchist and

Isaiah Thomas, printer, patriot and scholar, brought the *Massachusetts Spy* to Worcester when war broke out in 1775. *Courtesy American Antiquarian Society.*

an opponent of independence,[297] while his supporters tried to convince readers that the one-time mandamus councilor was devoted to "true republican principles."[298]

The prospect of having to choose between a candidate who had opposed the Revolution (Paine) and a candidate who had opposed the Constitution (Grout) finally became too much for Isaiah Thomas. The printer, who had been an active Whig, an ardent foe of the Regulators and a strong supporter of the new Constitution, on February 19 made his first published comment in an editorial obliquely endorsing Artemas Ward.

To Thomas, what was at stake was the fresh and fragile heritage of the American Revolution. Without using the Tory label, Thomas warned against "open and professed enemies of our country" who were trying to divide and conquer. Though Thomas did not name anyone, he endorsed a candidate who had been at the center of the struggle in the days when the spirit of liberty "rendered our arms victorious" and "pervaded our councils." Artemas Ward was the only candidate who fit that patriotic profile. After leaving the Continental army due to ill health, Ward had worked steadily as a member of the council—the executive arm of the Massachusetts government until the ratification of the state constitution in 1780.[299]

Thomas's meaning was not lost upon his readers, especially upon the supporters of Timothy Paine, who apparently felt that their man had beaten Judge Ward fair and square and should as a consequence be the consensus candidate among members of the reconstituted establishment. A week after the Thomas editorial, a writer warned "over zealous federalists" that they had better abandon their effort to revive Ward's candidacy. The writer urged the Ward men to "meet us half way and give their votes for Mr. Paine."[300]

A principal goal of the Paine candidacy was "reconciliation" among those General Lincoln had called "persons of the first character" in Worcester. The effort was not unrelated to Paine's election as state representative and his shared leadership of the Arminian secession, which had brought many of the surviving Loyalists into alliance with Arminian Whigs like Isaiah Thomas. Paine's congressional candidacy would further bind such men in common resolve to ensure that power would once again rest securely in the hands of men of property and learning.

Agrarian voters apparently agreed on what the stakes were, and they responded with such energy that Jonathan Grout was elected, becoming one of the few Antifederalists to serve in the first Congress. During the 1786 debates, votes on whether to participate in the conventions had been very close. They reflected Worcester's central place along the continuum from commercial centers to agricultural villages. In 1788–89, the town's ambivalence could hardly have been better expressed than it was by the 61 to 60 congressional vote between Paine and Grout in the shire town. In contrast, the voters of Petersham, Grout's agrarian hometown, gave their man 105 votes to Paine's 27 and Ward's 4. Meanwhile Lancaster, a market town with strong Loyalist and now Federalist tendencies, gave Paine 68 votes to Grout's 19 and Ward's 9.[301]

SECURING THE NEW ORDER

In 1790, Artemas Ward defeated Jonathan Grout in the election to the second Congress. Before the first ballot on October 4, a pro-Grout writer urged a large turnout, to settle a contest in which "the main struggle is whether the Farmers or the Lawyers in this county shall be represented." A Federalist writer dismissed with contempt "the vulgar objection against sending attornies at law."[302]

Ward and Grout were the clear leaders in the first round, and a second vote was set for November 26. In the apparent absence of a campaign effort by the agrarians, Ward won with 1,248 votes in the whole district, compared to 1,081 for Grout.[303] This time, the votes of Worcester's yeomen were clearly not mobilized. The number of votes cast in the town fell off by more than one-fourth. Artemas Ward received 53 Worcester votes to Jonathan Grout's 26. Thus, the man who had been forced by the bayonets of the Regulators to back away from his courthouse door was chosen to replace the agrarian spokesman from Petersham, the town in which the remnants of Daniel Shays's army had been scattered almost four years earlier.

In Worcester County, the agrarians were defeated, but not dead. Two years later, Grout defeated Ward during a first-round vote in November. The Federalists promptly agreed on a younger lawyer, Dwight Foster of Brookfield, as their new candidate and collected forty-one Worcester votes for him against eight for Samuel Lyman and one for Grout. Once again, with very little resistance from the voters of the shire town, a Federalist lawyer headed for New York to represent Worcester County.[304] Though not a Worcester resident, Foster was a fitting representative of the Federalist elite that had emerged in the shire town in the course of the 1780s. He would continue to serve as the district's representative for the rest of the 1790s, and then move on to the United States Senate.

Chapter 6

BEYOND FARMING (1790–1828)

It took decades after 1790 for Worcester to be slowly led away from its mentality as a traditional farming town, a community in which social or economic changes were unwelcome. As they had for generations, leaders with homes and business interests in the central village pursued one strategy after another to stimulate population growth and promote commercial and industrial development. During the 1790s, the advocates of development made some progress, but the pace then slowed. The residents of the village center—like citizens throughout the United States—divided into two fiercely antagonistic political parties. When partisanship receded after the War of 1812, the village center resumed its modernizing push. By the end of the 1820s, under a new generation of leaders, many of whom were born after the American Revolution, the "Port of Worcester" was linked by the Blackstone Canal to the world of Atlantic commerce. As so many of its promoters had long dreamed, Worcester was ready to move into an economic world beyond farming. Unexpectedly, the new era had been made possible by crews of Irish canal builders, people not included in the dreams of Worcester's boosters. Some of the Irish stayed on after the construction had been completed. Their presence reintroduced Worcester to ethnic and religious diversity, a change few members of the community were prepared to welcome.

FEDERALIST WORCESTER

In 1790, as Artemas Ward went off to Congress, and a post-Revolutionary order slowly settled over Worcester, some members of the community were in a better position than others to take advantage of the opportunities presented by the changing times. Timothy Bigelow, liberated from British captivity in the summer of 1776, had served honorably throughout the war and returned to Worcester as its most respected military hero. According to the official county record, he was "liberated" once again on April 1, 1790. This time, however, liberation was provided "By Deth." Bigelow had died the previous

Colonel Timothy Bigelow monument on Worcester Common, honoring Worcester's most distinguished Revolutionary War soldier. *Courtesy American Antiquarian Society.*

evening, at the age of fifty-one, in the Worcester County Jail. He had been committed six weeks earlier for failing to pay his debts.[305]

Bigelow had survived the challenges of war—including a 1781 court-martial that vindicated his conduct the night he was taken prisoner at Quebec.[306] In 1780, he had even been among the grantees of 23,040 acres in Vermont, where he had helped to found a town he named Montpelier.[307] But owning a piece of the Vermont wilderness did not allow Bigelow to surmount the economic perils of postwar life. He was never able to recover from the economic effects of ill-paid military service. Money he had borrowed to buy a farm on Jo Bill Road (now Institute Road) was already overdue by the time he returned to civilian life.[308] In the scarce-money, debt-ridden economy of the late 1780s, he had tried to resume his once-profitable trade as a blacksmith, with little success.[309] Timothy Bigelow had borrowed from the Salisbury brothers, as well as from Levi Lincoln, on whose claim he had been committed to jail. Lincoln eventually took possession of the Bigelow farm by foreclosure.[310]

The men who would shape the new era and profit from it would not, for the most part, be the artisans and farmers, men like Bigelow, who had brought down the colonial aristocracy. Instead, they would be men of commerce, like Salisbury, and men of the law, like Lincoln, who had moved to Worcester during the Revolutionary turmoil and were now poised to take advantage of the opportunities the infant republic afforded the enterprising and the bold. Allied with them were professional men and merchants who were prominent and strikingly prosperous members of the Chandler and Paine families.

It was not difficult for anyone visiting Worcester to locate these men and others striving busily to carry the town into a new era of commercial prosperity. They all lived and worked within walking distance of one another on Main Street. The Reverend Peter Whitney of Northborough, describing Worcester in 1793, remarked that "in the centre, in the compass of one mile, and mostly on one street are collected the county officers, a number of merchants and shop keepers, professional men, and mechanics of various sorts."[311]

When Whitney also noted that "the inhabitants of the outer parts of this town subsist by husbandry," he was referring to the majority of Worcester's population. The long-standing differences between the village center and the outlying farming districts persisted into the new era, as the men of business renewed their campaign to turn Worcester into an expanding center of trade. The town had hardly gained in population in the years since 1775, when the town had 1,925 inhabitants. By the first federal census in 1790, only 170 had been added, bringing the total to 2,095. Getting the town to grow more rapidly was at the top of the agenda of the Federalist gentlemen who provided much of the community's leadership in the 1790s.

As always, they paid great attention to improving the schools, which had been badly neglected during the Revolutionary upheaval. Despairing of adequate support from the town, in 1784 a group of leading figures in the center had formed a joint stock company to build and run a private school, probably with the expectation that it would receive public funding and serve as the town's grammar school as well.[312] In January 1787, Dr. Elijah Dix, merchant John Nazro and printer Isaiah Thomas signed an advertisement soliciting students on behalf of the school's proprietors, "a number of gentlemen in Worcester" who had, "for the purpose of instructing their children in the English, Latin, and Greek languages, erected a very commodious building, and provided an instructor, Mr. THOMAS PAYSON, late English preceptor of the Leicester Academy."[313] The two-story school was located on the west side of Main Street, about halfway between the meetinghouse and the courthouse.[314]

In 1789, at the suggestion of Timothy Paine and others, the town tried to lure something away from Leicester that was more important than Mr. Payson. The town offered an annual subsidy of forty pounds to Leicester Academy, chartered in 1784, if its trustees would move that institution to Worcester, undoubtedly into the proprietors' schoolhouse. This would have solved the perennial problem of providing a legally acceptable grammar school, and an academically respectable one as well. Yet the academy remained in Leicester.[315]

Paine was also a leader in an ambitious effort to lure a more significant institution to Worcester: the government of the state of Massachusetts. In 1792, he was one of the authors of a *Topographical Description of the Town of Worcester*, published in the Collections of Boston's new Massachusetts Historical Society. In the guise of a learned paper, the writers wanted to alert the elite readership of the new society to Worcester's advantages as a new, centrally located state capital, should the District of Maine succeed in its campaign to become a separate state. In 1793, the town tried to give the idea some impetus by granting land on the north end of the common "for the purpose of Erecting a State House on." The statehouse remained in Boston.[316] It was also in 1793 that Worcester, thanks again to merchants and professional men, joined such commercial centers as Boston, Stockbridge and Lancaster in becoming host to a Masonic lodge. Among the thirteen petitioners for the charter were a lawyer son of Timothy Paine, four merchant sons of John Chandler and one of Chandler's sons-in-law, also a merchant. The new lodge chose Isaiah Thomas as grandmaster. Most members were also members of the more cosmopolitan Second Parish. Aaron Bancroft, pastor of the parish and also a Chandler son-in-law, preached the sermon when the installation of officers was held in his church.[317]

Another Federalist initiative launched in 1793 came to fruition a decade later. The judges of the Court of Sessions decided that the second courthouse, opened in 1734, had become inadequate for the business of the growing county. They petitioned the state legislature for authority to impose the necessary taxes to build a new structure, but the plan was delayed while Worcester fought off one of the periodic attempts to divide the county. Authorization finally was secured, and construction on a site adjacent to the existing building began in 1801, under the supervision of a three-man committee led by Isaiah Thomas.

Worcester Federalists in 1796 also leaped at the opportunity to connect Worcester to the world of Atlantic commerce by building a canal along the Blackstone River from Worcester to Providence. This initiative was stymied in Boston when the state legislature refused to grant the company a Massachusetts charter. The General Court opted instead for a plan that promised to keep Worcester and the rest of the Massachusetts hinterland connected to the capital of Massachusetts rather than that of Rhode Island: a canal linking Boston to the Connecticut River. The plan was soon abandoned.[318]

The effort to tie Worcester commercially to the Atlantic was related to the fact that some Worcester entrepreneurs were taking some of the first steps in the development of Worcester as a manufacturing center. As in Great Britain and the United States in general, the leading edge of the Industrial Revolution came to Worcester in the form of textile production. In 1789, the Worcester Cotton Manufactory was organized by Daniel Waldo Jr., Samuel Brazer and other Worcester men, most of whom were members of the Second Parish and would later join the Morning Star Lodge or the Worcester Fire Society, another elite group of village center residents. The manufactory was built on the only waterway that flowed with some force through Worcester: the Mill Brook.

Rising in North Pond (later called Indian Lake), it flowed east of the central village, southeast of which it joined several other streams to form the Blackstone River. By the spring of 1789, a carding machine, spinning jenny and two looms were at work.[319] By summer, Samuel Brazer could announce the availability of Worcester-made cloth of a quality "superior to those imported," and summon customers to "give preference to the manufactures of their own country." Though in the spring of 1790 the company was advertising for an overseer, boys to serve as apprentices and "two or three journeymen weavers," by the late summer of 1790 it had apparently failed. [320]

At about the same time, Worcester's clockmaker, Abel Stowell, took two sons into partnership with him and began the manufacture of woolen goods.[321] Woolen or cotton fibers, before being spun into yard or thread, had to be combed or "carded." In response to the efforts at textile production in the region, in 1798 Samuel Denny opened a card factory on Mechanic Street in Worcester.[322] Denny undoubtedly had in mind not only recent Worcester initiatives, but also the burgeoning textile industry being organized at Pawtucket and other Blackstone Valley locations by the English immigrant Samuel Slater. The proposed Blackstone Canal would have provided Worcester a direct and profitable link to this network.

Even during the years of intense political partisanship, between 1800 and 1815, evidence accumulated in the village center of the industrialization that would in time transform Worcester as well as the region. In 1804, Peter and Ebenezer Stowell, who eventually had six water-powered looms in operation, began to weave fine carpets.[323] In 1810, John Earle and Erasmus Jones set up a wool-carding machine at a site known as Lincoln's Triphammer Shop east of the courthouse.[324] In 1812, the firm of Earle and Williams in the same area, perhaps at the same location, opened one of the earliest machine shops in Worcester to make machinery for spinning cotton and wool, carding machines and brass castings.[325]

THE REPUBLICAN ASCENDANCY

The Federalist leaders sometimes had to bring their projects before town meetings and ask for the approval of the voters. When that happened, they were subject to the long-simmering suspicions of the agricultural majority, as well as to the majority's perennial reluctance to pay taxes, especially for undertakings that seemed mainly to benefit the central village. Despite that handicap, for a decade or so after 1790 the Federalists had some success in achieving their objectives on issues such as fire protection, control of wandering livestock and school improvement. At the end of the 1790s, however, Federalist leaders found themselves confronted by the momentous decision of one of their most prominent members, Levi Lincoln, to set out on a different political course. Lincoln became a Jeffersonian Republican, and by the end of the 1790s he would lead the town out of the Federalist orbit. Worcester became a Republican citadel in a strongly Federalist county in a largely Federalist state.

Political partisanship dramatically changed the shape of Worcester's politics. Animosities in the town, as in Massachusetts and much of the nation, came to a peak during the War of 1812 and began to cool around 1815. The decade and more of Jeffersonian Republican ascendancy in Worcester slowed the progress of the central village and its business leaders, but after 1815, as influential men of both parties resumed regular cooperation in town affairs, reform efforts gained fresh momentum.

It is important to note that the relative slowdown in the development agenda between 1800 and 1815 was not due to the predominance of farmers among the Republican leaders of the town. In fact, party leadership came mostly from lawyers, merchants and tavern keepers, most of whom were undoubtedly sympathetic to the case for modernization. However, Republicans had to rely to a significant extent on the votes of Worcester's farmers. They seem in return to have provided the farmers, spread out in the "skirts," a useful means of resisting the future being prepared for them by the entrepreneurs who lived and traded along Main Street.

A mild portent of the intensely partisan future appeared in 1794, when Levi Lincoln, a Federalist, became a willing congressional candidate for the first time. He lost to fellow Federalist Dwight Foster in the district as a whole, but he won narrowly in Worcester, thirty-eight to thirty. Foster would win again in 1796 and 1798, beating Lincoln in Worcester the first time (sixty-six to forty-two), but losing to him the second (fifty-eight to sixty-nine).[326]

The increasing participation of Worcester voters, as well as Lincoln's growing constituency in the town, were signs that Worcester's most prominent lawyer was linking his local political ambitions to the partisanship developing in national politics.

There, the new federal government was becoming a bone of contention between elites from different sections of the country. Commercially oriented men, mostly from the Northeast, sought "energetic" government that would promote economic development. Men who had risen to prominence in agricultural regions, especially the South, worried that governmental activism at the national center would serve the ambitions of a grasping clique of businessmen rather than the simpler needs of a nation of farmers. By 1792, the competition had produced a bitter rivalry between George Washington's treasury secretary, Alexander Hamilton of commercial New York, and his secretary of state, Thomas Jefferson of agricultural Virginia. Their confrontation set the stage for the first national political alignments under the Constitution.

While the two cabinet secretaries held important and conflicting views concerning the nature of the Constitution and the economic future of the nation, what eventually mobilized large numbers of citizens behind Hamilton's Federalists or Jefferson's Republicans was controversy over foreign policy. War between England and the revolutionary French Republic began in 1793 and, due in large part to the imperial ambitions of Napoleon Bonaparte, continued until 1815. As the incipient American parties perceived them in the 1790s, the stakes in the European struggle could not have been higher. Both of the American parties accused their opponents of aligning themselves with a foreign power and of seeking to subvert the independence of the nation and its commitment to constitutional liberty. In the mid-1790s, the nation's official policy, set by George Washington, was neutrality in the war between the British and the French. Massachusetts, under the political influence of the commercial seacoast, inclined in the Federalist direction as partisan divisions appeared, and Worcester at first went along with the trend. The Federalist tide in Worcester politics reached its highest point in 1796 and 1797, pushed along by the 1796 presidential candidacy of John Adams, a Federalist who forty years earlier had been Worcester's schoolmaster. Federalist clerk of courts Joseph Allen received a virtually unanimous vote from the town as presidential elector, undoubtedly to cast his ballot for Adams. In the congressional race—still not clearly defined along partisan lines—Federalist Dwight Foster was victorious, within the town as well as in the district, over Levi Lincoln.[327]

The tide began to turn in 1798, when Lincoln outpolled Foster in Worcester, though he did not win in the congressional district as a whole.[328] Two turbulent years later, Thomas Jefferson was elected president of the United States over John Adams. What Jefferson called the "Revolution of 1800" also carried Levi Lincoln to Congress and helped solidify the movement that was transforming Worcester's politics. In 1800, even before true party battle lines had arrived on the state level,[329] Worcester cast 140 votes for Republican Elbridge Gerry against 35 for Federalist Caleb Strong. Strong carried the state with a thumping 73 percent of the vote, but he could attract only 19 percent in Worcester. The town's Republicans, rallying around Thomas Jefferson and Levi Lincoln, had reduced the Federalists to virtual insignificance as a local political force, even before Republicans statewide had begun to wage serious political war.

Lincoln had barely taken his seat in the seventh Congress before he resigned it to accept Jefferson's appointment as U.S. attorney general. Thanks to Federalism's continuing strength in Worcester County, Jabez Upham regained the congressional seat for his party a few months later, but he could only garner twenty-three votes in the town of Worcester against eighty-eight for the Republicans' John Whiting.[330] Lincoln had returned to exert whatever personal influence he could on Whiting's behalf.[331] In fact Lincoln, while serving in the part-time national post of attorney general, spent most of his time in Worcester, where he was for years the political "eyes and ears" of Thomas Jefferson. He also helped organize opposition to Isaiah Thomas's *Massachusetts Spy*, which had become a Federalist organ. Lincoln and his allies established a Republican alternative, the *National Aegis*, which began publication in December 1801.[332]

The Jeffersonian Republican takeover of town politics proceeded with remarkable speed and thoroughness. It took only two more years to purge Federalists from all significant town offices and from the position of state representative. Though they lived in a Federalist county in a Federalist state, Worcester voters excluded active Federalists from all offices within their reach for the next fifteen years.[333]

The tightly organized majority's careful control of the town meeting recalls the uncompromising political tactics employed by the town majority to expel the Loyalists from power in the 1770s, and later to purge the Bancroft men during the agrarian and parochial crisis of the 1780s. Levi Lincoln had not been in Worcester for the dramas of the early 1770s, and as a lawyer and a Bancroft supporter during the crisis of the late 1780s he had been among those excluded from office when his agrarian and orthodox townsmen again exercised rigid control over the meeting. Lincoln had learned his democratic lesson well. This time, as the power of Worcester's voters was consolidated and focused for the third time, Levi Lincoln had become the principal leader of the majority.

Federalists sputtered in disgust at proceedings such as those that unfolded in May 1802. First the town meeting voted to send only one representative to the House of Representatives in Boston; then it elected Republican Samuel Curtis. When Lincoln saw how easily Curtis had won, he persuaded the meeting to change its mind and send the two representatives the town was entitled to send. Republican Edward Bangs was then safely chosen to join Curtis in the legislature.

Because the selectmen supervised the voter lists, from 1803 onward Republicans had full control of an important political tool. The selectmen held an open meeting in 1807 to receive any complaints citizens might have about unjust exclusion from the lists, but no complainants appeared, perhaps because the session was held at Mower's tavern, which had become virtually the Republican Party headquarters in Worcester.[334] As partisan feelings over national politics continued to intensify, Levi Lincoln was elected lieutenant governor of Massachusetts in 1807 and 1808, and he became acting governor upon the death of James Sullivan in 1809. His presence in the Republican state administration only reinforced the grip Republicans held on politics in his hometown.

In 1807, Congress adopted, at the behest of President Jefferson, embargo laws intended to force concessions from the British, the French or both. While the nation waited for concessions, the embargo virtually shut down the foreign commerce of the United States. In 1808, the Boston town meeting protested the policy and asked Worcester and other towns to call meetings for the same purpose. In August, Worcester's selectmen replied in a letter defending the Jefferson administration's policies. A town meeting was unnecessary, they said, because the selectmen were themselves voicing "the sentiments of a large majority of the inhabitants of this town." Besides, they were sure the inhabitants would not consider it "satisfactory…on this occasion, at this season of the year, to be called together in town meeting."[335]

In 1809, the Worcester Federalists decided to mount a serious challenge in the March election meeting to the "flagrant and iniquitous" rule of the Republicans. Indeed, the qualifications of many potential Federalist voters were challenged—unfairly, in the opinion of the *Spy*, which further reported that even after excluding would-be voters, the Republicans prevailed only through parliamentary trickery employed by the Republican moderator, Edward Bangs.[336] The Republican version of these events said only that the Federalists had been treated with "merited contempt."[337] As it happened, Edward Bangs, the moderator, was also retiring after that meeting from the office of selectman. Rubbing salt in the Federalist wounds, the Republican-controlled meeting took the unprecedented step of voting "that the thanks of the town be given to Edward Bangs, Esq. for his long and faithful services in the office of selectman, to which he declined a re-election, and that the same be entered upon the records of the Town."[338]

The first American party system ironically took shape during a period in which most people regarded partisanship as a destructive influence in politics. Rather than embrace parties as legitimate vehicles for organizing public opinion, even the active participants in these early contests typically saw themselves as decent people forced by their malevolent opponents to fight fire with fire. Since their goal was to return to a world without parties, the only means to that end had to be the conversion—or the political annihilation—of their enemies. In such a charged ideological environment, political passions could rise to extreme heights. In 1836, two decades after the storm had subsided, Levi Lincoln's son, William Lincoln, still did not think it possible to discuss in his *History of Worcester* "the struggles of the great parties dividing the community" and "kindling strife in the relations of social life" during his youth. It would take at least another generation, he believed, before the story could be told with "independence and impartiality."[339]

Partisan furies reached their peak in Worcester, as in the state and nation, during the War of 1812. Even children in Worcester's streets were said to "rally themselves under the names of the two opposing parties, and to use the language…of invective and threatening." Samuel Austin, pastor of the First Church since 1790, declared that in Worcester "party interests" had been "pursued in many instances tumultuously, and without respect to law or decency.—Humanity is outraged. The elective franchise is in fact virtually taken from a portion of the citizens. They may neither speak, nor vote.— They must be silent, and content to be deprived of their privileges, or feel the smart of party resentment."[340]

In a series of *Farmer's Letters* written a decade earlier, Levi Lincoln had denounced the tendency of the orthodox Congregational clergy to act as an auxiliary force of the Federalist Party. Lincoln's criticisms were published in a new edition in 1812, partly as a response to a renewed spirit of political assertiveness among the clergy.[341] Samuel Austin of the First Church strode boldly onto the political stage. In a sermon in July 1812, Austin declared the war with Great Britain to be "against every precept of Christianity" because it was being "waged without adequate cause." It was, the pastor charged, the "war of a party" brought about "very much through the influence of men of an ungodly character."[342] Austin linked "infidel books" to political efforts "to bring down…the congregational ministers" by ending the system of taxation that supported them. Such efforts, he concluded, "have been demonstrated in publications, one of them domestic and very celebrated, and which, that the fame of its author might lose nothing by age, has recently had the honor of another edition."[343] In a footnote to the published sermon, Austin identified the infidel publication as Levi Lincoln's *Farmer's Letters* and added, "We forgive the writer. We pity him. We wish him well with all our heart. But we are ashamed that such an ebullition of despotism and malignity should ever have emanated from a press in New England."[344]

In contrast to the partisan rancors, both political and religious, that gripped Worcester in 1812, during that same year the American Antiquarian Society became a permanent institutional testimonial to the capacity of warring political leaders in Worcester to set aside their differences to establish an institution that would be an ornament to the community they were all trying to develop. In 1810 the printer, publisher and bookseller Isaiah Thomas had published his remarkable work of historical scholarship, *History of Printing in America*. In 1812, when he presented to the legislature a petition for the incorporation of

LINCOLN SQUARE, WORCESTER, MASS., WITH A VIEW OF THE NEW ANTIQUARIAN HALL, OLD AND NEW COURT HOUSES, AND UNITARIAN CHURCH.

This 1852 view of Lincoln Square, looking south, shows off the buildings of three prestigious Worcester institutions: the Unitarian Church (steeple), the old and new county courthouses and the American Antiquarian Society (right). *Courtesy American Antiquarian Society.*

a new learned society, Thomas was careful to place on the proposed board of directors leaders from both of the state's contending political parties.[345] With the society legally incorporated, in 1813 Thomas donated to it his historical library. Because wartime Boston was considered vulnerable to British attack, the library was left in Worcester, where it became the foundation of a collection that has made the American Antiquarian Society a world-renowned center for the study of early American history.[346]

The 1812 founding of the Antiquarian Society was not the only bipartisan effort to blossom during the height of partisanship. In that same year, Worcester Federalists and Republicans jointly petitioned the legislature to recharter the Worcester Bank. Led by Federalist Daniel Waldo Jr., the bank had been operating since 1804, but it had failed to win renewal from the Republican legislature of 1811.

Daniel Waldo and his son, Daniel, were the first two presidents of the Worcester Bank, chartered in 1804. *From the collections of the Worcester Historical Museum, Worcester, Massachusetts.*

Because the bank had become the main source of local credit, Republicans were defending an essential local institution, even if it happened to belong principally to one of the county's leading Federalists. Waldo in 1812 was president of the Worcester branch of the Federalist campaign organization known as the Washington Benevolent Society. That did not stop him from adding the name of Levi Lincoln II to the board of directors of the bank whose charter he succeeded in having renewed.[347]

The Center and the "Skirts": Fire Protection

Despite such instances of successful collaboration, the era of intense partisanship between 1805 and 1815 coincided roughly with a period of stagnation, as noted earlier, in the village center's campaign to bring Worcester up to its standards as a progressive business center. Of the many bones of community contention, the three that most frequently occupied the town meeting were fire protection, control of free-roaming livestock and the perennial issue of adequate public schools. In each of these struggles, the center achieved a degree of success in the 1790s and the early years of the new century, followed by little or no progress during a partisan decade, followed by new momentum as Federalist and Republican leaders rejoined one another as boosters of business development.

Village residents naturally differed from outlying farmers in their way of thinking about fire. A fire on a farm might bring suffering to a single family, but a fire in the center could spell disaster for any number of homes and businesses. The center's sustained effort to secure the town's help to cope with its special problem began on the night of January 26, 1786, when the Main Street house of Samuel Flagg burned to the ground.[348] Flagg and others petitioned the town to buy a fire engine,[349] but once a committee had estimated the cost, the town meeting rejected the idea.[350]

In 1792, Flagg and Dr. Elijah Dix, perhaps at their own request, were appointed the town's first fire wardens, presumably to look out for fire hazards and to supervise firefighting.[351] Another January fire, this one on Main Street in 1793, produced a more lasting response. The victims were Cornelius and Peter Stowell. Their weaver's shop was lost, along with woven cloth and stock.

On January 21, men of the center organized themselves into the Worcester Fire Society. The founders were prominent businessmen, the town's three physicians, as well as a cohort of lawyers, the register of deeds and the clerk of courts.[352] Missing from their ranks were all common tradesmen of the village center, such as the Stowells. The members of the Fire Society were setting themselves off as a business and professional elite, for reasons that soon became clear. The members equipped and organized themselves to respond to fires, but they were also taking upon themselves the task of providing guidance to Worcester in the matter of fire protection. In 1793, they got the town to buy "a good fire engine" and to build a shed on the common to house it, along with the town's hearse.[353]

Regardless of the diminishing party divisions, soon after the Main Street disaster the farmers rebelled once again against the Fire Society's apparently endless demands. This time the society wanted the town to build wells along Main Street to ensure an adequate supply of water for the engines. A committee appointed to consider the matter noted that "the town has been at a great expense to procure engines which will probably be beneficial only to a part of the inhabitants." It therefore found it "not expedient that those inhabitants who cannot expect to receive any advantage from those engines, should be subjected to any further expenses for wells in the middle of the town."

The town meeting agreed with its committee, in effect telling residents of the village that if they wanted wells, they—or the prosperous gentlemen of the Fire Society— would have to pay for them. It was nearly a decade later that the town took its next step toward adequate fire protection for the center, voting to buy and house a carriage to carry the fire hooks, saws and other apparatus used by the volunteer firefighters of the village center.

The Center and the "Skirts": Livestock Control

In the 1790s, the village center also tried, by getting control over wandering livestock, to free itself from one of the less desirable aspects of life in a farming community. From its earliest years, agricultural Worcester, like other towns, had allowed animals to roam freely. Crops and gardens were protected by enclosing them with fences. Further protection was provided by the requirement that swine carry a ring through their noses to prevent rooting and a yoke around their necks to prevent them from squeezing through small openings in fences. Fence viewers were annually appointed by the town to ensure that residents kept their enclosures in good repair, and field drivers and hog reeves responded to complaints about damage caused by browsing animals who managed to break through fences.

Foraging livestock did not complement the village center's effort to turn itself into an up-to-date marketing center. In the 1790s, men of the center began what turned out to be a long campaign to get untended animals out of circulation. As in other areas of contention, there was progress through the turn of the century, something of a standoff during the years of most intense partisanship, followed by renewed progress. On this front, however, the forces of commercial development managed in 1816 to achieve a final victory.

In March 1791, the town passed its usual vote "that the swine go at large the year ensuing being yoked and ringed according to law," but it added an unprecedented qualification: "excepting those belonging to the Center School Quarter."[354] The residents of the center would have to pen up their pigs. An effort to reconsider the vote was postponed, but it finally came to the floor again in April, and the old order was restored. Swine could once again roam the central village.[355]

In 1792, swine exclusion was voted again, but in narrower terms. The animals were banned from "the Main Street in the town from Mr. Samuel Chandler's farm house to Timothy Paine's Esqr. inclusively."[356] Samuel Chandler, son of the exiled Loyalist, had land on the west side of Main Street just south of the common. Timothy Paine's mansion was—and still is—north of the courthouse on what became Lincoln Street. In effect, Main Street from below the meetinghouse to above the courthouse had been declared a swine-free zone.

Skirmishes of this sort, involving at different times swine, horses, mules and cows, appeared on the town's agenda in 1792, 1800, 1801, 1805, 1814, 1815 and 1816.

In 1814, the swine were banished from the entire town, and this time the prohibition turned out to be permanent.[357] Twenty-three years into the animal control campaign, a resident or visitor would not find a pig roaming freely and legally on any of Worcester's roads, but might still bump into a cow ambling down Main Street under the protection of the law.

In 1815, just two years after their success against the swine, the livestock control forces seemed to have prevailed against the cows as well. The March meeting voted that no cattle, horses or mules "shall be suffered to go at large the current year in no part of the town."[358]

In May the town again freed its cows. However, it adopted new restrictions that demonstrated that the age of wandering livestock was nearing its end. The cows could go free in daylight, but the owner's name had to be branded on the cow's horns, or written on a strap around its neck, so that "the owner may be found in case of damage." In addition, no one could turn a cow loose without getting the permission of the selectmen, who were to give that permission only if they decided it was a matter of "necessity" for the owner of the cow. Furthermore, "no person" was to "have the benefit of turning more than one cow to feed in the highway the present season."[359] In effect, a person prosperous enough to own a cow, but too poor to maintain it, might get permission to let the cow roam, but he or she had to be prepared to pay for any damages the animal might cause.

In 1816, as if to commemorate the postwar softening of partisan hostilities, the twenty-five-year process finally came to its fated conclusion. Worcester voted to "restrain from going at large" all of its swine, cattle, horses and mules. For the first time, people coming to do business in the town would not have to contend with loose animals on the roads and highways.

THE CENTER AND THE "SKIRTS": SCHOOLS

Differences between the center and the "skirts" on matters of fire protection and animal control were mild compared to their conflicts over the issue that had perennially pitted them against one another: support of the public schools. In this as in previous generations, the source of the conflict was resistance to taxation, and the flash point was the legally required grammar school that provided boys with enough Latin and Greek to gain admission to college. In this arena of community conflict, the village center would achieve a dramatic victory in the years following the party divisions, gaining the power to levy its own taxes to support its own center schools, and also gaining supervisory control over the schools in the outskirts.

A long and frequently repetitive series of "solutions" was attempted, with attention sometimes focused on the grammar school, sometimes on the outlying English schools, sometimes on the center district's own English schools. Committees periodically stepped forth, studied the problems at hand (usually more financial than educational) and proposed optimistic reforms.

In 1823, a committee arose that seemed like all the others, but it was not. At a self-initiated meeting in August, "the inhabitants of the center school district" appointed a six-member committee to "report on the general concerns of said district."[360] Within weeks the committee was ready to report that "for several years past, the schools in this District have generally fallen below the common standard in the Commonwealth," and would not bear comparison with those in several neighboring towns. "Ought this state of things to be longer endured?" the committee asked. "Is it not reproachful to the Center District of the shire town in the county of Worcester?"[361] Calling the schools a reproach to the center, rather than to the whole town, further demonstrates the extent to which the center had developed a sense of its own identity.

The committee attributed the poor condition of the center schools to two factors: "the false notions of economy, which have introduced incompetent maballsters [masters]," and "the unaccountable neglect of parents to avail themselves" of the available services during periods when, thanks to voluntary contributions, competent teachers had been hired. The first problem could only be addressed with more money. The committee rejected "permanent reliance" on a system of voluntary contributions by wealthy individuals. It proposed two alternatives that could be pursued simultaneously: "to increase the general school tax for the benefit of the grammar school" and to "make assessment of the necessary additional sums upon the inhabitants of the district." The latter course would require an act of the legislature giving the center authority to tax its residents for its own schools.[362]

The year-round grammar school would be kept in the Center School House that had been purchased from the private proprietors. In addition, the English school operating in the building was to be continued, providing eight months of instruction each year. Both of these were to serve only boys. A "female school" was to be kept in each of the other two schoolhouses of the district for eight months, and a third female school "of a higher order," also for eight months, was to be created to serve "the scholars most advanced from the other female schools."[363]

Following publication of this report, the reformers began to pursue a state law granting taxing powers to the center. Meanwhile, the possibility of increasing the town's funding for the grammar school was explored by John Davis, a rising young lawyer, member of the Second Parish and since 1822 son-in-law of Aaron Bancroft. Davis and others, late in 1823, submitted a petition asking the town what it would do to place the grammar school "on a more respectable footing," in particular whether it would "increase the school tax for the benefit of the grammar school, and to what amount."

John Davis, like his friend
Levi Lincoln II, was a power
in Massachusetts politics.
For a time Lincoln's law
partner, he began a nine-year
career in the U.S. House of
Representatives in 1824 and
then returned to Massachusetts
to succeed Lincoln as governor
in 1833. He was reelected in
1834, and the next year was
chosen by the legislature to
represent Massachusetts in
the U.S. Senate. He won the
governorship in 1841 and 1842.
In 1847, he was sent back to
the Senate, from which he
retired in 1853. *Courtesy American
Antiquarian Society.*

While the town was considering this proposal, the center continued its efforts to acquire a legal identity in the state legislature. On the last day of 1823, on its own authority, the district chose a board of overseers with the powers and responsibilities suggested by the committee in August.[364] In January 1824, the legislature authorized the inhabitants of the Center School District to raise by taxation funds in addition to any raised by the town to support the schools in their district, and to regulate those schools as they saw fit.[365]

Ironically, the legislation did not turn control of the grammar school—the focus of so much concern about "respectability"—over to the center. That institution remained the responsibility of the whole town of Worcester, and it therefore remained under the authority of the selectmen. The reformers thus were undoubtedly gratified, but not satisfied, when the town in March 1824 adopted the funding proposal John Davis had introduced in December, raising the appropriation for the grammar school as well as all other schools.

The center promptly went about the business of establishing its English schools, including the female schools. Those seeking higher educational standards faced the continuing challenge of a grammar school under the authority of selectmen, and schools in the outlying districts were still being run by neighborhood committees. In March 1826, the legislature changed the rules for the whole state, providing that in each community a central school committee should hire all teachers and otherwise supervise the schools. In Worcester, the reformers were ready to seize the opportunity. When the whole town on April 3 elected its new centralized committee, it chose three members of the clergy and two others. All five were members of the center district's board of overseers.[366]

In April 1827, the new committee reported on its efforts "in the introduction of a new order of things."[367] That involved delicate meetings with residents of the outskirts, who were now going to be supervised by a central school committee. Concerning the great question of the grammar school, the committee reported that its first consideration after taking the school out of the hands of the selectmen had been to consider "how it might be raised to the character which it ought to sustain." For the grammar school, the committee recruited a master and tightened up attendance rules. The committee closed its 1827 report with confidence "in regard both to the Latin School in particular, and the other Schools generally, that they are, by the common consent of all, in altogether an improving state."[368]

TOWARD "THE PORT OF WORCESTER"

In two ways, the Worcester Country Agricultural Society, organized in 1819, symbolized a new era of public life in the community. It displayed the new spirit of cooperation that had developed between former political antagonists, and it incorporated the victory of the town center over the farmers of the outskirts. Men of the center, evenly balanced between the two parties, joined with prominent political figures living throughout Worcester County to form an elite society that would pursue strategies by which the "yeomanry" might improve its agricultural practices. The society would sponsor cattle shows and other competitions to reward improvements in livestock, produce and manufactures. The members of the society would be gentlemen of public prominence, men who owned farms, but were increasingly engaged in commerce, the professions and manufacturing.[369]

Arch-Republican Levi Lincoln, arch-Federalist Daniel Waldo Jr. and Republican Edward Bangs, on behalf of the society, successfully petitioned the legislature for incorporation and for state subsidies to support its work. The first president of the Agricultural Society was Levi Lincoln.[370]

During the very successful campaign to gain control of the schools, men of the center had also been busily about the task of tidying up the common, building Worcester's first new town hall, accomodating the desire of the Agricultural Society to be provided with appropriate quarters and—the livestock having been excluded—getting more control over the human use of the center's streets and sidewalks.

In 1816, the town had taken a step toward the industrial era's more disciplined use of time by agreeing to have the bells in the church towers rung daily at noon.[371] In 1823, in response to a petition from Levi Lincoln II and others, the town voted to remove the pound on the common that had once been reserved for detained livestock,[372] and it gave

The meetinghouse, home of both town and church, became an exclusively religious building and shared the common with the town hall, erected in 1825. *Courtesy American Antiquarian Society.*

the center school district permission to move its schoolhouse on the common a distance to the southeast, to the corner of the old burying ground, opposite the Baptist church.[373] These steps were apparently related to an effort of the Worcester County Agricultural Society to clear space on the common in order to put up its own building, a proposition the town agreed to in 1823.[374]

In 1824, faced with a demand from the First Parish for payment if the town continued to use its meetinghouse for municipal business, the town voted to build a new town hall.[375] Whether the town or the First Parish owned the original meetinghouse and the common land on which it stood proved to be a contentious issue that was not finally addressed until the 1890s. Worcester's new town hall, erected adjacent to the south meetinghouse, at the corner of Main and Front Streets, was ready for its first town meeting on May 2, 1825.[376] The Agricultural Society was granted the use of the north hall on the second floor for its meetings and for exhibiting manufactured items during its annual Cattle Show and Exhibition of Manufactures. In return for giving up its claim to the common land, the society would not have to pay rent. In effect, the Agricultural Society had gotten the town to provide the space it needed, and it could now enjoy the facilities free of charge.

As they celebrated the erection of their new municipal building, town leaders took additional steps to bring a businesslike sense of order to the central village. In 1824,

Worcester County Cattle Show
AND
Exhibition of Manufactures.

THE Trustees of the Agricultural Society of the County of Worcester, desirous that the County should derive the earliest practicable advantages from the influence of the Institution, and from the liberality of the Legislature in aid of its objects, announce to the Publick their determination to have a *Cattle Show* and *Exhibition of Manufactures*, at Worcester, on *Thursday* the *seventh day of October next*, at 9 o'clock, A. M.—and they propose the following Premiums to be awarded for excellence on that occasion.

For Stock.

Household Manufactures.

For Agricultural Improvements.

For Agricultural Experiments.

For Domestick Manufactures.

A poster promoting the Worcester County Agricultural Society's 1819 exhibition. *Courtesy American Antiquarian Society*.

the selectmen were instructed to take proper care of the trees growing "in the Centre School district."[377] Front yards were banned from most of Front Street in 1825, in the interest of the free movement of people, horses and vehicles. To more clearly separate public ways from private lots, a committee was also established to ascertain the precise bounds of all streets and roads in the town.[378] In 1826, the time-honored but awkward practice of allowing men to pay their highway taxes by laboring on the roads and bridges was abandoned; all future taxes were to be "paid in money."[379] An 1828 report found that Main Street was generally obstructed by encumbrances and recommended that the surveyors of highways be ordered to remove them "so soon as they can be removed without great and disproportionate expense or loss to the town or individuals."[380] In that same year, the town adopted new bylaws; several to keep the "foot or sidewalks" of the town free of obstructions, one to punish anyone who tied horses or cattle to trees planted along the public streets "for shade & ornament" and another to punish anyone allowing a "horse gelding or other beast to go in an immoderate gait" in the streets of Worcester.[381]

The perceived need to assert order in the central village was related to the fact that by the 1820s the population of Worcester was, at last, growing at a fairly brisk pace. During the two decades between 1790 and 1810, Worcester's population had grown by 23 percent, to a total of 2,577 people. During the years from 1810 to 1830, however, it grew by 62 percent to 4,172. The town's growth during the 1820s was largely due to hopes raised by the revived project of building a canal to connect Worcester to Providence, and via Narragansett Bay to the world of Atlantic commerce. The idea first broached in the 1790s was finally brought to fruition between 1821 and 1828. Most of the Federalist leaders who had hailed the project in the 1790s did not survive to see it, but the building of the Blackstone Canal finally spurred the commercial and manufacturing growth they had labored ceaselessly to stimulate.

As in the 1790s, in 1821 it was the merchants in Providence who launched the canal project, and Worcester boosters and investors enthusiastically offered their support. By 1824, the Blackstone Canal Company had received charters from both states, issued stock and granted its first contruction contracts. Although the Providence investors had hired Benjamin Wright, chief engineer of the Erie Canal, to supervise the project, Wright would not be finished with the Erie for another year. The men of Rhode Island, too impatient to wait, gathered their own crews and equipment and set out to build. The 1824 building season soon turned into disaster. The people who had the expertise, the experience and the equipment to succeed in such a project were busy in New York, completing the great canal linking Lake Erie to the Hudson River. Many of them were Irish contractors and skilled workers who had learned their business in England, Scotland and Wales before being recruited to build the Erie Canal. They would in time come to the rescue of the Blackstone Canal, and some of them, by remaining in Worcester, would bring to an end its history as an exclusively Protestant community.

In the summer of 1824, the ambitious Rhode Island builders had penetrated only a few miles from Providence before they ran up against rising land and intersecting waterways that stymied them. They failed repeatedly to run a dry inner lining, called a "prism," over bogs and streams. By late summer, construction had been halted and some contractors were abandoning the project. Heavy rains in the autumn damaged much of what had been accomplished, and a dam burst in December destroyed most of the prism that remained.[382]

Benjamin Wright in the spring brought his chief assistants and a number of contractors from the now completed Erie Canal. All of the contractors were Irish. They issued calls for their own subcontractors, who brought their Irish Catholic crews to build the Blackstone.[383] By 1826, when around one thousand men were at work on the canal, 80 percent of them were Irish.[384] In 1826, Benjamin Wright awarded contracts for twenty-three miles of the canal to be built from Worcester south to Uxbridge. Contracts for the largest and most complex stretches, including the section in Worcester, were won by Irish contractor Tobias Boland. When Boland visited the town in January 1826 to meet with local leaders and consider possible routes for the canal, he set off two years of feverish anticipation and preparation for Worcester's new economic era.[385]

The Irish crews arrived in Worcester on July 4, 1826. As soon as they began their work, the value of land along the route of the canal in Worcester shot up, and commercial offices began to be built on its banks. Freight and storage facilities, stables, stores, inns, taverns and many new residences crowded in. In 1828, as the opening of the canal neared, farmers who could afford to do so hired extra help to maximize the harvests they anticipated selling to distant customers. Tons of anthracite coal mined in Worcester were piled alongside granite from Worcester quarries and bricks from the town's two new brickyards.[386]

The Irish were prohibited from residing within the central village they were doing so much to transform. Indeed, they might have been prevented from coming to Worcester at all had the company not responded to local complaints by threatening to move the northern terminus south to Millbury. Opposition in Worcester was overcome when the company gave assurances that the Irish would come into the central village only to carry out their work on the canal. The workers were settled in a shantytown east of the village, in the Pine Meadows region near Washington Square.[387] Although Worcester leaders expected the strangers to leave once their work had been finished,[388] Tobias Boland and many of the hundreds of Irish Catholics he had brought to Worcester chose to stay on.

In 1828, the publication of the first Worcester Village Register further underlined the sharpening sense of differentiation between the central village and the rest of the community.[389] The register listed the town's lawyers, physicians, merchants, manufacturers and a wide variety of artisans. It was, in effect, a census of the nonfarmers of Worcester. In keeping with its commercial character, the register also listed the schedule of mail and passenger stagecoaches serving the town. A second edition appeared in 1829, as did a Worcester Village Directory accompanied by a map of the center, which was bounded on the north by Lincoln Square, on the west by Main Street, on the south by Green and North (now Franklin) Streets and on the east by Grafton and Summer Streets. Other than sketches of public buildings, the most conspicuous feature on the map was the Blackstone Canal, with its terminus between Central and Thomas Streets.[390]

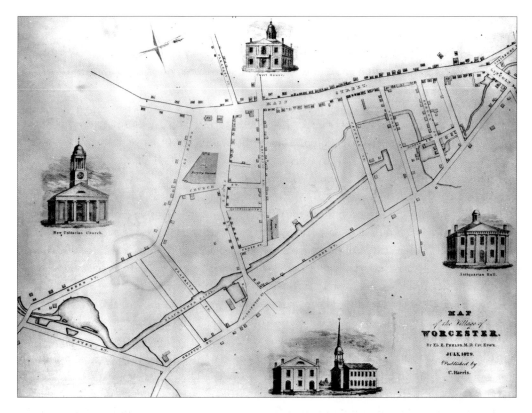

Above: Map of the central village of Worcester as the Blackstone Canal arrived in 1828. *Courtesy American Antiquarian Society*.

Below: A retrospective painting done around 1888 by Frederick G. Stiles, showing the Blackstone Canal's northern basin as it might have looked in a more pastoral era. *Courtesy American Antiquarian Society*.

A History of Worcester

On October 8, 1828, the packet boat *Lady Carrington* became the first vessel to travel the entire length of the canal from Providence to Worcester. The local newspapers began reporting canal activities under a printed box headlined "The Port of Worcester," and a flag flew around the clock, indicating that Worcester had become a port of entry to the United States.[391]

It was a heady time, especially for the elite of the central village. Recovered from the divisions of the party era, a new generation of Worcester leaders was enjoying conspicuous success in the "era of good feeling." Most conspicuous among them was Levi Lincoln II, who was nominated by both parties for the governor's office in 1825 and elected to the first of eight consecutive terms as governor of Massachusetts.

Nearly a century had passed since Worcester's designation as the shire town of a new county in 1731. During all of those years, owners of substantial property in the community, especially those with business interests in the central village, had worked to turn their town into something more culturally progressive and more economically rewarding than an isolated farm town. As events would show, the Blackstone Canal was not the answer to their dreams, yet it was the canal that triggered the most crucial single event in Worcester's transformation into a major industrial city. As soon as Worcester and its surrounding countryside began its economic partnership with Providence, Boston interests launched plans to reconquer their hinterland by building a rail line to Worcester. The railroad, which came to town in the 1830s, would turn out to be the key to Worcester's destiny for the next century. By the time the town hailed the *Lady Carrington*, Worcester had taken important steps toward a world beyond farming.

Chapter 7

INDUSTRY AND INSURGENCY
(1828–1848)

The comfortable gentlemen who welcomed the canal boats into Worcester had many reasons to be confident about the economic future of their community and about their continuing role as its leaders. Mostly lawyers or commercial men, they associated with one another in the Worcester Fire Society, the Worcester Agricultural Society, the American Antiquarian Society, the Morning Star Lodge of Masons and often as members of the Second Parish, whose seventy-year-old pastor, Aaron Bancroft, had become the first president of the American Unitarian Association in 1825.

Most prominent in public affairs were the town's lawyers, and the most prominent among them was Levi Lincoln II. After serving as Speaker of the Massachusetts House of Representatives, as lieutenant governor and as an associate justice of the Supreme Judicial Court, Lincoln was elected governor each year from 1825 to 1832.[392] He was a consensus candidate, first nominated by the Republicans but also accepted by the Federalists as their party faded into insignificance. Later, as a member of the Whig Party, Lincoln served several terms in Congress, was appointed collector of the Port of Boston and served in the state senate before becoming Worcester's first mayor in 1848.[393]

John Davis, for a time Lincoln's law partner, began a nine-year term in the U.S. House of Representatives in 1824, then returned to Massachusetts to succeed Lincoln as governor in 1833. He was reelected in 1834, and the next year was chosen by the legislature to represent Massachusetts in the U.S. Senate. In 1840, Davis was persuaded to leave the Senate to run again for governor. He was narrowly defeated, but won the governorship in 1841 and 1842. In 1847, he was sent back to the Senate, from which he retired in 1853.[394]

In their family connections, Levi Lincoln II and John Davis—both Unitarians—personified the blending of the post-Revolutionary aristocracy of merchants and lawyers with the pre-Revolutionary ruling class of lawyers, court officials and great landowners. Lincoln's mother was Martha Waldo, which made him the grandson of the eminent merchant and banker Daniel Waldo and of Waldo's wife, Rebecca Salisbury Waldo. Rebecca was the sister of two other eminent merchants, Samuel and Stephen Salisbury.[395]

Levi Lincoln II, after serving as Speaker of the Massachusetts House of Representatives, lieutenant governor and an associate justice of the Supreme Judicial Court, was elected governor each year from 1825 to 1832. He later served several terms in Congress and served in the state senate before being elected Worcester's first mayor in 1848. *Courtesy American Antiquarian Society.*

Levi Lincoln II was married to Penelope Winslow Sever, whose mother was a daughter of John Chandler, the last patriarch of the pre-Revolutionary aristocracy.[396] John Davis was married to Eliza Bancroft, daughter of the Reverend Aaron Bancroft and Lucretia Chandler Bancroft, who was also a daughter of John Chandler.[397] Worcester's two most eminent Whig lawyer-politicians of the decades between 1820 and 1850 were married to granddaughters of the Loyalist leader who had died in exile.

Behind Lincoln and Davis marched a phalanx of young lawyers, some of whom made the Worcester County bar second in reputation only to that of Boston. Looking back many years later, a female member of the town aristocracy recalled the lawyers of greatest renown and their ability to attract to their offices law students "from far and wide," with the happy result that "there were always plenty of young men in society for partners at balls and parties."[398]

Young men "in society," as well as their more established elders, were caught up in the spirit of "improvement"—personal, social and national—that was characteristic of the age. The Worcester Agricultural Society, despite its name, from its inception in 1818 had taken a deep interest in the promotion of manufacturing. The society's annual Cattle Show and Exhibition of Manufactures, followed by the Agricultural Ball,[399] quickly became a highlight of Worcester's social year. "If agriculture be the life's blood of the people," the society was told by its first president, the first Levi Lincoln, "the arts of Manufacture

This dress of taffeta and crewel started life with the Paine family in 1773 and was made over for a granddaughter to wear to the Cattle Show Ball in 1830 or 1831. *From the collections of the Worcester Historical Museum, Worcester, Massachusetts.*

constitute the real independence of the nation."[400] By the 1830s, Levi Lincoln II and other lawyers and merchants controlled the directorships not only of the Worcester Bank, incorporated in 1804, but also of a series of new banks opened to respond to the credit needs of a rapidly developing community.[401] Worcester's established leaders were eager to encourage manufacturing in their midst, little dreaming that they were opening up their town to forces that would find a variety of ways to challenge their rule.

Canal, Railroads and Social Separation

The Blackstone Canal suffered from weaknesses that might have proven fatal even if Boston capitalists had not sent out a railroad to compete with it within a few years. Because the canal at some places flowed within the banks of Blackstone River and at other places followed a channel of its own, the supply of water needed to carry boats was not under the full control of the canal operators. The Blackstone was the source of water power for small- and middle-sized industries up and down the forty-five-mile length of the Blackstone Valley. When the water supply was scarce, the canal competed for it with mill owners. These early industrialists so resented the boatmen's competition for their power source that they sometimes had cartloads of stones dumped in the canal to obstruct the passage of freight and passengers.[402] The New England weather also took its toll, since passage could be blocked by ice, sometimes for months.

In 1834, the canal's peak year, 5,336 tons of goods were brought into Worcester, while 826 tons were carried out.[403] The discrepancy between the imports and exports during the brief career of the canal indicates that Worcester merchants were right to welcome it. They had substantially increased their role as suppliers to smaller shopkeepers in the towns throughout the region. Much of their supply was now coming from Providence rather than Boston, a diversion of Worcester County's trade that brought a quick response from the Massachusetts capital.

In 1831, the legislature incorporated the Boston and Worcester Railroad.[404] By 1833 contractors, many of them Irish, and workers, most of them Irish, had brought the railway halfway along its forty-four-mile, gradually rising course to Worcester. In 1834, as it approached Worcester's eastern border, the route had to take a sharp detour to the south to go around Lake Quinsigamond. Once west of the lake, the line turned north, running between the lake and the eastern flank of Sagatabscot Hill. At some points there was only a narrow separation between the hill and the shore of the lake. Cuts had to be made through the solid granite, with picks, shovels and black blasting powder the only tools. An especially deep cut was needed when the road finally turned west again to resume its direct course into the village. While Irish workers blasted their way through the hill, track was being laid from the town center out to Sagatabscot. To satisfy the owners, who wanted very badly to open the road early in 1835, some contractors kept their men working on the cut as an early winter settled in late in 1834.

Soon after the start of 1835, disaster struck at the deep cuts. One worker was crushed to death in a rock slide; two others were killed in a black powder explosion; three more

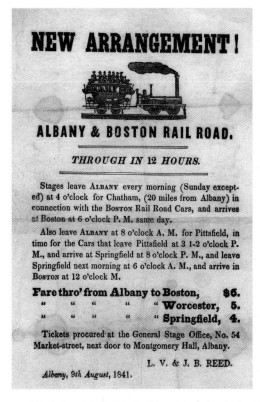

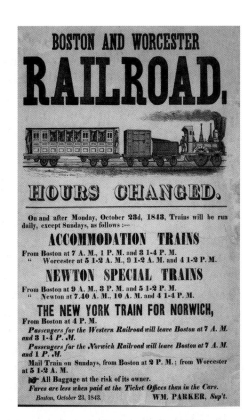

Handbills, distributed to keep travelers informed about routes and fares, reveal some of the conditions passengers faced. *Courtesy American Antiquarian Society.*

were crushed in another rock slide; and early in February, an Irish worker fell from the icy rocks to his death. Another crew, working in a March snowstorm, was killed in a powder blast. On the same day another faulty explosion rained rock down on the railroad shanty camp, injuring women and children, some of them seriously.

To protest the dangerous conditions, the exasperated workers put down their tools. For their rebellion they were dismissed and ordered out of the cuts and the camps. When they refused to move or to be moved, Irish contractors Tobias Boland and William Lomasney, at the behest of company officials, came out from the village of Worcester with the pastor of the Irish immigrants, the Reverend James Fitton. The mediation of these authorities resulted in improved conditions and better pay for the workers, while the women and children were moved to the relative safety of the Irish settlements at Pine Meadow, on the eastern edge of the town center.[405] The railroad opened for public travel on July 6, 1835, setting off a grand celebration in Worcester.[406]

The "Deep Cut," through which trains still travel between Worcester and Boston, had a profoundly different impact on the lives of the privileged than it did on those of the Hibernian workers. One woman recalled many years later that the country town into which the railroad had been introduced was still a quiet place, free of "the shrill whistles and electric bells, that now make a pandemonium of any place in the vicinity of a

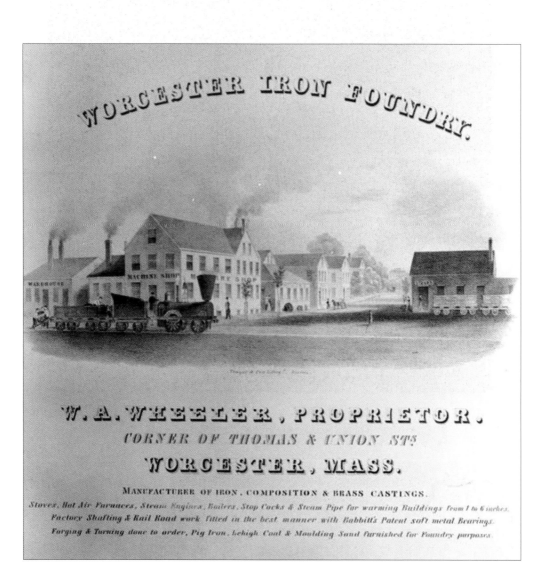

Stephen Salisbury II, son of prominent Revolutionary-era hardware merchant Stephen Salisbury, rose to become one of Worcester's leading landowners and financiers. *Courtesy American Antiquarian Society.*

Opposite above: The collision between the old and the new could be on the minds of each individual in this 1845 engraving. *Courtesy American Antiquarian Society.*

Opposite below: William A. Wheeler's machine shop at Thomas and Union Streets in the 1840s was portrayed as an isolated, almost bucolic site specially served by a railroad. *From the collections of the Worcester Historical Museum, Worcester, Massachusetts.*

factory or a railroad." In those peaceful days the cut "used to serve the useful purpose of notifying us when our friends coming from Boston, were nearing Worcester." She and her family "used to hear the reverberation as the train passed through the 'Deep Cut,' and thus knew when it was time to be ready to greet the expected guests."[407]

The railroad connection to Boston was the first in a series of ties that gave Worcester greatly improved access to raw materials and markets, and in so doing launched it definitively on its career as a major inland manufacturing center. The Western Railroad, linking Worcester to Springfield, began regular operations on October 1, 1839. The Norwich and Worcester connected the town to New London, Connecticut, from which boats traveled regularly to New York City, in 1840.[408] In 1847, Worcester gained a new tie to Providence in the form of the Providence and Worcester Railroad, signaling the impending death of the Blackstone Canal Company.[409] In that year, the Worcester and Nashua Railroad also tied the town to southern New Hampshire.[410]

Placing Worcester at the center of a new transportation network stimulated further population growth. During the 1820s, when the Blackstone Canal was built, the population rose to 4,172, a gain of 41 percent. During the 1830s, with the new railroad connections, the total went up to 7,947. In the 1840s, after the introduction of industrial steam power,[411] Worcester's population grew by a striking 127 percent, reaching 17,049 in 1850. Though there had been few manufacturing jobs in Worcester in 1820, 47 percent of the workforce was engaged in manufacturing by 1840.[412]

During the canal and early railroad years, Worcester began to experience a pattern of cooperation among creative artisans and imaginative capitalists that would give a distinctive and long-lasting cast to its economic and civic culture. Worcester's preeminent antebellum industrialist, Ichabod Washburn, was a major figure in shaping that culture. Trained in Leicester as a blacksmith, he moved to Worcester in 1819 with a small loan from Daniel Waldo,[413] and in 1820 began to handcraft woolen machinery and lead pipe. In 1822, as the demand for woolen machinery increased, he acquired a new partner and was soon employing thirty men in the production of wire carding machinery as well as "lead aqueduct." The manufacture of wire finally settled Washburn's future. He invented a wire-block to greatly improve the rate at which wire could be drawn through a die. He then contracted with Stephen Salisbury II, one of the town's largest landholders, for the construction of a wireworks on what became Grove Street.

To provide water power for the factory he was going to rent to Washburn, Salisbury dammed the Mill Brook as it ran through his property, creating Salisbury Pond. Before the advent of the industrial steam engine, Salisbury's capital and Washburn's technical ingenuity had launched what would become Worcester's largest manufacturing enterprise.[414] Farther south on the Mill Brook, Salisbury built the Court Mills at Lincoln Square, a building on Prescott Street for the Ames Plow Company and other large factory buildings on Union Street.[415] In these and similar structures, Salisbury and like-minded landowners provided working space and power—water power, horse power and steam power—to skilled artisans with limited capital, ambitious men who needed the opportunity to try out the ideas that might make their fortunes. The availability of these facilities was to a considerable extent responsible for the unusual diversity of products that became characteristic of Worcester manufacturing by the middle of the nineteenth century.[416]

The central village of Worcester, for so long a court and marketing center, expanded and took on a new character during the 1830s and 1840s, separating into an elite West Side and an East Side populated mostly by people who labored on the canal and the railroads, in the markets and manufacturing shops that sprang up beside them or on other construction projects in the growing community. The Irish canal workers had been confined to a camp near Washington Square, east of the common, in an area known as Pine Meadow or the Meadows, a district that had long been home to much of the town's black population. During the 1830s and 1840s, Irish settlement spread to an area south and slightly west of the Meadows. The new neighborhood, in and around what became Green Street, soon earned the nickname Scalpintown for the rough behavior of some of its residents.[417]

There the Irish established community institutions, including in 1832 Christ Church, the first Catholic house of worship in western Massachusetts. For the education of boys, in 1826 the Reverend James Fitton established, on Pakachoag Hill in southern Worcester, Mount St. James Academy, which would evolve into the College of the Holy Cross. St. John's Parish, which registered over three hundred adult members in 1840,[418] moved its worship services in 1845 from the inadequate Christ Church structure to the new St. John's Church, which still stands on Temple Street.[419] By 1846, the area around Temple Street, Water Street and the southern part of Summer Street was becoming the hub of a low-value residential district. Meanwhile, low-value residences that used to be interspersed among expensive residential and commercial buildings in the central village were disappearing.[420]

First an academy, then a college, the Catholic institution atop "Mount St. James" sent signals of Irish progress and permanence. *Courtesy American Antiquarian Society.*

Before 1830, the homes of most members of the Worcester elite were located on Main Street, on streets facing the common or in the Lincoln Square area.[421] These residences did not establish exclusive neighborhoods. The homes of the wealthy stood alongside the dwellings of more humble folk, as well as a wide variety of business establishments and churches. By 1830, however, commercial development had driven Main Street property values beyond the reach of most of the workers, artisans and small tradesmen who were being attracted to the town. Competition for desirable land pushed people with lower incomes to the side streets and promoted a process of residential segregation by class that would become a prominent feature of social life in Worcester.[422]

As the economy expanded in the 1830s and 1840s, affluent newcomers joined with Worcester families of new wealth to fill in quickly the available residential sites on Main Street and around the common.[423] Since the areas east of Main Street were filling up with railroad tracks, commercial and manufacturing establishments and the homes of workers, families seeking high-value residential space near the village center had to look west, to the crest of the ridge running parallel to Main Street.[424]

For generations, the only road running west from Main Street had been Pleasant Street, the old "Road to Paxton." This changed in 1830, when Charles Allen, a prominent lawyer, built Pearl Street. Not long after, Levi Lincoln II built what became known as Elm, Chestnut and Walnut Streets, all leading west from Main Street into his extensive property holdings.[425] In 1835, Lincoln had a Greek Revival mansion built for his family on Elm Street. The following year, Stephen Salisbury II had a splendid home built on Highland Street, just south of Lincoln's holdings. [426]

Lincoln could choose to whom he would sell the very desirable lots in his newly emerging high-value neighborhood. The attractiveness of the area was enhanced by the availability of an exceptional local architect, Elias Carter, who designed both the Lincoln and Salisbury homes and in the next two decades added elegant homes on the West Side for the Waldo, Kinnicutt and Foster families. Carter also designed and built homes for other prominent families on the southern extension of the western ridge, known as Nobility Hill.[427] Some high-value homes continued to be built near Lincoln Square, but the momentous migration of the elite into what would become known as the exclusive West Side had begun.[428]

The clustering of the poorest residents east of the town center and the gradual movement of the wealthier families to the west was just one manifestation of the changing social composition of Worcester. As the population came to be made up mostly of new arrivals, members of the traditional elite began to feel some discomfort with the new arrangements, or lack of arrangements. Their social and political influence had, to a significant extent, rested upon their personal acquaintance with the farmers, artisans, shopkeepers and others who made up their small community. Now the town was filling up with strangers.

While John Davis was governor in the early 1840s, his wife, Eliza Bancroft Davis, heard "complaints made in the town, that people were not intimate with each other, that they kept in certain sets, and did not mingle with their fellow townsmen." Her

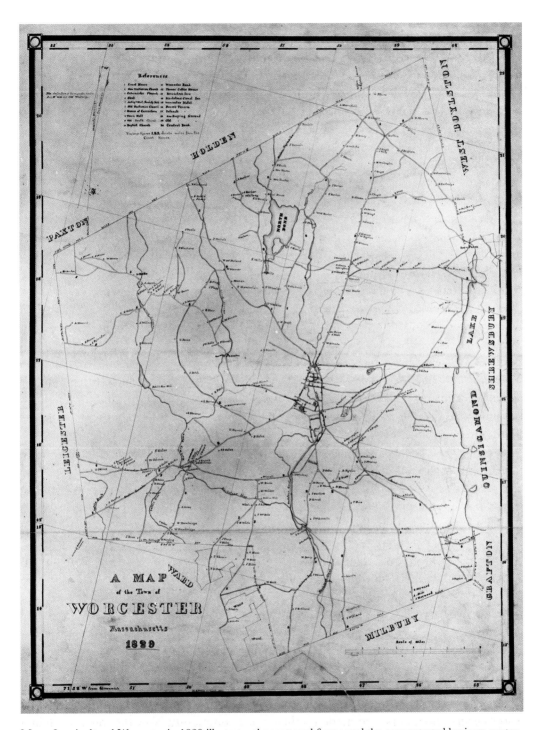

Map of agricultural Worcester in 1829 illustrates the scattered farms and the concentrated business center of the town. *Courtesy American Antiquarian Society*.

first reaction was to exclaim, "How can 7,000 people expect to be intimate with each other?" Nevertheless, "Mrs. Governor Davis" felt a duty to at least try to alleviate the problem. So she sent out word that her home would be open to the people of the town on certain evenings, "and that she would be glad to see her fellow townspeople on those dates, in order that those who desired to do so might become acquainted with each other."

The gesture was, according to one witness, "a perfect failure." On another occasion, special efforts were made to attract to the Agricultural Ball people who did not habitually associate with the town's first families. Some newcomers responded to the invitation, but "one set of people danced at one end of the hall, and another at the other end, both strangers to each other."[429]

Of particular concern to many of Worcester's established leaders was the moral and intellectual condition of the many young male workers migrating to the town in search of the opportunities promised by the canal and the railroads. In 1829, John Davis and "prominent citizens from various towns in the county" met to lay plans for the Worcester Lyceum, which was formally created in November "for mutual instruction and improvement."[430] Like such institutions in other towns, the Lyceum was envisioned as a means of transcending class lines, or of preventing such lines from developing in the first place.[431] It provided educational programs, especially weekly lectures from October to March in town hall. For a modest charge, young men "of good moral character" had access to "all the advantages and means of improvement of the Institution," including by 1836 a library of five hundred volumes and "a good chemical apparatus."[432]

Though the Lyceum was supposed to be an agency promoting self-improvement and economic mobility, at one of its meetings in 1837 Edward D. Bangs raised an issue that would soon widen the separation between Worcester's wealthiest families and the rest of the community.[433] The son of Edward Bangs, one of the first Levi Lincoln's closest political and professional collaborators, Edward D. Bangs was one of the closest political and professional collaborators of the second Levi Lincoln. In his 1837 Lyceum address, Bangs deplored the dilapidated condition into which the town of Worcester had allowed its public cemeteries to fall.[434]

Bangs had no plan for rescuing the existing graveyards, but he had an idea for a new one: private ownership. Within months of his speech Daniel Waldo had purchased a nine-acre tract on the road later known as Grove Street, and announced his intention of donating it for a private cemetery. A corporate charter was quickly granted to the "proprietors of Rural Cemetery." With names like Waldo, Davis, Bangs, Barton, Salisbury, Paine, Lincoln, Jennison and Rice, the first board of corporators embodied the Worcester establishment. The first forty-eight lots were soon sold to the highest bidders at public auction.[435] The wealthiest families of Worcester were providing for themselves in death an exclusive neighborhood not unlike the one they were creating for themselves in life.

ANTIMASONRY AND THE MECHANICS

The state of political parties in Massachusetts during the 1830s and 1840s for a time insulated the lawyer-led Worcester elite from challenges bubbling up from below. The first national party system, created in the 1790s by Federalists and Republicans, had given way after the War of 1812 to an "era of good feeling." Though Federalists in Massachusetts continued for some years to show the party flag, it was the decline in organized partisanship that had allowed Levi Lincoln II to win the governor's office in 1825 as a consensus candidate.

In some parts of the nation, the Jacksonian era called forth a significant challenge to ruling economic elites. In Worcester, however, the challenge was more rhetorical than real. A Jacksonian newspaper, the *Worcester County Republican*, appeared in 1829, attacking the "oligarchy" and the "nobility of this village."[436] In 1831, the paper printed a letter complaining that lawyers, doctors, merchants and ministers had been admitted with no difficulty to the Worcester Agricultural Society's Ball, while "a farmer or mechanic… would stand a poor chance against the body aristocratic in Worcester."[437]

Despite its appeal to groups with grievances, the Jacksonian Republican (Democratic) Party in Worcester was led principally by entrepreneurs on the rise, men who sought not to challenge the emerging industrial order but to share in its rewards. At least ten Democratic leaders in Worcester were involved in the leadership of the new Central, Citizen's and Quinsigamond Banks.[438] Many were self-made businessmen who resented the social, economic and political advantages long enjoyed by the lawyers and the older, established property owners.[439] Far from being a threat to the local aristocracy, Worcester's most prominent Democratic leader, Isaac Davis, was among the first incorporators of the elite Rural Cemetery.[440]

The Democrats may have been none too threatening, but beginning in 1829, members of the traditional leadership of Worcester faced a very real and unexpected political challenge in the form of the Antimasonic movement. Antimasonry arose in western New York following the 1826 kidnapping and probable murder of William Morgan, a stonemason who with a partner had been planning to publish an exposé of freemasonry and its secret ways. Morgan's partner emerged from imprisonment in a Masonic lodge and spread word of the vigilante actions Masons had taken to prevent public exposure. When Morgan could not be found, alarmed communities formed citizens' committees to look into the operations and influence of the secret fraternities. A series of trials that began in 1827 did not produce justice, nor did they produce adequate information about what had happened to Morgan. Masons used their official positions and their influence to block effective legal action, apparently placing their oaths of Masonic loyalty above their duties as citizens. Political protest in 1828 began sweeping Antimasons into office in western New York, and Antimasonry soon spilled over into Massachusetts and other Northern states.[441]

The movement was politically innovative in ways that would soon transform American politics. Because they were seeking the destruction of what they regarded as a dangerous aristocracy, the Antimasons could not adopt the traditional political course of appealing to local leaders—who were often Masons—to exercise their influence over their neighbors. Instead, the reformers appealed directly to entire communities. They went past established local leaders to "agitate" at the grass roots. They asked people to judge for themselves, to accept individual conscience as a trustworthy inner guide to the needs of public morality. They organized for political action at the polls, forming the first important third party in the nation's history and holding the first national nominating convention. Once elected to office in Massachusetts and other states, the Antimasons pioneered in the use of legislative public hearings to investigate and to publicize.[442] In these and other ways, they were pointing the way toward a more democratic political order.

In Worcester County, Masonic institutions had been spreading rapidly during the 1820s. There were nineteen lodges in 1829—one-third of them chartered since 1820— with a total membership of around two thousand men.[443] In the town of Worcester, the Morning Star Lodge dated back to 1793. The Worcester Chapter, Royal Arch Masons— for men who had attained freemasonry's highest degree—was chartered in 1823.[444]

Antimasonic candidates were never able to attract more than 20 percent of the vote in Worcester.[445] On the state level, in 1829 and 1830 Antimasons continued to support Levi Lincoln II, a National Republican but not a Mason, for governor while they nominated their own candidates for the legislature.[446] Most Antimasons in Massachusetts were further alienated from their National Republicans allies in 1832 when the Republicans nominated Henry Clay, a Mason, for president. A state convention of Antimasons, meeting in Worcester in September 1832, nominated Samuel Lathrop for governor.[447] Levi Lincoln, in his final run for the office, again defeated both Lathrop and Marcus Morton with relative ease.[448]

Opponents of Andrew Jackson in 1834 organized the Whig Party, naming themselves after the old British antimonarchist faction to emphasize their opposition to "King Andrew." National Republicans of Massachusetts, as they were evolving into Whigs, finally came up with a strategy to mollify the Antimasons. After Governor John Davis had recommended "a voluntary surrender of the Masonic institution," a convention of Masonic National Republicans met in Worcester to renounce the charters their lodges had been granted by the state,[449] thus separating the Masonic bodies from any formal association with the government. Similar conventions were then held around Massachusetts.[450] Most Antimasons in Worcester joined the Whigs.[451] Their experience in organizing an anti-aristocratic political movement based on an appeal to conscience, however, would not be forgotten.

TEMPERANCE AND THE MECHANICS

The evangelical spirit of the times also gave new energy to efforts to control or eliminate the use of alcohol. To the extent that it mobilized ordinary citizens in campaigns for reform that lacked the blessing of the legal-commercial elite, the temperance movement had an insurrectionary character in Worcester and elsewhere. Like other forms of insurgency, its center of support lay among the employers and workers streaming into

Worcester to find their places in the new industrial economy. Temperance reformers were responding to the process of industrialization and to the commercialization of agriculture, but they were not traditionalists yearning for a return to simpler and better times. They were instead men and women seeking to advance the process of social and economic change by eliminating a widespread form of irrational behavior that they saw as an impediment to progress.[452]

Initially, temperance reformers focused their attention on changing individuals, persuading them to sign pledges of total abstinence from the consumption of "ardent spirits." In time, many turned to the legal prohibition of all sales of alcohol as the only adequate way to rid society of the suffering, vice and crime associated with intoxication. In both phases of the movement, Worcester's traditional elite was reluctant to become followers in a crusade that was being led largely by evangelical clergymen, industrial employers and skilled workers.

Nationally, the American Temperance Society was launched in 1826 under the leadership of young clergymen.[453] The first temperance society in Worcester was founded by the Reverend Rodney Miller and members of the First Congregational Church in 1830. Concern over intemperance was already so widespread that a town society was formed in May 1831, and by 1832 it could claim almost half the adult population of Worcester as subscribers.[454]

In 1834, feeling was mobilized enough for the town meeting to advise the selectmen not to recommend to the county commissioners licenses for the sale of ardent spirits by anyone other than innkeepers. The effect was to prohibit in Worcester the sale of liquor by the bottle, while innkeepers continued to serve their customers by the glass.[455] With this victory in hand, the temperance forces raised their sights for 1835. In town meeting on March 23, by a vote of 325 to 272, the town advised the selectmen not to recommend licenses for any retailers or innkeepers.[456]

The innkeepers responded by closing their doors, claiming that they could not operate profitably while providing only rooms and meals to travelers.[457] The town during that spring of 1835 was awaiting with great anticipation the opening of the Boston and Worcester Railroad. The possibility that Worcester would be without accommodations for visitors produced the backlash the innkeepers were undoubtedly seeking. Pro-license forces held a large public meeting that urged the selectmen to ignore the advice of the town meeting and approve licenses for innkeepers. Two days later the selectmen complied, issuing certificates of approbation to six innkeepers. The town's official policy was reversed on April 13, when the meeting voted to reconsider the vote of March 23.[458]

In general, support for continued licensing came most conspicuously from the merchants, lawyers and court officials, while clergymen, manufacturers and many mechanics strongly supported the temperance crusade. The pro-license men were alarmed by this effort to change traditional behavior by legal means, especially when that effort was in the hands of voluntary organizations brought together by individuals outside the ruling circle. Since their own social rank was based on traditional customs and institutions, the lawyers and merchants were much more favorably inclined toward gradual change and moderate reform over which they could continue to preside.[459]

The manufacturers and mechanics, on the other hand, were succeeding on their own in the new and growing industrial sector, and they were quite willing to join together in voluntary organizations to advance the material and moral improvement of the community in which they hoped to make their prosperous futures.[460] This power of the temperance crusaders to mobilize people politically had been demonstrated in 1840, when the Whig Party in the United States carried out its innovative "Log Cabin" campaign on behalf of its presidential nominee, William Henry Harrison. Stirring up an unprecedented outburst of electioneering across the nation, Whigs organized local Log Cabin committees to promote extravagant displays of loyalty to Harrison.

The Worcester Whigs welcomed new Log Cabin activists into the fold, but the recruits were often young men whose backgrounds and political experiences differed significantly from those of the National Republicans, the original base of the Whigs. Among the new Whig activists, supporters of temperance outnumbered pro-liquor advocates seven to one. Many also came from the ranks of Antimasonry. Unlike the traditional National Republican/Whig leadership, these men belonged largely to the emerging evangelical middle class, which included many mechanics. They had participated in evangelically inspired political insurgencies. They had experience in appealing to conscience over the heads of the established local leadership.[461] Although their efforts in the Log Cabin campaign bolstered the efforts of the established Whigs, it would not be long before the differences between the two groups would become dramatically evident.

The creation in 1842 of the Worcester County Mechanics Association was not put forth as an act of political insurgency. The association nevertheless embodied a growing sense of distinction—and distance—between leaders of the industrial sector of the economy and the town's older leadership. In its origins, the association bore a superficial resemblance to the Worcester Lyceum, which had been created in 1829 for the moral and educational well-being of young men, especially those employed in the new manufacturing shops. The first president of the Lyceum, the Reverend Jonathan Going, was an active temperance leader,[462] as were the secretary, Anthony Chase, and executive committee member Ichabod Washburn. The temperance spirit was also in the air in 1841, when Chase and Washburn joined a group of men, most of them industrial employers, to consider a new organization for the "Moral, Intellectual, and Social improvement" of the increasingly numerous class of mechanics.[463]

The Mechanics Association, founded by those men and others the following year, was thus aimed at the personal and vocational uplift of its members. However, it was also perceived by many of those members as a means of setting themselves apart as an occupational and social group. The mechanics, including those who were employers, wanted to distinguish themselves from two other groups. One was old Worcester—the farmers, lawyers and merchants of the pre-industrial community; the other was the less skilled members of the industrial workforce, the growing population of laborers as well as the ambitious but still rising types to whom membership in the Lyceum was open. The distinguishing mark of the mechanics was their technical skill. Membership in the new association was explicitly limited to "operative and master mechanics and manufacturers."[464]

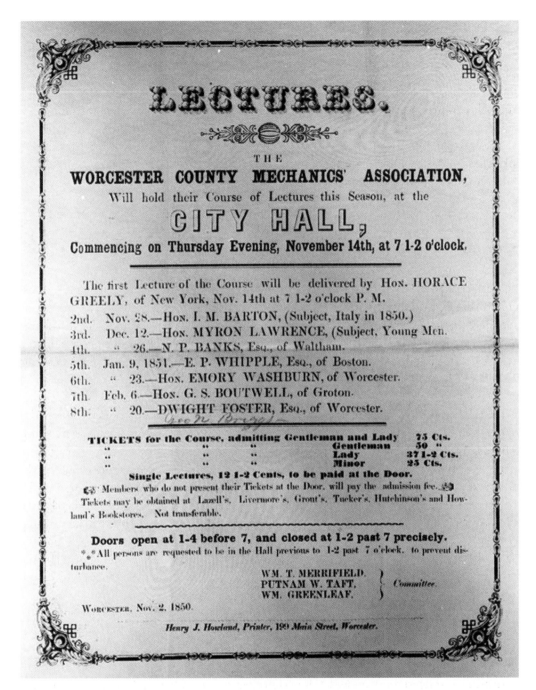

The businessmen who boosted the Mechanics Association, like many leaders of the era, placed great importance on moral and intellectual self-improvement. *Courtesy American Antiquarian Society.*

Though the Mechanics Association was supposed to be a nonpolitical society, the members' dissatisfaction with the political status quo in Worcester was recorded as early as December 1842, when they sponsored a debate on the question, "Are the laboring classes in our community enjoying their full share of influence?" After discussion, the "sense of the meeting" was that the laboring classes "do not enjoy their full share of influence."[465] In September of the momentous year 1848, the association presented its Mechanics Fair, the first under its own auspices rather than those of the gentry in the Worcester Agricultural Society. In the Mechanics Association, as in party politics, in Antimasonry and in temperance reform, the men in the shops—both employers and workers—were finding means of asserting themselves separately from—and sometimes in opposition to—the traditional local aristocracy.

Antislavery and Women's Rights

Of all the reform movements carried out in the spirit of evangelical reform, the battle against slavery eventually had the greatest impact on the politics of Worcester and of the nation. Opposition to slavery had been part of Worcester's public culture at least since the town meeting denounced the institution during the Revolutionary turbulence of the 1760s. In 1819, a county convention—led by Worcester lawyers—adopted spirited resolutions opposing the admission of Missouri to the Union as a slave state.[466]

By the era of the Blackstone Canal, antislavery sentiment had taken institutional form in Worcester as the local branch of the American Colonization Society, made up of many of the same merchants and lawyers who associated with one another as National Republican leaders. John Waldo Lincoln, brother of Levi Lincoln II, was a leader of the society,[467] and prominent Congregational ministers were among its members.[468] Founded nationally in 1817, the Colonization Society sought to address both the problem of slavery and what it saw as the incompatibility of the races. Its goal was to encourage African Americans, including emancipated slaves, to migrate from the United States. In 1822, the society founded Monrovia (later Liberia) on the west coast of Africa to receive the migrants.

In the 1830s, the local antislavery movement took on a new tone as the Worcester followers of William Lloyd Garrison began to organize. Garrison—an Antimason—had begun his antislavery career as a colonizationist. He changed his mind, partly due to the adamant opposition of free black Americans to the idea that the races could never live side by side in freedom in the United States.[469] Garrison launched his newspaper, the *Liberator*, in 1831 with a ringing call for immediate emancipation. As the Antimasonic insurgency was gaining strength, Worcester's traditional leaders found themselves dealing with a second appeal, emanating from outside their circle of influence, for immediate and radical change.

The colonizationists took steps to resist. Although Garrison had followers in the town, Garrisonian speakers had no easy time making their views heard in Worcester. They tried repeatedly to use church buildings for their talks, but they encountered stiff and sustained opposition. In August 1832, Arnold Buffum, a lecturer for Garrison's New England

Antislavery Society, found that in Worcester the Colonization Society had "as far as possible barred every door against light and truth."[470] When the Garrisonians did start to gain access to churches, it was the Baptist church that was first opened to them, and then the new building of the Methodists, who had formed a religious society in Worcester in 1834.[471] The doors of the Congregational churches remained barred, with one very important exception. In January 1836, a group separated on friendly terms from the two orthodox Congregational churches—the First Church and the Calvinist Church (founded in 1820)—to form a new society, which they named Union Church. In 1837, their new pastor, the Reverend Jonathan Woodbridge, found himself at odds with the majority of his church members, who wanted to open their building to antislavery lecturers. At his request, Woodbridge was dismissed.[472] The leading lay member of Union Church was the mechanic, industrialist, temperance advocate and future founder of the Mechanics Association, Deacon Ichabod Washburn.[473] Through his influence, the Congregational establishment's wall of defense against the Garrisonians had been breached.

The issue of women's rights became a particularly important one among the Worcester abolitionists. At the first Anti-Slavery Convention of American Women, held in New York City in May 1837, Abby Kelley was one of two hundred delegates from nine Northern states. By participating in the first public political meeting of women in the United States,[474] Kelley and her colleagues were violating a powerful national taboo against overt female participation in public life. A former and future resident of Worcester, the twenty-six-year-old Kelley was an admirer of Angelina Grimké, who had repudiated her heritage as a member of a prominent family of South Carolina slaveholders and, with her older sister Sarah, had begun to give antislavery talks before closed meetings of women.[475] While in New York, Kelley invited the Grimkés to visit Lynn, where she was then a teacher and an active member of the Lynn Female Anti-Slavery Society. The sisters agreed to begin their upcoming tour in Lynn. To Angelina Grimké's surprise, a large number of sympathetic men took seats in the Lynn Methodist Church, and she found herself for the first time speaking before a mixed—what was then called a "promiscuous"—audience of a thousand people.[476] Another taboo had been broken, and the Grimké sisters thereafter continued to speak before audiences made up of both men and women.

In 1839, Abby Kelley began what became a heroic career as an antislavery lecturer and defender of women's equality. More moderate abolitionists saw the advocacy of gender and racial equality as, at best, politically damaging distractions from the campaign against slavery. A showdown between the Garrisonians and the moderates came at the 1840 meeting in New York of the American Anti-Slavery Society, and it came over the issue of female participation. The Garrisonian presiding officer nominated Abby Kelley to serve on the business committee, which would set the convention's agenda. After loud, prolonged and acrimonious debate, Kelley's nomination was sustained by the convention. The following day, over three hundred male delegates withdrew to form a competing organization, the American and Foreign Anti-Slavery Society.[477] Led by such figures as Lewis and Arthur Tappan, the new organization soon formed the Liberty Party to take the antislavery issue into national politics.

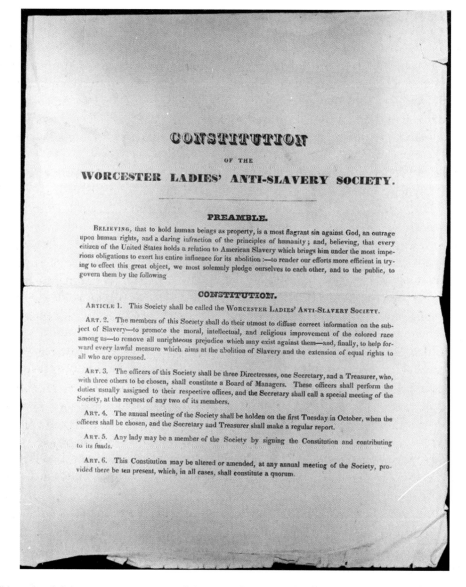

This undated document captures some of the moral fervor that underlay the Garrisonian doctrine of reform through "moral suasion." Worcester became a center of abolitionist activity. *Courtesy American Antiquarian Society.*

1848: The "Temperance Party" Insurgency

Since 1722, Worcester had governed itself through open town meetings, with elected selectmen carrying most of the administrative burden. The rapid rate of overall population increase may have impressed the town fathers with the need for more efficient and effective government, but they seem to have been paying particular attention to what was happening among the Irish settlers.

The small but stable Irish community that had remained in Worcester following the completion of the Blackstone Canal had come largely from economically advanced areas in the east of Ireland. Beginning in 1844, Irish contractors on the Worcester and Nashua Railroad began recruiting unskilled workers from the western counties of their homeland, young men of the peasantry with little of the literacy[478] or the experience of the world that had characterized the earlier settlers.[479] The rough new arrivals who made their way into the Irish neighborhoods in Worcester were soon attracting attention for disorderly and criminal behavior.[480]

In June 1847,[481] the pioneer Irish community in Worcester also began to feel the dramatic impact of the Great Famine that had befallen Ireland in 1845 and 1846. Between 1845 and 1850, Worcester's Irish population exploded from around 600 people to over 3,200.[482] Like the railroad workers, the famine migrants were often from the west of Ireland, deeply impoverished, with few skills and little education. By 1850, almost half the Irish in Worcester were illiterate.[483] Added to the existing tensions between the early Irish and the railroad newcomers, the famine migration overwhelmed the institutions the immigrant community had begun to build.[484] Irish neighborhoods were soon under the control of street gangs carrying on their own reign of terror.[485]

During 1847, the Worcester establishment came to the conclusion that the town should petition the legislature for a city charter. The "most urgent, and probably, the prevailing motive" behind that course of action, according to Levi Lincoln II, was "the organization of a vigilant and efficient Police." The need for "firm and energetic…restraints," Lincoln said, had arisen from the fact that in the course of only a few years, "a homogeneous population almost purely agricultural, of native citizens of the place, personally known to each other" had been "succeeded by vast accessions of new residents, engaged in all the varied pursuits and occupations of business, and by a constant influx of transient persons of every description and character." The town had to become a city with an effective police force because "the unprotected, in their very feebleness, should find the shield of law their security. Property should be held in safety, order and quiet maintained by authority, and morality and virtue enforced by rules of sobriety."[486]

In the formal proceedings required to secure the city charter, the influential men of the community acted as town fathers were traditionally expected to act: in unison. On November 8, 1847, John Milton Earle, editor and publisher of the *Worcester Spy*, moved that the town meeting appoint a committee of ten to petition the legislature for a city charter. The committee quickly selected was an embodiment of the town's traditional leadership. Nine of the ten members belonged to the Worcester Agricultural Society, eight were lawyers and nine were active in either the Whig or Democratic Parties.[487] After the legislature and the governor had granted the request of the committee, on March 18, 1848, Worcester voters accepted the new city charter by a vote of 1,026 to 487. The resistance to city government expressed by nearly one-third of the voters foreshadowed what would happen when it came time to elect officers for the new city government.[488]

The charter provided for a powerful board of aldermen that would share many administrative functions with the mayor. The town was divided into eight wards, each of which would be represented by an alderman elected by voters throughout the city. While the mayor and the aldermen would be elected citywide, each ward would also choose for itself a group of "ward officers," including three common councilors, three members of the school committee, a warden, a clerk, three inspectors, a member of the board of overseers of the poor and an assistant assessor.[489] Reflecting the tradition of shared power and responsibility embodied in the town meeting, the new system called for the voters annually to choose 112 public officials, in addition to the mayor.

The election process adopted by the town as it became a city seemed also to rest on the traditional hope that consensus could be worked out in advance of any votes being cast. In each ward, voters attended an open meeting to nominate their own ward officers. In each case, they nominated only one candidate each for the offices that would be filled in the election. The ward meetings also chose delegates to attend a citywide meeting where candidates for the at-large offices of mayor and aldermen would be selected.[490] The delegates at the citywide meeting put together a ticket, "nominated at the meetings of citizens, called without distinction of party."[491]

When it became known that sixty-five-year-old Levi Lincoln II, the personification of the old aristocracy, would be the establishment's candidate for mayor, the "men in the shops" began talking about an alternative.[492] For a mayoral candidate they turned to the Reverend Rodney Miller, former pastor of the First Congregational Church. Miller, along with the ardent abolitionist Reverend George Allen, had administered the Lord's Supper at the consecration of Ichabod Washburn's Union Church in 1836.[493] Miller had been the president of the city's first temperance society in 1830.[494] It was around Miller and under the temperance banner that the opposition to Lincoln and to the leadership he represented took shape.

In 1844, Miller had been dismissed from his church after a pastorate of seventeen years. His critics at that time claimed that "the number and wealth of the Parish" had become "so reduced, as to render it embarrassing, if not impracticable to sustain his ministry." The First Church had been the town's only church until the 1780s, and by the 1840s its members were clearly anxious about the diminishing stature of their congregation. Miller, they concluded, did not have the talents needed "to sustain and promote the best interests of this ancient Parish, in the prominent position it occupies amongst the Congregational Churches and Parishes in this part of the Commonwealth."[495]

Rejected by an "ancient" institution that laid claim to a "prominent position" in the community, Rodney Miller in 1848 was still in Worcester, perhaps unemployed, boarding on Belmont Street, close to the railroads, the factories and the workers who were searching for an effective means of resisting claims to prominence based on antiquity. His Temperance Party candidacy seems to have surprised J.S.C. Knowlton, owner and editor of the *Democratic Worcester Palladium*, which prided itself on its contact with the laboring classes. Knowlton pointed out that the Miller supporters had "no peculiar claim" to the temperance label, since the insurgency involved "but a small part of the intelligent and substantial portion" of the new city's temperance advocates.[496] Besides Miller, the temperance organizers nominated a slate of aldermanic candidates.[497]

When the city's first vote for mayor was taken, although Lincoln came out on top, the dismissed pastor received 44 percent of the vote against the former governor and congressman. Lincoln may or may not have perceived this substantial objection to his election as evidence that new people with new perspectives were looking for new leadership in Worcester. He was certainly not about to conclude that the ways of the past were becoming obsolete. As he concluded his inaugural address, the new mayor recalled valuable citizens who in his lifetime had helped "to form the character of the town and to build it up." He listed "the Chandlers, and Paines, and Allens, and Greens, and elder Lincolns (Levi and Abraham), Thomas, Heywood, Curtis, Bangs, Flagg, Mower, Salisbury, Austin, Bancroft, Waldo."[498] Lincoln's list of model citizens constituted a passable index of the leadership of post-Revolutionary, pre-industrial Worcester. With the exception of the printer Isaiah Thomas, no mechanic or manufacturer occupied a sufficiently high place in Lincoln's esteem to be included among those who had given Worcester its character and helped to build up the town.

1848: The "Free Soil" Insurgency

Another sequence of events unfolding in 1848 revealed even more clearly the substantial resistance that had been building up against the established political order in Worcester, at least since the opening of the Blackstone Canal in 1828. Ten days after Lincoln's inauguration as mayor, by a seven-vote margin a Whig caucus in the Worcester district selected as its delegate to the party's national convention Charles Allen, a prominent attorney and until recently a member in good standing of the Whig establishment. Allen, however, had become a "Conscience Whig," insisting that his party take a frank and determined stand against the extension of slavery into new territories and states. In Massachusetts, "Conscience Whigs" were contrasted with "Cotton Whigs," who made up the conservative mainstream of the party. Sustained by great manufacturers of cotton goods, the Cotton Whigs were individuals who, whatever their disapproval of slavery, did not want peaceful and profitable relations with the South disturbed by political agitation.[499]

The Worcester Whig caucus that selected Charles Allen as its delegate also adopted two provocative resolutions. One declared that what really separated Whigs from their opponents was their "uncompromising opposition to any further extension of slavery over any territory of the United States." The other expressed the opinion that "no candidate for the Presidency can receive the electoral vote of Massachusetts who is not publicly known to be opposed to the extension of slavery over territory now free."[500]

On June 7, the Whig National Convention in Philadelphia nominated General Zachary Taylor in the hope that the hero of the Mexican War, running with Millard Fillmore of New York and without a party platform, might rise above the increasingly bitter sectional divide. Taylor was, however, a wealthy Louisiana slaveholder who owned additional plantations in Mississippi. Charles Allen rose to address the convention. Claiming to speak for Massachusetts, Allen shouted above the roar of opposing voices that he could not "consent that this shall go forth as the unanimous voice of this convention…We declare the Whig party of this Union this day dissolved."[501]

As Allen made his way back to Worcester, some of his friends organized a city hall meeting for June 21 of citizens unhappy with the presidential nominations of both Taylor and Democrat Lewis Cass. City hall—as town hall was named upon the adoption of the city charter—was the largest meeting space in the city; it was packed and overflowing as Allen stepped to the podium. "The great men of the city were not there," wrote a still-enthused eyewitness forty years later. "The press had not advocated it. The clergymen were cold. The merchants and professional men passed it by."[502]

Who had packed the hall to hear the rebellious delegate? "The men from the shops… were there to express their sovereign will…[D]isregarding the wishes and advice of those to whom they had been accustomed to trust the management of their political interests, they had resolved to take matters into their own hands, and had come out to do their work themselves."[503]

The mechanics were in charge of the meeting. The speech Allen gave the crowd when he arrived was not an abolition speech. Allen's address was mostly about who governed Worcester. It was the speech his listeners wanted to hear.

At the Whig convention, Allen revealed, Massachusetts delegates had been asked whether Zachary Taylor could win in their districts. When Allen answered that Taylor could not win in Worcester County, a party leader contradicted him, saying he had heard differently about political sentiment in Worcester. Allen said he asked who had given such assurances. The answer: "Governor Lincoln."

To the mechanics assembled in city hall, Allen shouted, "Am I right, or was he?" The men from the shops erupted at this "challenge against the man who held the first place in the respect and regard of the citizens of Worcester," and they "endorsed the bold and self-reliant man who stood before them."[504] Allen's next local target was the city's other Whig giant, former Governor John Davis, who was then serving in the United States Senate. Davis had, according to Allen, written a letter supporting Zachary Taylor. "If Governor Davis denies that I have spoken the truth of him, I will prove it. If Governor Lincoln denies that I have spoken the truth of him, I will prove it."[505]

A bit later the "earnest form" of Charles Allen's brother, the Reverend George Allen, pushed forward to propose a ringing resolution "that Massachusetts wears no chains and spurns all bribes; that Massachusetts goes now and will ever go for free soil and free men, for free lips and a free press, for a free land and a free world."[506] The meeting adopted that and other defiant resolutions. A Free Soil convention attracted eight thousand men from across Massachusetts to Worcester on June 28, giving the city a claim to being the birthplace of the Free Soil Party.[507]

The Whigs, despite defections by the Free Soilers, carried on a vigorous fight in the fall of 1848. In September, Levi Lincoln II welcomed into his Elm Street mansion a distant relative, Congressman Abraham Lincoln of Illinois, who had come to address a large Whig rally at city hall.[508] On November 6, Daniel Webster spoke for Taylor and Fillmore at another city hall rally presided over by Mayor Lincoln. During the Webster address, however, the streets outside were teeming with Free Soilers from the city and the county who had streamed in for a torchlight procession with bands and banners in support of their presidential candidate, Martin Van Buren.[509]

The election was held two days later. In Worcester County, the Free Soil candidate received 43 percent of the total vote, making Worcester the only county in the state won by the Free Soil presidential ticket. The vote in the city was 1,489 for the Free Soil candidate, 589 for the Whig and 284 for the Democrat—strong evidence that Free Soil was drawing its support from former Democratic as well as former Whig voters. Allen had not won a majority in the whole district, but he defeated the incumbent, Charles Hudson, in a special election in January 1849, to take the seat that had been occupied from 1825 to 1841 by John Davis and Levi Lincoln. Fifty Free Soil men also took seats in the Massachusetts House of Representatives, twenty of them from Worcester County.[510]

The combined Whig and Democratic forces of Worcester had suffered a spectacular defeat. After a generation of false starts, the "men in the shops," rallying behind the cause of Free Soil, had triumphed in a major political confrontation with the aristocracy of lawyers and merchants who had ruled Worcester since the Revolution. They could now cast their eyes on the prestigious local seats held by the mayor and aldermen and could believe confidently that they might fill them themselves. That is precisely what they did in the municipal election of 1849. Henry Chapin became the Free-Soil mayor, and the entire Free Soil slate took office with him. That was, of course, not the end of the story, but it marks the closing of this history.

Readers will please be kind enough to forgive the sudden stop. It might have been more courteous to put the story, and possibly the reader, to rest at a quieter moment in the proceedings. That would, however, not be faithful to 1848, to the Free Soilers, to the Irish and those who feared them and to the economic and moral tensions of the period, especially to the clamor caused by Americans trying to puzzle out what should be done about slavery and industrialization. The new city of Worcester was not born into quiet times. The momentum of the Free Soilers has already carried us past our closing date and into 1849. We must desist, but we cannot be stopped from imagining our way back to 1849 and trying to understand more and better. Once there, we may sense the rising of the storm that would not be stilled, and we know that yonder, beyond the limits of this history, lies a terrible, swift sword.

NOTES

CHAPTER 1

1. Gookin, *Historical Collection*, 65–85.
2. Lincoln, *History of Worcester*, 17, 27.
3. Salisbury, *Manitou and Providence*, 7, 23, 30; Cronon, *Changes in the Land*, 86; Leach, *Flintlock and Tomahawk*, 1; Cook, *Indian Population*, 58.
4. Simpson and Simpson, introduction to *Diary*, 2.
5. Gookin, *Historical Collection*, 14.
6. Cronon, *Changes in the Land*, 52.
7. Ibid., 80, 63.
8. Salisbury, *Manitou and Providence*, 183–85.
9. Anon., "A True Account of the Most Considerable Occurrences," 279.
10. Malone, *Skulking Way of War*, 7, 14; Salisbury, *Manitou and Providence*, 221–22; Jennings, *Invasion of America*, 220–25.
11. Salisbury, *Manitou and Providence*, 224.
12. Washburn, "Seventeenth-Century Indian Wars," 90; Leach, *Flintlock and Tomahawk*, 161–65.
13. Massachusetts Colony, *Records of the Governor*, 55.
14. Vaughan, *New England Frontier*, 245–46.
15. Gookin, *Historical Collection*, 63.
16. Gookin, *Daniel Gookin*, 61–71.
17. Ibid., 72–81.
18. Ibid., 128–29, 111–14.
19. Rice, "Records of the Proprietors," 12, 13, 14. Although the committee, in its October 1668 report, announced that the proposed plantation at Quinsigamond was "now called WO[R]CESTER," variations of "Quinsigamond" continued to be used until the General Court made "Worcester" official in 1684.

20. Lincoln, *History of Worcester*, 7; Rice, "Records of the Proprietors," 23; Bodge, *Soldiers In King Philip's War*, 105; Lincoln, *History of Worcester*, 9.

21. Gookin, *Historical Collection*, 79–87.

22. Lincoln, *History of Worcester*, 365.

23. Ibid., 10–11.

24. Gookin, *Historical Collection*, 17; Lincoln, *History of Worcester*, 365.

25. Blake, "Incidents of the First and Second Settlements," 74.

26. Rice, "Records of the Proprietors," 21, 22, 26; Lincoln, *History of Worcester*, 17, 20.

27. Weiss, "Patterns and Processes," 16.

28. Hubbard, "Present State," 58; Washburn, "Seventeenth-Century Indian Wars," 92–93; Leach, *Flintlock and Tomahawk*, 24–35.

29. Easton, "Relacion of the Indian Warre," 12; Leach, *Flintlock and Tomahawk*, 42–43.

30. Leach, *Flintlock and Tomahawk*, 69–70.

31. Temple, *History of North Brookfield*, 76; Bodge, *Soldiers in King Philip's War*, 105.

32. Temple, *History of North Brookfield*, 76.

33. Leach, *Flintlock and Tomahawk*, 73–74; Temple, *History of North Brookfield*, 31, 33, 77–78; Ellis and Morris, *King Philip's War*, 86.

34. Leach, *Flintlock and Tomahawk*, 66; Hubbard, "Present State," vol. 1, 86; Metcalf, *Annals of Mendon*, 62.

35. Temple, *History of North Brookfield*, 79.

36. Ibid., 78–81.

37. Gookin, "Historical Account," 447; Temple, *History of North Brookfield*, 82, 86; Leach, *Flintlock and Tomahawk*, 80.

38. Temple, *History of North Brookfield*, 83–84.

39. Hubbard, "Present State," vol. 1, 88; Leach, *Flintlock and Tomahawk*, 72; Ellis and Morris, *King Philip's War*, 79–81.

40. Temple, *History of North Brookfield*, 100.

41. Leach, *Flintlock and Tomahawk*, 226; Easton, "Relacion of the Indian Warre," 13.

42. Eliot, "Petition from Rev. John Eliot," 297.

43. Salisbury, "Red Puritans," 31.

44. Eliot, "Petition from Rev. John Eliot," 297.

45. Hubbard, "Present State," vol. 1, 237–38.

46. Gookin, "Historical Account" 450–51.

47. Ibid., 451.

48 Ibid., 467–74.

49. Gookin, *Daniel Gookin*, 156; Massachusetts Court of Assistants, *Records of the Court of Assistants*, vol. 1, 71–73.

50. Bodge, *Soldiers In King Philip's War*, 267–68.

51. Gookin, "Historical Account," 467, 478–79.

52. Mather, *Brief History*, 104.

53. Washburn, "Seventeenth-Century Indian Wars," 94; Leach, *Flintlock and Tomahawk*, 61, 85, 113, 117.

54. Ibid., 84, 94; Leach, *Flintlock and Tomahawk*, 126–31; Jennings, *Invasion of America*, 312.

55. Rowlandson, "Narrative of the Captivity," 122–23; map in Lincoln, *Narratives*, following 123.

56. Leach, *Flintlock and Tomahawk*, 179; Gookin, "Historical Account," 508.

57. Leach, *Flintlock and Tomahawk*, 181; Gookin, "Historical Account," 508.

58. Leach, *Flintlock and Tomahawk*, 213–14; anon., "True Account."

59. Anon., "True Account," 278–79; Drake, *Biography and History*, 262–63.

60. Ellis and Morris, *King Philip's War*, 267–68.

61. Church, *Diary*, 154, 156; Ellis and Morris, *King Philip's War*, 274.

62. Ellis and Morris, *King Philip's War*, 281, 284.

63. Leach, *Flintlock and Tomahawk*, 243; Ellis and Morris, *King Philip's War*, 288.

64. Leach, *Flintlock and Tomahawk*, 245; Ellis and Morris, *King Philip's War*, 237–38.

65. Anon., "Indian Children," 271–73.

66. Ibid., 273.

67. Order of the General Court, appended to "Indian Children," 273; Leach, *Flintlock and Tomahawk*, 246.

68. Lincoln, *History of Worcester*, 365.

Chapter 2

69. Ibid., 28, 367–68.

70. Wall, *Reminiscences*, 20.

71. Rice, "Records of the Proprietors," 33.

72. Ibid.

73. Ibid., 32; Gookin, *Daniel Gookin*, 3; Rice, "Records of the Proprietors," 32, 42; Martin, *Profits in the Wilderness*, 24–25.

74. Rice, "Records of the Proprietors," 32; Aldrich, "The Bench and the Bar," 1422.

75. Blake, "Incidents," 74–75.

76. Rice, "Records of the Proprietors," 13; Lincoln, *History of Worcester*, 32; Gookin, *Daniel Gookin*, 106–10.

77. Rice, "Records of the Proprietors," 15.

78. Weiss, "Patterns and Processes," 18.

79. Rice, "Records of the Proprietors," 40–42.

80. Blake, "Incidents," 76–77.

81. Lincoln, *History of Worcester*, 32. Wing's mills were located just north and west of what is now Lincoln Square. Blake, "Incidents," 84–91; Rice, "Records of the Proprietors," 44.

82. Blake, "Incidents," 87–90.

83. Kinnicutt, "Historical Notes," 278.

84. Ibid.; Rice, "Records of the Proprietors," 48–49.

85. Blake, "Incidents," 95.

86. Aldrich, "The Bench and the Bar," 1422–23; Nutt, *History of Worcester* I, 214–15; Rice, "Records of the Proprietors," 59.

87. Lincoln, *History of Worcester*, 41–42. Unless otherwise specified, biographical information used in this chapter is from "Early Settlers. Their Ancestry and Descendants," in Nutt, *History of Worcester* 1, 43–270.

88. Lincoln, *History of Worcester*, 41; Nutt, *History of Worcester* 1, 215. Although Lincoln and Nutt both refer to Adonijah Rice as the "first white child" born in Worcester, some Anglo-American children must have been born during the two decades of the second settlement.

89. Ulrich, *Midwife's Tale*, 6.

90. Ibid., 189.

91. Scholten, *Childbearing*, 27–28.

92. Rice, "Records of the Proprietors," 65–140; Powell, *Puritan Village*, 133–38.

93. Rice, "Records of the Proprietors," 113, 115, 139.

94. Weiss, "Patterns and Processes," 23.

95. Lincoln, *History of Worcester*, 45; Butler, *Walking in the Way*, 7.

96. Lincoln, *History of Worcester*, 164; Spears, *Old Landmarks*, 127.

97. Lincoln, *History of Worcester*, 45–47; Perry, *Scotch-Irish*, 9; Nutt, *History of Worcester*, 1, 128. The estimated proportion of Scotch-Irish in Worcester is based on the following: when the first town meeting was held in 1722, John Gray was elected to the five-man board of selectmen. When pews and seats were assigned in the meetinghouse in 1724, none of the fifteen enclosed pews, reserved for leading taxpayers, went to the Scotch-Irish, but seventeen of the thirty-eight open seats were assigned to them. When the seating was done again in 1733, forty-one of eighty-nine open seats went to the Scotch-Irish. (Rice, "Early Records," 10, 28, 84–86.)

98. Perry, *Scotch-Irish*, 10, 12; Russell, *A Long Deep Furrow*, 138; Lincoln, *History of Worcester*, 191. Fitzgerald remained in Worcester at least until 1722. (Perry, *Scotch-Irish*, 13.)

99. Lincoln, *History of Worcester*, 164.

100. Ibid., 164–65.

101. Ibid., 164.

102. Ibid., 165.

103. Ibid., 50, 164.

104. The background of the settlers is drawn from Nutt, *History of Worcester* 1, 43–270. The membership of the factions is derived from Rice, "Early Records." The town records (mostly the record of the town meeting) for 1722 to 1753 were published as "Early Records," Book I (1722–29) and Book II (1740–53), in Volume 2 of the *Collections of the Worcester Society of Antiquity*. They are here cited as "Early Records I" and "Early Records II." The records for 1754 to 1848 appeared as "Town Records" in Volumes 4, 8, 10, 11 and 15 of the *Collections*. They will be cited as "Town Records," followed by the *Collections* volume and page numbers. When a date in the text indicates the source of the evidence, no additional citation will be provided.

105. Unless otherwise noted, all information concerning officeholding and actions of the town meeting are from the "Early Records" for the dates cited.

106. Rice, "Early Records I," 15.

107. Lincoln, *History of Worcester*, 166.

108. Ibid., 51.

109. Ibid., 52–53.

110. Ibid., 54–55.

111. Ibid., 55–57.

112. Ibid., 57; Mathews, *Expansion of New England*, 86; Lincoln, *History of Worcester*, 167; Shipton, *Biographical Sketches*, 3, 339. Eliot's son had married Gookin's daughter. Their son, John, was Mary Eliot Burr's father.

113. Perry, *Scotch-Irish*, 13.

114. Rice, "Records of the Proprietors," 107; Nutt, *History of Worcester* vol. 1, 162; Massachusetts General Court, *Journals of the House*, vol. 6, 226.

115. Massachusetts General Court, *Journals of the House*, vol. 8, 4, 174; vol. 9, 4, 208.

116. Ibid., vol. 8, 217; Shipton, *Biographical Sketches*.

117. Lincoln, *History of Worcester*, 58.

CHAPTER 3

118. Unless otherwise specified, all information concerning county officeholding is from Whitmore, *Massachusetts Civil List*, or anon., "Register of Civil Officers, 205–11.

119. Bowen, *History of Woodstock* vol. 1, 16; Gookin, *Historical Collection*, 80–81; Chandler, *Chandler Family*, 16–23.

120. Chandler, *Chandler Family*, 42–47.

121. Information on council membership from Whitmore, *Massachusetts Civil List*.

122. Brennan, *Plural Office-Holding*, 34-35; Chandler, *Chandler Family*, 51, 121.

123. Rice, "Early Records I," 83.

124. Rice, "Records of the Court of General Sessions," 24.

125. Ibid., 95–98.

126.Ibid., 30–31, 42.

127. Lincoln, *History of Worcester*, 342.

128. Ibid.; Rice, "Records of the Court of General Sessions," 26–29.

129. Rice, "Records of the Court of General Sessions," 53.

130. Rice, "Early Records I," 49–50.

131. The complaint was signed by Phineas Heywood (son-in-law of Deacon Nathaniel Moore), Gershom Rice Jr., Benjamin Flagg Jr. and Palmer Goulding. Worcester County Mass. Papers, Box 1, folder 6.

132. Rice, "Early Records I," 107; Lincoln, *History of Worcester*,192; Perry, *Scotch-Irish*, 13.

133. Worcester County Mass. Papers, Box 1, Folder 6, AAS; Lincoln, *History of Worcester*, 192; Perry, *Scotch-Irish*, 13; Rice, "Records of the Court of General Sessions," 122, 141–42.

134. Rice, "Early Records I," 107–08.

135. Massachusetts General Court, *Journals of the House*, ix, 15, 78, 218.

136. Lincoln, *History of Worcester*, 47, 192; Perry, *Scotch-Irish*, 17. Though Lincoln did not specifically assign a date to this event, the placement of his account may initially leave the impression that the event occurred around 1718; many subsequent writers have used that date. However, Lincoln also linked the destruction of the meetinghouse directly to the Scotch-Irish emigration from Worcester and the founding of Pelham, which occurred in the late 1730s. Lincoln returned to the subject in his "Ecclesiastical History" section (192), and placed the demolition of the meetinghouse between the hiring of William Johnston (post-1731) and the petition to the town for tax relief, which was acted upon in 1737.

137. McClellan, *Early Settlers of Colrain*, 18; Parmenter, *History of Pelham*, 13–15.

138. Parmenter, *History of Pelham*, 15.

139. Ibid., 13–37.

140. Of the forty-one Scotch-Irish men assigned seats in the Worcester meetinghouse in 1733, at least sixteen became settlers of Pelham by the early 1740s. Of the twenty-nine original Scotch-Irish proprietors of Pelham, twenty-two were from Worcester.

141. Rice, "Early Records I," 84–86; names of early Pelham settlers are in Parmenter, *History of Pelham*, 77–86; Pelham proprietors are listed in Parmenter, 17; Worcester church membership from Church Record Book, 1745–1790, Worcester, Mass. Old South Church Records, Box 1, Folder, 1, AAS; Nutt, *History of Worcester* 1, 28.

142. Whitefield, *George Whitefield's Journals*, 152–65, 474–75; Lincoln, *History of Worcester*, 168.

143. Lincoln, *History of Worcester*, 168–69.

144. William Lincoln in 1837 hinted strongly that David Hall and the New Lights were principally responsible for the revolt against Burr in Worcester. (Lincoln, *History of Worcester*, 169.) That interpretation, which differs from the one presented here, has been regularly repeated in subsequent accounts.

145. Worcester, Mass. Old South Church Records (AAS), Box 2, Folder 1.

146. The details of the town's actions can be traced in the "Early Records" and those of the church in the Church Record Book, 1745–90, Worcester, Mass. Old South Church Records, Box I, Folder 1 (AAS). Biographical information about ministerial candidates, including their theological inclinations, can be found in Shipton, *Biographical Sketches*, and in Dexter, *Biographical Sketches*.

147. Shipton, *Biographical Sketches*, vol. 10, 380; Church Record Book, 1745–90, Worcester, Mass. Old South Church Records, Box I, Folder 1 (AAS).

148. Lincoln, *History of Worcester*, 173, 174, 223.

149. Rice, "Early Records II," 61.

150. Rice, "Early Records II," 83, 98, 123, 124.

151. Adams, *Diary and Autobiography*, vol. 3, 263.

152. Ibid., vol.1, 42–44.

153. Maccarty Family Papers, AAS.

154. For Pakachoag petition, see Rice, "Early Records II," 11, 15.

155. Leach, *Arms for Empire*, 227.

156. Pencak, *War, Politics, & Revolution*, 120; Leach, *Arms for Empire*, 231; Lincoln, *History of Worcester*, 61.

157. Hanna, "New England Military Institutions," 19, 31, 68–69.

158. Leach, *Arms for Empire*, 246–47; Schutz, *William Shirley*, 115–16.

159. Leach, *Arms for Empire*, 401.

160. Hunt, *American Anecdotes*, 225. This account, which quotes from an unidentified writing of John Adams, links these events to the news of Braddock's defeat on July 9, 1755. The commotion seems more likely to have occurred after the fall of Fort William Henry in 1757. Adams reported that the militia marched for the frontier, but they "were all stopped and countermarched before they reached Fort William Henry." Fort William Henry did not exist at the time of Braddock's defeat. It was built following a battle two months later on Lake George.

161. Lincoln, *History of Worcester*, 65; biographical details from Nutt, *History of Worcester*, 1, 43–270 and Rice, "Worcester Births, Marriages and Deaths."

162. Lincoln, *History of Worcester*, 64.

163. Leach, *Arms for Empire*, 437; Lincoln, *History of Worcester*, 65; Adams, *Diary and Autobiography*, vol. 3, 266–67.

164. Rice, "Town Records IV," 22; Chase, "Baldwin-Eaton Estate," 103; Adams, *Diary and Autobiography*, vol. 3, 265.

165. Adams, *Diary and Autobiography*, vol. 3, 265; Rice, "Town Records IV," 63, 71, 80, 87, 96; Goodwin, *Town Officer*, 250.

166. Doolittle, *Doolittle Family*, vol. 1, 165–67.

167. For Doolittle's deism, see Adams, *Diary and Autobiography*, vol. 3, 265.

168. Adams, *Diary and Autobiography*, vol. 3, 265.

169. Ibid., vol. 3, 269–70.

170. Doolittle, *Doolittle Family*, vol. 1, 166; Rice, "Town Records IV," 71, 79.

171. Massachusetts General Court, *Journals of the House*, vol. 42, 215, vol. 43, 303.

172. Rice, "Early Records II," 131; Rice, "Town Records IV," 9, 81.

173. *Boston Gazette*, March 31, 1766, 3.

CHAPTER 4

174. Province Tax List, Worcester, Mass. Records, Box 1, Folder 1, AAS. The other slaveholders were Jacob Hemenway, Samuel Mower and Samuel Brooks.

175. Howe, *Genealogy of the Bigelow Family*, 43, 74–79.

176. Lincoln, *History of Worcester*, 73–74.

177. Johnson, "Worcester in the War," 16–21; Nichols, "Samuel Salisbury," 46–48.

178. Brown, *Revolutionary Politics*, 57.

179. Rice, "Town Records IV," 201–02.

180. Miller, *Origins of the American Revolution*, 330.

181. Worcester, Mass. American Political Society Records, 1773–76 (AAS).

182. Province Tax List for 1770, Worcester, Mass. Records, Box 1, Folder 1, AAS.

183. American Political Society Records, 4.

184. These calculations are based on the ages of the twenty of twenty-six protestors and the twenty-five of thirty-one APS founders whose ages were traceable in Nutt, *History of Worcester*, vol. 1, 43–270, and for Nathan Baldwin's age, in Baldwin, *Baldwin Genealogy*, 619.

185. American Political Society Records, 17–19; Lincoln, *History of Worcester*, 79–80.

186. The record of the meeting, made by by Clark Chandler, does not specifically state that the instructions reported by the committee were adopted by the town. Given the Whig control of the rest of that day's business, it seems all but certain that the town did adopt the report.

187. Of 256 Worcester property owners taxed by the province in 1770, only 23 (9 percent) had property with an assessed value of more than £100. There were 157 (61 percent) with fewer than £50. Included among those were 94 (37 percent) with less than £25. The median holding among property owners assessed was £38, one-ninth the size of the estate of John Chandler (£346). Province Tax List for 1770, Worcester, Mass. Records, Box 1, Folder 1, AAS.

188. Massachusetts Provincial Congress, "Conventions of Worcester County" in *Journals of Each Provincial Congress*, 636. The proceedings of the county conventions are appended to the journals of the Provincial Congress, those for Worcester County appearing on 627–52. Unless otherwise indicated, all information concerning the convention is from this source, for the date(s) indicated in the text.

189. Rice, "Town Records IV," 230. The text of the protest and the signatures are on 231–33.

190. American Political Society Records, 15.

191. Lincoln, *Journals of Each Provincial Congress*, 628.

192. American Political Society Records, 17.

193. Lincoln, *History of Worcester*, 92, 94.

194. Fifty-two men had signed the protest, and forty-three had recanted, leaving nine rather than five failing to recant. The discrepancy in the numbers may be due to the fact that some signers of the protest were not from Worcester.

195. Lincoln, *History of Worcester*, 92. The manuscript record book is in the keeping of the Worcester City Clerk.

196. Matthews, "Documents," 472.

197. Note penciled by Nathaniel Paine in AAS copy of Lovell's *Worcester in the War*, 10: "The Paine house referred to above was not completed till after the war began. Tim Paine lived on Lincoln St. near Lincoln Square in a house still standing—1897."

198. Matthews, "Documents," 476–77.

199. Patterson, *Political Parties*, 96.

200. "Conventions of Worcester County," 633n.

201. Matthews, "Documents," 478.

202. American Political Society Records, 26.

203. Alden, *General Gage*, 213–14.

204. "Conventions of Worcester County," 635n.

205. Ibid., 635–37.

206. Ibid., 638.

207. Ibid., 639, 641, 642.

208. Ibid., 642.

209. Ibid., 643–44; Gross, *Minutemen*, 59.

210. American Political Society Records, 27.

211. Andrew McFarland Davis, *Confiscation*, 115, 224.

212. Shipton, *Biographical Sketches*, vol. 17 (1975), 101; vol. 16 (1971), 330; vol. 12 (1962), 60.

213. Ibid., vol. 12 (1962), 60, 295; vol. 17 (1975), 70–71, 580–83.

214. Lincoln, *History of Worcester*, 106.

215. Lincoln, *History of Worcester*, 108–10.

216. Flexner, *Washington*, 60; *Massachusetts Spy*, July 5, 1775, 3.

217. American Political Society Records, 29.

218. Ibid., 36.

219. Lincoln, *History of Worcester*, 229.

220. U.S. Revolution Collection, AAS, Box 2, Folder 1.

221. American Political Society Records, 40.

222. Stark, *Loyalists of Massachusetts*, 139.

223. Ibid., 142.

224. Ibid., 143–44.

225. Davis, "Historical Notes on the Letter," 142–45.

226. Shipton, *Biographical Sketches*, vol. 16 (1971), 331; vol. 12 (1962), 61.

227. Deposition of Nathan Baldwin, October 14, 1777, U.S. Revolution Collection (AAS), Box 2, Folder 6.

228. "Capt. Lovell's Reasons"; Deposition of David Chadwick, October 14, 1777, U.S. Revolution Collection, Box 2, Folder 5. Clifford K. Shipton. *Biographical Sketches*, vol.16 (1971), 331.

229. In May 1776, the law was changed to allow three representatives to towns with 220 voters, and authorizing another representative for each additional 100 voters. Dalton et al., *Leading the Way*, 47.

230. Howe, *Genealogy of the Bigelow Family*, 78; Lincoln, *History of Worcester*, 279.

231. The details of the Lovell affair can be followed in depositions in the U.S. Revolution Collection (AAS), Box 2, Folders 4, 5 and 6.

232. Petition, undated, U.S. Revolution Collection, Box 2, Folder 4.

233. Massachusetts General Court, *Journals of the House*, vol. 53, 115.

234. U.S. Revolution Collection (AAS), Nathan Baldwin Deposition, Box 2, Folder 6.

CHAPTER 5

235. Except where otherwise noted, this account is based on Chandler, *American Criminal Trials*, vol. 2, 1–58.

236. Chandler, *American Criminal Trials*, 12.

237. Maccarty, *The Rev. Mr. Maccarty*, 1, 2.

238. Chandler, *American Criminal Trials*, 42.

239. Ibid.

240. Ibid., 43.

241. Ibid., 34.

242. Ibid., 34.

243. Ibid., 49.

244. Ibid., 50.

245. Maccarty, *The Rev. Mr. Maccarty*, 3.

246. Rice, "Town Records XVI," 360–61.

247. Ibid., 382.

248. Ibid., 395.

249. Ibid., 321, 324–5, 331.

250. The names of the recruits are in Lovell, *Worcester in the War*, 124. With one exception, the names do not appear on Worcester tax lists available for the period.

251. Salisbury Family Papers (AAS), box 4, folder 3.

252. Lovell, *Worcester in the War*, 124.

253. Rice, "Town Records XVI," 340.

254. Gross, *Minutemen*, xx.

255. Cushing, "Cushing Court," 118–44; MacEacheren, "Emancipation," 289–306.

256. Ibid., 124–25.

257. Ibid., 133.

258. Lovell, *Worcester in the War*, 9.

259. There were 142 men on the 1778 tax list who had not been taxed in Worcester eight years earlier; only 52 of the new taxpayers had family names that had not been present in Worcester in 1770. Five years later, 97 new men appeared on the 1783 tax list, but only 39 of them had surnames names that were new to Worcester.

260. In 1770, fifty-eight people appeared on a state tax list as holders of trading stock, money or "faculty," a term used to designate the special earning capacity of men like lawyers or doctors. (Province Tax List, 1770, Worcester, Mass. Collection, Box 1, folder 1). On a 1778 town tax list, sixty-six individuals were assessed under "faculty."

261. Lincoln, *History of Worcester*, 230.

262. Ibid., 286.

263. Shipton, *Biographical Sketches*, 14, 238.

264. Davis, *Confiscation*, 96, 210.

265. Nutt, *History of Worcester*, vol. 1, 253.

266. Rice, "Town Records XVI," 322.

267. The following account is based on Moynihan, "Meetinghouse vs. Courthouse," 34–54.

268. Lincoln, *History of Worcester*, 201.

269. Rice, "Town Records XXVIII," 27, 33.

270. Ibid., 35–36.

271. Worcester, Mass. First Unitarian Church Records (AAS), Box 1, Folder 3.

272. The incorporators are listed in First Unitarian Church Records, Box 1, Folder 3. Seven of the incorporators had signed the 1774 Loyalist protest; the eighth Loyalist was Timothy Paine.

273. The members of the Second Parish and its church are listed in First Unitarian Church Records, Box 1, Folder 1. Biographies of college graduates and lawyers are in Lincoln, *History of Worcester*, chapters 13 and 14.

274. Rice, "Town Records XXVIII," 51, 95–97, 99–103.

275. Hall, *Politics Without Parties*, 113–22, 194–203.

276. Rice, "Town Records XXVIII," 12, 21–23.

277. Ibid., 86.

278. Lincoln, *History of Worcester*, 134–38.

279. Letters on both sides appeared regularly in *Worcester Magazine* during these months.

280. Rice, "Town Records XXVIII," 85.

281. Ibid., 86–89.

282. One of the three, Eli Chapin, was named as an incorporator in the legislation establishing the Second Parish. However, he had petitioned the General Court not to include his name. (First Unitarian Church Records, Box 1, Folder 3.)

283. Wall, *Reminiscences*, 44. Bigelow's inn was on what is now East Mountain Street, near the border with Shrewsbury. Baird was also a farmer.

284. *Worcester Magazine*, December 1786, 452.

285. Massachusetts Archives, 189: 83–84.

286. Rice, "Town Records XXVIII," 101.

287. Massachusetts Archives, 189: 83–84; jail records, Worcester County Mass. Papers, Box 2, Folder 1, AAS.

288. Baird's appeal for bond, endorsed by the governor's council, is in Massachusetts Archives 189: 184.

289. Szatmary, *Shays' Rebellion*, 101–05. Szatmary's assertion that the Regulators wanted the weapons in Springfield in order to overthrow the state government (99–100) is based entirely on a highly dubious report printed in the ardently anti-Regulator *Massachusetts Centinel* on January 17, 1787. The report was attributed to a former Continental army officer from New York who had visited Shays to collect a debt. It provides the only evidence supporting the proposition that Shays intended to march on Boston and overthrow the government. Even if Shays uttered the words attributed to him, they may have amounted to nothing more than bluster—or bluff.

290. Rice, "Town Records XXVIII," 107.

291. Ibid., 130.

292. Massachusetts Convention, *Debates and Proceedings*, 87–92.

293. Rice, "Worcester District in Congress," 79; Massachusetts Convention, *Debates and Proceedings*, 91; Brooke, *Heart of the Commonwealth*, 235.

294. Lincoln, *History of Worcester*, 136.

295. One appeal to Ward's supporters came in the form of a letter calling upon all who had voted for candidates other than Paine and Grout to unite behind Paine, since they all would rather see him elected than Grout. ("A Voter for Worcester District," *Massachusetts Spy*, January 22, 1789.)

296. "An Old Man," *Massachusetts Spy*, January 22, 1789, 2.

297. "Politicus," *Massachusetts Spy*, February 26, 1789, 2.

298. "An Elector," *Massachusetts Spy*, February 26, 1789, 2.

299. Martin, *Profits in the Wilderness*, 240–41.

300. "A Yeoman of Worcester District," *Massachusetts Spy*, February 26, 1789, 2.

301. *0*, March 5, 1789, 2.

302. "Z.Z.," *Massachusetts Spy*, September 30, 1790, 2; anon., *Massachusetts Spy*, September 23, 1790, 2.

303. *Massachusetts Spy*, December 30, 1790, 3.

304. Rice, "Town Records XXVIII," 213, 233.

CHAPTER 6

305. Worcester Jail Records, Worcester County, Massachusetts Collection (AAS), Box 2, Folder 1; Crane, "History of the Jo Bill Road"; Hersey, *History of Worcester*, 412

306. *Massachusetts Spy*, March 15, 1781.

307. Lincoln, *History of Worcester*, 280.

308. Farnsworth, "Shays' Rebellion," 34.

309. Lincoln, *History of Worcester*, 280; Worcester Jail Records.

310. Farnsworth, "Shays' Rebellion," 34; Worcester Jail Records; Crane, "History of the Jo Bill Road," 209.

311. Whitney, *History of the County*, 27–28.

312. Lincoln, *History of Worcester*, 302.

313. *Worcester Magazine*, January 1787.

314. Glasgow, "Educational History," 2, 1815.

315. Rice, "Town Records XXIX," 157; Whitney, *History of the County*, 103.

316. Paine, "Topographical Description," 112–16; Rice, "Town Records XXIX," 234.

317. Nason, *Centennial History*, 8, 10, 14, 21; Kring, *Fruits of Our Labors*, 52. The petitioners referred to were Nathaniel Paine; Nathaniel, Clark, Samuel and Charles Chandler; and John Stanton.

318. Lincoln, *History of Worcester*, 339.

319. Brooke, *Heart of the Commonwealth*, 274.

320. Washburn, *Industrial Worcester*, 17.

321. Ibid., 24.

322. Ibid., 23.

323. Ibid., 24.

324. Ibid., 25.

325. Ibid., 26.

326. Rice, "Town Records XXIX," 312, 356.

327. Ibid., 312.

328. Ibid., 356.

329. Formisano, *Transformation of Political Culture*, 108.

330. Rice, "Town Records XXXII," 19.

331. Quarrey, "Political Party Organization," 5.

332. Lincoln, *History of Worcester*, 333.

333. Active Federalists who between 1812 and 1820 joined the Washington Benevolent Society are listed in Worcester County Mass. Collection, Miscellaneous Materials, Octavo Volume #2, AAS.

334. Quarrey, "Political Party Organization," 18.

335. The letter was published in the *National Aegis*, August 24, 1808. Lincoln, *History of Worcester*, 155.

336. *Massachusetts Spy*, March 22, 1809, quoted in Quarrey, "Political Party Organization," 19.

337. *National Aegis*, March 22, 1809, quoted in Quarrey, "Political Party Organization," 19.

338. Rice, "Town Records XXXII," 175.

339. Lincoln, *History of Worcester*, 152.

340. Austin, *Sermon preached*, 12.

341. Austin, *Apology of Patriots*, 28.

342. Austin, *Sermon preached*, 16.

343. Austin, *Apology of Patriots*, 28.

344. Ibid., 28, 29.

345. Brooke, *Heart of the Commonwealth*, 268.

346. Shipton, *Biographical Sketches*, 82.

347. Brooke, *Heart of the Commonwealth*, 281–83.

348. Lincoln, *History of Worcester*, 360.

349. Rice, "Town Records XXVIII," 70.

350. Ibid., 72.

351. Rice, "Town Records XXIX," 204.

352. Gaskill, "Civic and Political History," 1437–38.

353. Rice, "Town Records XXIX," 234, 255.

354. Ibid., 179.

355. Ibid., 183.

356. Ibid., 204.

357. Rice, "Town Records XXXIV," 285.

358. Ibid., 310.

359. Ibid., 319.

360. Worcester, "Report of a Committee of the Centre School District in Worcester, 1823," reprinted as "Appendix to the School Report." *City Document No. 27* (1873), 165, 168.

361. Ibid., 166.

362. Ibid., 167.

363. Ibid.
364. Ibid., 169.
365. "Worcester Center School District, 1828," 169.
366. Rice, "Town Records XXXVII," 231.
367 Ibid., 254–57.
368. Ibid., 257.
369. Brooke, *Heart of the Commonwealth*, 268.
370. Lincoln, *History of Worcester*, 325.
371. Rice, "Town Records XXXIV," 333.
372. Rice, "Town Records XXXVII," 174.
373. Ibid., 183.
374. Ibid., 180–82.
375. Ibid., 198.
376. Ibid., 211.
377. Ibid., 202.
378. Ibid., 216.
379. Ibid., 230.
380. Ibid., 88–95.
381. Ibid., 296–97.
382. Powers, "Invisible Immigrants," 100–02.
383. Ibid., 104–06.
384. Ibid., 111.
385. Ibid., 113, 123.
386. Ibid., 146.
387. Ibid., 143, 144.
388. Ibid., 144.
389. *Worcester Village Register*, Worcester, 1828 [published by the Worcester Talisman].
390. Anon., *Worcester Village Directory*.
391. Powers, "Invisible Immigrants," 150.

CHAPTER 7

392. Lincoln, *History of Worcester*, 368; Nutt, *History of Worcester*, vol. 2, 173.
393. Formisano, *Transformation of Political Culture*, 82.
394. Gaskill, "Civic and Political History," 1444.
395. Nutt, *History of Worcester*, vol. 1, 172, 221, 254.
396. Ibid., 173.
397. Kring, *Fruits of Our Labors*, 238
398. Sturgis, "Old Worcester, IV," 80.
399. Tymeson, *Rural Retrospect*, 8–9.
400. Quoted in Brooke, *Heart of the Commonwealth*, 304.
401. Brooke, *Heart of the Commonwealth*, 341.

402. Washburn, *Industrial Worcester*, 51.
403. Gaskill, "Civic and Political History," 1432.
404. Lincoln, *History of Worcester*, 341.
405. Powers, "Invisible Immigrants," 269–72.
406. Gaskill, "Civic and Political History," 1442.
407. Sturgis, "Concerning Schools," 256.
408. Washburn, *Industrial Worcester*, 53.
409. Ibid., 51, 56.
410. Ibid., 56.
411. Ibid., 48.
412. Tyrrell, *Sobering Up*, 92.
413. Nutt, *History of Worcester*, vol. 3, 60.
414. Washburn, *Industrial Worcester*, 142–45.
415. Nutt, *History of Worcester*, vol. 1, 221–22.
416. Washburn, *Industrial History*, 292–300.
417. Powers, "Invisible Immigrants," 235–37, 242–53.
418. Ibid., 277.
419. Ibid., 278.
420. Weiss, "Patterns and Processes," 71.
421. Ibid., 56.
422. Ibid., 63–64.
423. Ibid., 79.
424. Ibid., 79.
425. Ibid., 82.
426. Tymeson, *Rural Retrospect*, 4.
427. Weiss, "Patterns and Processes," 83–84.
428. Ibid., 86.
429. Sturgis, "Concerning Schools," 253.
430. Paine, "Societies, Associations, and Clubs," 1527; Lincoln, *History of Worcester*, 330.
431. Brooke, *Heart of the Commonwealth*, 310.
432. Lincoln, *History of Worcester*, 330.
433. Tymeson, *Rural Retrospect*, 27.
434. Ibid., 27–28.
435. Ibid., 28–38.
436. Brooke, *Heart of the Commonwealth*, 311.
437. Quoted in Brooke, *Heart of the Commonwealth*, 311.
438. Ibid., 318.
439. Ibid., 318–19.
440. Tymeson, *Rural Retrospect*, 34.
441. Formisano, *Transformation of Political Culture*, 201; Bullock, *Revolutionary Brotherhood*, 277–78.
442. Ibid., 283–85, 298–302.

443. Brooke, *Heart of the Commonwealth*, 326.

444. Paine, "Societies, Associations, and Clubs," 1534–35.

445. Brooke, *Heart of the Commonwealth*, 332.

446. Formisano, *Transformation of Political Culture*, 204–05.

447. Ibid., 210.

448. Ibid.

449. Brooke, *Heart of the Commonwealth*, 354.

450. Formisano, *Transformation of Political Culture*, 215–16.

451. Ibid., 216.

452. Tyrrell, *Sobering Up*, 6.

453. Ibid., 58–62.

454. Ibid., 92.

455. Rice, "Town Records XV," 37–38.

456. Ibid., 61.

457. Tyrrell, *Sobering Up*, 94.

458. Rice, "Town Records XV," 63.

459. Tyrrell, *Sobering Up*, 95–99.

460. Ibid., 101.

461. Brooke, *Heart of the Commonwealth*, 359–60.

462. Tyrrell, *Sobering Up*, 68–69.

463. Worcester County Mechanics Association Records, vol. 3, 1.

464. Ibid., vol. 3, 14.

465. Ibid., vol. 3, 19.

466. Gaskill, "Civic and Political History,"1440.

467. Buell, "Workers of Worcester," 61.

468. Brooke, *Heart of the Commonwealth*, 362.

469. Benjamin Quarles, *Black Abolitionists*, 19.

470. Mooney, "Antislavery in Worcester County," 8.

471. Ibid., 11, 28.

472. Smalley, *Worcester Pulpit*, 443–45.

473. Nutt, *History of Worcester*, 60.

474. Sterling, *Ahead of Her Time*, 44–45.

475. Ibid., 40.

476. Ibid., 52.

477. Ibid., 104–05.

478. Powers, "Invisible Immigrants," 310.

479. Ibid., 296–97.

480. Ibid., 300.

481. Ibid., 358.

482. Ibid., 331.

483. Ibid., 333–34.

484. Ibid., 331.

485. Ibid., 358.

486. Lincoln, *Address of Hon. Levi Lincoln*, 7.

487. Brooke, *Heart of the Commonwealth*, 371.

488. Chasan, "Civilizing Worcester," 25–26.

489. *Daily Spy*, March 3, 1849, 2.

490. *Massachusetts Spy*, April 5, 1848, 2.

491. Ibid., April 12, 1848, 2.

492. Chasan, "Civilizing Worcester," 27.

493. Lincoln, *History of Worcester*, 223.

494. Smalley, *Worcester Pulpit*, 220.

495. Printed communication, March 2, 1844, Worcester, Mass. Old South Church Collection, Box 1, Folder 7, American Antiquarian Society.

496. Quoted in Chasan, "Civilizing Worcester," 27.

497. City Records, vol. 1 (City Hall), 29–30.

498. Lincoln, *Address of Hon. Levi Lincoln*, 20.

499. Rice, "Worcester County in the Free-Soil Movement," 1661.

500. Ibid.

501. Ibid., 1662.

502. Ibid., 1663.

503. Ibid.

504. Ibid., 1664.

505. Ibid., 1665.

506. Ibid.

507. Ibid., 1667–78.

508. Southwick, *150 Years of Worcester*, 33.

509. Rice, "Worcester County in the Free-Soil Movement," 1669.

510. Ibid.

BIBLIOGRAPHY

MANUSCRIPT COLLECTIONS CITED

American Antiquarian Society
   Chandler-Ward Family Papers.
   Maccarty Family Papers.
   Miscellaneous Mss. Collection.
   Salisbury Family Papers.
   U.S. Revolution Collection.
   Worcester, Massachusetts, American Political Society Records, 1773–76.
   Worcester, Massachusetts, First Unitarian Church Records.
   Worcester, Massachusetts, Old South Church Records.
   Worcester, Massachusetts, Records.
   Worcester County, Massachusetts, Papers.

Worcester County Records, Court of General Sessions of the Peace, Worcester County Courthouse.

Worcester Historical Museum
   Worcester County Mechanics Association Records.

BOOKS AND PERIODICALS

Adams, John. *Diary and Autobiography of John Adams*. Edited by Lyman H. Butterfield. 4 vols. New York: Atheneum, 1964.

Alden, John R. *General Gage in America*. Baton Rouge: Louisiana State University Press, 1948.

BIBLIOGRAPHY

Aldrich, Charles F. "The Bench and the Bar." Chap. 2 in *History of Worcester County, Massachusetts*, edited by Duane Hamilton Hurd. 2 vols. Philadelphia: J. Lewis and Co, 1889.

Anonymous. *Abstracts of Early Worcester Land Titles.*Worcester: Worcester Society of Antiquity, 1907.

————. "Indian Children Put to Service, 1676." *New England Historical and Genealogical Register* 8 (1854): 271–73.

————. "Register of Civil Officers in the County of Worcester." *Worcester Magazine and Historical Journal* 2 (1826): 205–11.

————. "A True Account of the Most Considerable Occurrences that Have Happened in the Warre between the English and the Indians in New England" (orig. pub 1676). In *The Old Indian Chronicle*, edited by Samuel G. Drake. Boston: S.A. Drake, 1867.

————. *Worcester Village Directory*. Worcester: Worcester Talisman, 1828.

Austin, Samuel. *The Apology of Patriots: or The Heresy of the Friends of the Washington Peace Policy Defended: Sermon on the National Fast, Aug. 20, 1812.* Published by request. Worcester: Isaac Sturtevant, 1812.

————. *Sermon preached in Worcester, Massachusetts, on the occasion of the special fast, July 23d, 1812; Published from the press, by the desire of some who heard it, and liked it, by the desire of some who heard it, and did not like it, and by the desire of others who did not hear it, but imagine they should not have liked it, if they had.* Worcester: Isaac Sturtevant, 1812.

Baldwin, Charles Candee. *The Baldwin Genealogy from 1500 to 1881.* Cleveland, 1881.

Bancroft, Aaron. *The World Passeth Away.* Worcester, 1811.

Blake, Francis. "Incidents of the First and Second Settlements of Worcester." *Proceedings of the Worcester Society of Antiquity for the Year 1884.* Bound in *Collections of the Worcester Society of Antiquity* 6 (1885).

————. "Some Worcester Matters, 1689–1743." *Proceedings of the Worcester Society of Antiquity for the Year 1885* (1886), 21–23. Bound in *Collections of the Worcester Society of Antiquity* 7 (1888).

Bodge, George M. *Soldiers in King Philip's War.* Boston: printed for the author, 1906.

Bowen, Clarence Winthrop. *The History of Woodstock, Connecticutt*. 8 vols. Norwood, MA: Plimpton Press, 1926–43.

Brennan, Ellen. *Plural Office-Holding in Massachusetts, 1760–1780*. Chapel Hill: University of North Carolina Press, 1945.

Brooke, John L. *The Heart of the Commonwealth: Society and Political Culture in Worcester County, Massachusetts, 1713–1861*. Cambridge [England]: Cambridge University Press, 1989.

Brookfield. *Vital Records of the Town of Brookfield, Massachusetts to the End of the Year 1849*. Worcester: F.P. Rice, 1909.

Brown, Richard D. *Revolutionary Politics in Massachusetts: The Boston Committee of Correspondence and the Towns, 1772–1774*. Cambridge: Harvard University Press, 1970.

Buell, Charles C. "The Workers of Worcester: Social Mobility and Ethnicity in a New England City." PhD diss., New York University, 1974.

Bullock, Chandler. "High Points in Early Worcester Politics." *Worcester Historical Society Publications* 1 (1930).

Bullock, Stephen C. *Revolutionary Brotherhood: Freemasonry and the Transformation of the American Social Order, 1730–1840*. Chapel Hill: University of North Carolina Press, 1996.

Butler, Charles Evans. *Walking in the Way: A History of the First Congregational Church in Worcester, 1716–1982*. Worcester: Commonwealth Press, 1987.

Chandler, George. *The Chandler Family*. Worcester, 1883.

Chandler, Peleg W. *American Criminal Trials*. 2 vols. Boston: T.H. Carter, 1844.

Chasan, Joshua. "Civilizing Worcester: The Creation of Institutional and Cultural Order, Worcester, Massachusetts, 1848–1868." PhD diss., University of Pittsburgh, 1974.

Chase, Charles A. "The Baldwin-Eaton Estate." *Collections of the Worcester Society of Antiquity* 21 (1905).

Church, Benjamin. *Diary of King Philip's War, 1675–1676*. With an introduction by Alan and Mary Simpson. Chester, RI: Pequot Press, 1975.

Cook, Sherburne F. *The Indian Population of New England in the Seventeenth Century*. Berkeley: University of California Press, 1976.

———. "The Significance of Disease in the Extinction of the New England Indians." *Human Biology* 45 (1973): 485–93.

Crane, Ellery B. "History of the Jo Bill Road." *Proceedings of the Worcester Society of Antiquity* 18 (1902).

Cronon, William. *Changes in the Land: Indians, Colonists, and the Ecology of New England.* New York: Hill & Wang, 1983.

Cushing, John D. "The Cushing Court and the Abolition of Slavery in Massachusetts: More Notes on the 'Quock Walker Case.'" *The American Journal of Legal History* 5 (1961): 118–44.

Dalton, Cornelius, John Wirkkala and Anne Thomas. *Leading the Way: A History of the Massachhusetts General Court, 1629–1980.* Boston: Office of the Massachusetts Secretary of State, 1984.

Davis, Andrew McFarland. "Alphabetical List of Partners in the Land Bank of 1740." *New England Historical and Geneological Register* 50 (1896): 187–97, 308–17.

———. *The Confiscation of John Chandler's Estate.* Boston: Houghton Mifflin, 1903.

———. "Historical Notes on the Letter [of Lucretia Chandler Bancroft]." *Proceedings of the American Antiquarian Society* 14 (1901): 143–45.

———."The Land Bank Mortgages in Worcester County." *Proceedings of the American Antiquarian Society* 16 (1903): 85–90.

Dexter, Franklin B. *Biographical Sketches of the Graduates of Yale College with Annals of the College's History.* 6 vols. New York: H. Holt, 1885–1912.

Doolittle, William Frederick. *The Doolittle Family in America.* 2 vols. Cleveland, 1901–08.

Drake, Samuel G. *Biography and History of the Indians of North America, from its first discovery.* Boston: Benjamin B. Mussey & Co., 1851.

———. *The Old Indian Chronicle.* Boston: S.A. Drake, 1867.

Easton, John. "A Relacion of the Indian Warre." In *Narratives of the Indian Wars*, edited by Charles H. Lincoln. New York: C. Scribner's Sons, 1913.

Eliot, John. "A Petition from Rev. John Eliot against selling Indians for slaves." *New England Historical and Genealogical Register* 6 (1852).

Ellis, George W., and John E. Morris. *King Philip's War.* New York: The Grafton Press, 1906.

Farnsworth, Albert. "Shays' Rebellion." *Massachusetts Law Quarterly* 12 (1927).

Flexner, James T. *Washington: The Indispensible Man.* Boston: Little, Brown, 1974.

Formisano, Ronald P. *The Transformation of Political Culture: Massachusetts Parties, 1790s–1840s.* New York and Oxford: Oxford University Press, 1983.

Gaskill, Francis A. "Civic and Political History." Chap. 180 in *History of Worcester County, Massachusetts*, edited by Duane Hamilton Hurd. 2 vols. Philadelphia: J. Lewis and Co., 1889.

Glasgow, Edward B. "Educational History." Chap. 183 *History of Worcester County, Massachusetts*, edited by Duane Hamilton Hurd. 2 vols. Philadelphia: J. Lewis and Co., 1889.

Goodwin, Isaac. *The Town Officer.* Worcester: Dorr and Howland, 1825.

Gookin, Daniel. "An Historical Account of the Doings and Sufferings of the Christian Indians in New England." *Transactions of the American Antiquarian Society* 2 (1836): 447.

———. *Historical Collection of the Indians in New England.* Spencer, MA: Towtaid, 1970.

Gookin, Frederick William. *Daniel Gookin, 1612–1687: Assistant and Major General of the Massachusetts Bay Colony.* Chicago: privately printed [R.R. Donnelly], 1912.

Gross, Robert A. *The Minutemen and Their World.* New York: Hill & Wang, 1976.

Hall, Van Beck. *Politics Without Parties: Massachusetts, 1781–1791.* Pittsburgh: University of Pittsburgh Press, 1972.

Hanna, Archibald. "New England Military Institutions, 1693–1750." PhD diss., Yale University, 1950.

Hersey, Charles. *History of Worcester, Massachusetts from 1836 to 1861.* Bound with a corrected edition of William Lincoln, *History of Worcester, Massachusetts.* Worcester: Charles Hersey, 1862.

BIBLIOGRAPHY

Howe, Gilman Bigelow. *Genealogy of the Bigelow Family*.Worcester, 1890.

Howland, Henry. *The Worcester Almanac, Directory and Business Advertiser, for 1848*. Worcester: Henry Howland, 1848.

Hubbard, William. "The Present State of New England." In *The History of the Indian Wars in New England*, edited by Samuel G. Drake. 2 vols. Roxbury: W.E. Woodward, 1865.

[Hunt, Freeman]. *American Anecdotes: Original and Select*. 2 vols. Boston: Putnam and Hunt, 1830.

Hurd, Duane Hamilton, ed. *History of Worcester County, Massachusetts*. 2 vols. Philadelphia: J. Lewis and Co., 1899.

Hutchinson, Thomas. *The History of the Colony and Province of Massachusetts-Bay*. Edited by Lawrence Shaw Mayo. 3 vols. Cambridge: Harvard University Press, 1936.

Jennings, Francis. *The Invasion of America: Indians, Colonialism, and the Cant of Conquest*. Chapel Hill: University of North Carolina Press, 1975.

Johnson, Donald E. "Worcester in the War for Independence." PhD diss, Clark University, 1953.

Kinnicutt, Lincoln N. "Historical Notes Relating to the Second Settlement of Worcester." *Proceedings of the American Antiquarian Society* 16 (1916).

Kring, Walter Donald. *The Fruits of Our Labors: The Bicentennial History of the First Unitarian Church of Worcester, 1785–1985*. Worcester: First Unitarian Church, 1985.

Leach, Douglas E. *Arms for Empire: A Military History of the British Colonies in North America, 1607–1783*. New York: Macmillan, 1970.

————. *Flintlock and Tomahawk: New England in King Philip's War*. New York: Macmillan, 1958.

Lincoln, Charles H, ed. *Narratives of the Indian Wars*. New York: C. Scribner's Sons, 1913.

Lincoln, Levi, [II]. *Address of Hon. Levi Lincoln...April 17, 1848*. Worcester: n.p.,1848.

Lincoln, William. *History of Worcester, Massachusetts*. Worcester: M.D. Phillips, 1837.

————. *History of Worcester, Massachusetts*. 2 vols in 1. Worcester: Charles Hersey, 1862.

Lincoln, William, ed. *The Journals of Each Provincial Congress of Massachusetts in 1774 and 1775.* The proceedings of the county conventions are appended to the journals of the Provincial Congress, those for Worcester County appearing on 627–52.

Lovell, Albert A. *Worcester in the War of the Revolution.* Worcester, 1876.

Maccarty, Thaddeus. *The Rev. Mr. Maccarty Account of the Behaviour of Mrs. Spooner.* Worcester, 1778.

MacEacheren, Elaine. "Emancipation of Slavery in Massachusetts: a Reexamination, 1770–1790." *Journal of Negro History* 55 (1970): 289–306.

Malone, Patrick M. *The Skulking Way of War: Technology and Tactics Among the New England Indians.* Lanham, MD: Madison Books, 1991.

Martin, John Frederick. *Profits in the Wilderness: Entrepreneurship and the Founding of New England Towns in the Seventeenth Century.* Chapel Hill: University of North Carolina Press, 1991.

Massachusetts Colony. *Records of the Governor and Company of the Massachusetts Bay in New England.* 5 vols in 6. Boston: William White [printer to the Commonwealth], 1853–54.

Massachusetts Convention, 1788. *Debates and Proceedings in the Convention of the Commonwealth of Massachusetts…which Finally Ratified the Constitution of the United States.* Boston: W. White [printer to the Commonwealth], 1856.

Massachusetts Court of Assistants. *Records of the Court of Assistants of the Colony of the Massachusetts Bay, 1630–1692.* Edited by John Noble and John F. Cronin. 3 vols. Boston: County of Suffolk, 1901–28.

Massachusetts General Court, House of Representatives. *Journals of the House of Representatives of Massachusetts.* 50 vols. Boston: Massachusetts Historical Society, 1919–90.

Massachusetts Province. *The Acts and Resolves, Public and Private, of the Province of the Massachusetts Bay.* Edited by Abner Cheney Goodell, et al. 21 vols. Boston, 1869–1922.

Massachusetts Provincial Congress. *The Journals of Each Provincial Congress of Massachusetts in 1774 and 1775 and of the Committee of Safety, with an appendix containing the proceedings of the county conventions.* Edited by William Lincoln. Boston: Dutton and Wentworth [printers to the state], 1838.

BIBLIOGRAPHY

Massachusetts Secretary of the Commonwealth. *Massachusetts Soldiers and Sailors of the Revolutionary War*. 17 vols. Boston: Wright and Potter Print. Co., 1896–1908.

Mather, Increase. *A Brief History of the Warr with the Indians in New-England*. Boston: John Foster, 1676.

Mathews, Lois Kimball. *The Expansion of New England: The Spread of New England Settlement and Institutions to the Mississippi River 1620–1865*. Boston: Houghton Mifflin, 1909.

Matthews, Albert. "Documents Relating to the Last Meetings of the Massachusetts Royal Council, 1774–1776." *Publications of the Colonial Society of Massachusetts* 32 (1937).

McClellan, Charles H. *The Early Settlers of Colrain, Mass.* Greenfield, MA, 1885.

Meagher, Walter J., and William J. Grattan. *The Spires of Fenwick: A History of the College of the Holy Cross, 1843–1963*. New York: Vantage Press, 1966.

Metcalf, John G. *Annals of the Town of Mendon, from 1659 to 1880*. Providence, RI: E.L. Freeman, 1880.

Miller, John C. *Origins of the American Revolution*. Boston: Little, Brown and Company, 1943.

Mooney, James E. "Antislavery in Worcester County, Massachusetts: A Case Study." PhD diss., Clark University, 1971.

Morgan, Edmund S. *The Puritan Family*. Boston: Trustees of the Public Library, 1944.

Moynihan, Kenneth J. "Meetinghouse vs. Courthouse: The Struggle for Legitimacy in Worcester, 1783–1788." In *Shays' Rebellion: Selected Essays*, edited by Martin Kaufman, Westfield, MA: Westfield State College, 1987.

Nason, Edward S. *A Centennial History of Morning Star Lodge*. Worcester: The Lodge, 1894.

Nichols, Charles L. "Samuel Salisbury—A Boston Merchant in the Revolution." *Proceedings of the American Antiquarian Society*. n.s. 35 (1926).

Norton, Mary Beth. "The Evolution of White Women's Experience in Early America." *American Historical Review* 89 (1984): 593–619.

Nutt, Charles. *History of Worcester and Its People*. 4 vols. New York: Lewis Historical Publishing Company, 1919.

Paine, Nathaniel. "Societies, Associations, and Clubs." Chap. 184 in *History of Worcester County, Massachusetts*, edited by Duane Hamilton Hurd. 2 vols. Philadelphia: J. Lewis and Co., 1889.

Paine, Timothy, William Young, Edward Bangs and Sanuel Stearns. "A Topographical Description of the Town of Worcester." *Collections of the Massachusetts Historical Society* 1 (1792): 112–16.

Parmenter, C.O. *History of Pelham, Mass.* Amherst, 1898.

Patterson, Stephen. *Political Parties in Revolutionary Massachusetts.* Madison: University of Wisconsin Press, 1973.

Pencak, William. *War, Politics & Revolution in Provincial Massachusetts.* Boston: Northeastern University Press, 1981.

Perry, Arthur Latham. *Scotch-Irish in America.* Boston, 1891.

Potter, Burton W. "Col. John Murray and His Family." *Collections of the Worcester Society of Antiquity* 24 (1908).

Powell, Sumner C. *Puritan Village; the Formation of a New England Town.* Middletown, CT: Wesleyan University Press, 1963.

Powers, Vincent. "Invisible Immigrants: The Pioneer Irish of Worcester, Massachusetts, 1826–1860." PhD diss., Clark University, 1976.

Quarles, Benjamin. *Black Abolitionists.* New York: Da Capo Press, 1969.

Quarrey, Mike. "Political Party Organization in Worcester, 1800–1809," typescript, American Studies Seminar Research Papers, American Antiquarian Society, 1980.

Rice, Franklin P., ed. "Early Records of the Town of Worcester," Book 1: 1722–39. *Collections of the Worcester Society of Antiquity* 2 (1881).

———. "Records of the Court of General Sessions of the Peace for the County of Worcester." *Collections of the Worcester Society of Antiquity* 5 (1882).

———. "Records of the Proprietors of Worcester, Massachusetts." *Collections of the Worcester Society of Antiquity* 3 (1881).

———. "Town Records." *Collections of the Worcester Society of Antiquity* 4 (1882), 8 (1890), 10 (1891), 11 (1893), 15 (1895).

————. "Worcester Births, Marriages and Deaths." *Collections of the Worcester Society of Antiquity* 12 (1894).

————. "The Worcester District in Congress." *Collections of the Worceser Society of Antiquity* 9 (1890).

Rice, William W. "Worcester County in the Free-Soil Movement." Chap. 201 in *History of Worcester County, Massachusetts*, edited by Duane Hamilton Hurd. 2 vols. Philadelphia: J. Lewis and Co., 1889.

Rowlandson, Mary. "Narrative of the Captivity of Mrs. Mary Rowlandson, 1682." In *Narratives of the Indian Wars*, edited by Charles H. Lincoln. New York: C. Scribner's Sons, 1913.

Russell, Howard S. *A Long Deep Furrow: Three Centuries of Farming in New England*. Hanover, NH: University Press of New England, 1976.

Salisbury, Neal. *Manitou and Providence: Indians, Europeans, and the Making of New England, 1500–1643*, New York: Oxford University Press, 1982.

————. "Red Puritans: The 'Praying Indians' of Massachusetts Bay and John Eliot." *William &Mary Quarterly* 3d series, 31 (1974): 27–54.

S[altonstall], N [athaniel]. "The Present State of New England." In *Narratives of the Indian Wars*, edited by Charles H. Lincoln. New York: C. Scribner's Sons, 1913.

Salwen, Bert. "Indians of Southern New England and Long Island, Early Period." In *Northeast*, edited by Bruce Trigger. Vol. 15 of *The Handbook of North American Indians*, edited by William C. Sturtevant. Washington, D.C: Smithsonian Institution, 1978.

Scholten, Catherine. *Childbearing in Ameriican Society, 1650–1859*. New York: New York University Press, 1985.

Schutz, John A. *William Shirley: King's Governor of Massachusetts*. Chapel Hill: University of North Carolina Press, 1961.

Shepard, Thomas. "The clear sun-shine of the Gospel breaking forth upon the Indians in New-England." Reprinted in *Collections of the Massachusetts Historical Society* 3d series, 4 (1834).

Shipton, Clifford K. *Biographical Sketches of those who attended Harvard College*. 18 vols. Cambridge: Harvard University Press, 1933–75.

Smalley, Elam. *The Worcester Pulpit*. Boston: Phillips, Samson and Company, 1851.

Snow, Dean R. *The Archaeology of New England*. New York: Academic Press, 1980.

Southwick, Albert B. *150 Years of Worcester: 1848–1998*. Worcester: Databooks, 1998.

———. *Once Told Tales of Worcester County*. Worcester: Databooks, 1994.

Spears, John Pearl. *Old Landmarks and Historic Spots of Worcester, Massachusetts*. Worcester: Commonwealth Press, 1931.

Stark, James H. *The Loyalists of Massachusetts and the Other Side of the American Revolution*. Boston: J.H. Stark, 1910.

Steele, Richard C. *Isaiah Thomas*. Worcester: Worcester Bicentennial Commission, 1975.

Sterling, Dorothy. *Ahead of Her Time: Abby Kelley and the Politics of Antislavery*. New York and London: W.W. Norton and Company, 1991.

Sturgis, E.O.P. "Concerning Schools for Girls in Worcester in Former Days." *Proceedings of the Worcester Society of Antiquity* in *Collections of the Worcester Society of Antiquity* 19 (1903).

———. "Old Worcester, IV." *Proceedings of the Worcester Society of Antiquity* in *Collections of the Worcester Society of Antiquity* 18 (1902).

Szatmary, David P. *Shays' Rebellion: The Making of an Agrarian Insurrection*. Amherst: University of Massachusetts Press, 1980.

Temple, J.H. *History of North Brookfield, Massachusetts*. North Brookfield: published by town, 1887.

Tymeson, Mildred McClary. *Rural Retrospect: A Parallel History of Worcester and Its Rural Cemetery*. Worcester, 1956.

Tyrrell, Ian. *Sobering Up: From Temperance to Prohibition in Antebellum America, 1800–1860*. Westport, CT: Greenwood Press, 1979.

Ulrich, Laurel Thatcher. *A Midwife's Tale: The Life of Martha Ballard, Based on Her Diary, 1785–1812*. New York: Knopf, 1990.

Updegraff, Harlan. *Origins of the Moving School in Massachusetts*. New York: Teachers College, Columbia University, 1908.

Vaughan, Alden. *New England Frontier: Puritans and Indians, 1620–1675.* Revised edition. New York and London: Norton, 1979.

Wall, Caleb. *Reminisences of Worcester.* Worcester, 1877.

Washburn, Charles G. *Industrial Worcester.* Worcester: The Davis Press, 1917.

Washburn, Wilcomb E. "Seventeenth-Century Indian Wars." In *Northeast*, edited by Bruce Trigger. Vol. 15 of *The Handbook of North American Indians*, edited by William C. Sturtevant. Washington, D.C.: Smithsonian Institution, 1978.

Weiss, Edwin Theodore, Jr. "Patterns and Processes of High Value Residential Districts: The Case of Worcester, 1713–1970." PhD diss., Clark University, 1973.

Whitefield, George. *George Whitefield's Journals.* Edinburgh: Banner of Truth Trust, 1978.

Whitmore, William H. *The Massachusetts Civil List for the Colonial and Provincial Periods, 1630–1774.* Albany: J. Munsell, 1870.

Whitney, Peter. *The History of the County of Worcester.* Worcester: Isaiah Thomas, 1793.

Willard, Joseph. *Willard Genealogy.* Boston: Willard Family Association, 1915.

[Wilson, John]. "The Day-Breaking, if not the Sun-Rising of the Gospell with the Indians in New-England." *Collections of the Massachusetts Historical Society* 3rd series, 4 (1834).

Worcester. "Report of a Committee of the Centre School District in Worcester, 1823," reprinted as "Appendix to the School Report City Document No. 27, 1873.

Yarrington, Hollis Roger. "Isaiah Thomas, Printer." PhD diss., University of Maryland, 1970.

INDEX

A

Abenaki 29
Adams, John 55, 56, 58, 59, 60, 66, 81, 82, 92, 113
Adams, Samuel 61, 62, 66, 67
Aix-la-Chapelle 57
Algonquian 14, 18
Allen, Charles 138, 151, 152
Allen, George 150, 152
American Antiquarian Society 115, 129
American Political Society 67, 68, 69, 70, 72, 73, 76, 79, 82, 83, 87
Amherst, Jeffrey 58
Andros, Edmund 35
aristocracy 47, 49, 60, 77, 79, 82, 88, 93, 95, 103, 109, 129, 130, 141, 146, 150, 153
Arminianism 53, 54
Arminius, Jacob 53
Ashland 19, 25
Athol 27
Auburn 20, 56
Austin, Samuel 115

B

Baird, Daniel 99, 100, 101, 102
Baldwin, Nathan 59, 61, 62, 66, 67, 80, 82
Bancroft, Aaron 95, 97, 120, 129, 130
Bancroft, David 58
Bancroft, Lucretia Chandler 130
Bangs, Edward 114, 122, 140
Barre 27, 93

Battle of Worcester 33
Belcher, Jonathan 51
Bell Hill 58
Belmont Hill 58
Bigelow, David 65, 89, 92, 99, 100, 102, 103
Bigelow, Joshua 64, 65, 66, 69, 72, 73, 74, 79, 86, 88, 95
Bigelow, Timothy 67, 69, 72, 73, 79, 80, 81, 82, 83, 86, 107, 108
Blackstone Canal 107, 111, 125, 126, 128, 132, 136, 146, 149, 151
Boland, Tobias 126, 133
Bourne, Shearjashub 41
Brazer, Samuel 110
Brookfield 14, 20, 23, 29, 36, 89, 90, 106
Brown, Luke 58
Burr, Isaac 42, 43, 52, 53, 55

C

Calvin, John 38
Cambridge 19, 23, 55, 81
Canton 19, 25, 29
Chabanakonkomon. *See* Webster
Chandler, Clark 68, 71, 73, 74, 80
Chandler, Gardiner 58, 77, 94
Chandler, John 41, 45, 46, 47, 48, 49, 50, 51, 54, 56, 57, 58, 60, 63, 68
Chandler, John, Jr. 58, 61, 62, 64, 65, 66, 68, 71, 72, 73, 77, 80, 83, 94, 97, 110, 130
Chandler, Lucretia 97
Chandler, Mary Church 80
Chandler Hill 58

INDEX

ABOUT THE AUTHOR

Kenneth J. Moynihan is professor emeritus of history and chair of the history department at Assumption College in Worcester. A 1962 graduate of Assumption Preparatory School, he holds a bachelor's degree from the College of the Holy Cross and master's and doctoral degrees from Clark University. He was a member of the Assumption faculty from 1970 to 2007. The author of a number of articles in professional journals and books, he also writes a weekly newspaper column, published from 1976 to 1998 in *Worcester Magazine* and since then in the *Worcester Telegram and Gazette*.